D1245144

# THESIS PROJECTS IN SCIENCE AND ENGINEERING

# THESIS PROJECTS IN SCIENCE AND ENGINEERING

## A COMPLETE GUIDE FROM PROBLEM SELECTION TO FINAL PRESENTATION

## Richard M. Davis

SCHOOL OF ENGINEERING
AIR FORCE INSTITUTE OF TECHNOLOGY

ST. MARTIN'S PRESS
NEW YORK

LIBRARY OF CONGRESS CATALOG CARD NUMBER: 78–65255
*Copyright © 1980 by St. Martin's Press, Inc.*
ALL RIGHTS RESERVED.
Manufactured in the United States of America.
32109
fedcba

For information, write St. Martin's Press, Inc.,
175 Fifth Avenue, New York, N. Y. 10010

COVER DESIGN: Notovitz and Perrault Design
TYPOGRAPHY: Judith Woracek

CLOTH ISBN: 0–312–79964–0
PAPER ISBN: 0–312–79963–2

# PREFACE

This book is intended to help students pursuing graduate degrees in science and engineering develop and carry out their thesis projects—from the selection of the problem through the submission of the final draft of the report. Primarily it addresses the needs of candidates for the master of science (MS) degree, but it should prove helpful to candidates working on doctoral dissertation projects as well, especially those who have not carried out a master's thesis project. The book should provide some perspective on each of the main steps involved in a thesis project and, I hope, help students both to avoid common snares and to accomplish some of the things that must be done along the way. Someone who has completed several research projects will already be familiar with most of these things. But for most MS students and some doctoral candidates, the thesis project is their first substantial research effort. It is new territory—the proper steps and potential problems that are familiar to advisors are new to them.

There are important differences between master's and doctoral projects that should be recognized. In a master's thesis project, a degree candidate undertakes to solve a real, but limited, research problem in his professional field. He is expected to define the project effectively and to plan and carry out the research in a sound and responsible manner. He must demonstrate that he can use some of the tools of his profession and that he understands the significance of the results of the research. The project is then described in a report that presents and interprets his efforts. Throughout the project he maintains fairly close contact with his thesis advisor, who oversees his efforts and provides guidance and direction where necessary. In developing and carrying out the project, the student is learning to do research, but his project need not produce a substantial contribution to his field.

In a doctoral dissertation project, the candidate undertakes to solve a more substantial and demanding problem. He must define the problem and plan and carry out the research with much less guidance from his advisor and committee. In fact, as the project develops he will tend to relate to his advisor and committee members more as a colleague than a student. Like an MS candidate, he must describe his project and present and interpret the results of his research in his dissertation. But in his oral examination, he is expected to defend his method and his interpretation of the meaning of his results to a far greater extent than is an MS candidate. The dissertation project is a demonstration that the candidate can plan and carry out original creative research independently, and the results of the project are expected to have significance in his field. Although the problem may be highly specialized, the time necessary to solve it is usually much longer than that required in an MS thesis project. Because the problem is more complex, the candidate must draw upon a greater breadth of understanding in his field in solving it; and because he must demonstrate that he can perform independent research, he must exercise his own initiative and demonstrate professionalism to a greater extent than is expected in an MS project.

In some respects, the difference is more one of degree than of kind. In a master's project, the student is learning to do research; in a doctoral project, he demonstrates that he can do independent research. This may seem to be a fine distinction, but it is a very real one. Overall, however, the primary steps in the projects are much the same: selection and definition of a suitable project, planning and carrying out the research, and producing an acceptable report that effectively describes the research and presents and interprets the results.

Much of this book reflects ideas and comments made by the 1,500 or more students who have participated in my own thesis seminars over the past sixteen years, and I certainly want to acknowledge their very substantial contribution to it. Furthermore, in preparing the text I have drawn upon the combined experience of about forty thesis advisors and several other specialists who read all or parts of the draft and supplied dozens of helpful suggestions and comments. Together these advisors hold advanced degrees from twenty-six different universities and have guided over 1,200 thesis projects—and that's a lot. All of them should be acknowledged individually, but I hesitate to name any for fear of the inadvertent omission of others.

I do, however, want to make special acknowledgment of the following people who allowed me to use their material as examples in this book:

| | |
|---|---|
| Johnny L. Berg | Tommy J. Kent |
| Richard L. Bloom | Jeffrey L. Kiner |
| Guion S. Bluford, Jr. | John W. Lukes |
| Donald L. Corwin | Donald T. Palac |
| Frank S. Fazekas | Ray G. Pope, Jr. |
| David W. Fleeger | Charles P. Pritzlaff |
| Ronald G. Fraass | Donald E. Pusch |
| M. K. Greenway, Jr. | Richard A. Ray |
| James H. Havey, Jr. | William H. Reeve |
| Kenneth K. Hunt | Max A. Stafford |
| David J. Irwin | John M. Santiago, Jr. |
| J. Gregory Jolda | Jerry L. Stinson |
| John T. Karem | Robert R. Summers |

| Larry E. Taylor | Stephen J. Wanzek |
| George W. Trever | Donald B. Warmuth |
| Thomas E. Walsh, Jr. | Warren B. Watkinson |

They may have missed a comma here and there, but they present their material well. And nothing that I could write could better illustrate the subject matter.

Finally, special acknowledgment is due the patience and professionalism of Joyce Barnes, who typed the text and helped with many details in the preparation of the manuscript. As I have indicated in the book, a good typist can make the difference between happiness and ulcers, and Mrs. Barnes is one of the best.

Richard M. Davis

# CONTENTS

# LIST OF SAMPLE THESIS PAGES

# NOTES ON TERMINOLOGY

The word "thesis" is sometimes used to refer to the research project that a student undertakes when earning an advanced degree and sometimes to the report that results. Because both the project and the report are discussed throughout this book, the following ground rules have been established. The project itself will be referred to as the "thesis project" or simply the "project." The report will generally be referred to as the "thesis" (a common usage). In passages in which a distinction between the project and the report is emphasized, the latter will simply be called the "report."

In some schools, the school year is divided into quarters; in others, it is divided into semesters. In this book, all references are to quarters. If your school operates on a semester basis, read "semester" wherever the term "quarter" appears in the text.

In some schools, completed thesis projects are assigned letter grades; in others, they are rated on a "pass-fail" or "acceptable-unacceptable" basis. In this book, references are to evaluation of the project rather than to the specifics of either scale.

# THESIS PROJECTS IN SCIENCE AND ENGINEERING

# Introduction

A thesis project is usually defined as a learning experience in which a student carries out an independent research effort in his field and presents the results in a full formal report (thesis). In carrying out the research, the student should develop competence in handling project-sized problems and contribute something original to his field. But while almost everyone who undertakes a thesis project hopes to do something significant, the student does not have to produce a major contribution to human knowledge in order to qualify for an MS degree. Major contributions just aren't that numerous—few master's projects (or doctoral or other research projects) produce them. Rather, the student is expected to demonstrate that he can effectively define and limit a problem in his technical field, locate and evaluate pertinent publications, plan what must be done to solve the problem, and schedule and carry out the necessary research. Then he must produce a full formal report describing the research effort in sufficient detail that someone else in his technical field can read it and understand what the problem was, what the student did, what resulted, and what it all means.

Three points should be clearly understood at the outset. First, the thesis project is supposed to be an independent research effort. Although a faculty member acts as an advisor, the research is planned and carried out by the student. The advisor generally oversees what the student plans and does, and he makes suggestions from time to time about the project; but, as far as possible, the project must remain the student's work. The student, not the advisor, is learning to plan and carry out research.

Second, the problem may not be solved or, perhaps, fully solved in the course of the research project. Certainly, most students intend to find the answers to their project problems, and probably most do. But finding the answer is not always possible—unanticipated delays may occur, promising methods do not always produce results, and unforseen intermediate problems arise. In such cases, the project may be rated as excellent work if a sound approach was followed, resourcefulness and creativity were demonstrated in the research, and there was consistent, diligent effort throughout.

Third, the written report (thesis) is not the primary objective of the project, but a necessary end result—as are project reports on almost any other research, whether academic, industrial, or governmental. The research is intended to solve a problem in the professional field concerned (generally, that's what any research is—a search for new knowledge or the answer to a problem), and the report is the last major step in the sequence. Preparation of the report usually requires a considerable amount of time and effort, and specifications regarding it may be stringent, but it is the information reported that is the primary object of the project.

There is a very real satisfaction in completing a research project and reporting the outcome to your professional peers. The entire foundation of knowledge built by your previous academic work is coupled with the time and effort that went into the project itself to produce your first real contribution to your professional field, and however limited the application of your conclusions may be, you have added something to the information available in your field. When a project has been completed, most people feel that the result was well worth the effort expended and the uncertainties and frustrations encountered along the way. If your entire project seems to be a bore, you have certainly picked the wrong topic for your research and possibly even the wrong field for your life's work.

A thesis project is a substantial undertaking. It requires careful analysis and planning to determine what must be done, to do it, and to complete an acceptable report. It also takes consistent effort over quite a few months, as well as imagination and the ability to overcome unforeseen obstacles. But it isn't an impossible task. Thousands of students undertake thesis projects each year, and most of them complete their projects acceptably and more or less on time. This book is intended to help you complete yours. Of necessity, some of the discussion contained is rather general, and some does not apply to all projects. You may be able to skip some of the suggested procedures or do some things differently than suggested here. But you should read the entire book before you decide how to handle your project. And the earlier in the project you read it, the more potential help it may be to you.

Because every project is unique, because each advisor has his own way of working with students, and because different departments and universities have different requirements, there is no universally "right" way to do most things involved in a thesis project. But the overall sequence is usually much the same. This book is intended to provide perspective on the project as a whole, to alert you to the kinds of things that will be expected of you in the course of your project, and to tell you about some of the things that must be planned for and accomplished. It is meant to help you determine what must be done, develop a plan for getting it done, accomplish it, and fulfill related university requirements.

The sequence in the first part of the book corresponds roughly to the order in which things are done on a typical thesis project. It begins with the selection of a research problem and then moves on to limiting the problem, carrying out the research, writing the report, preparing the drafts, and making the oral presentation. Because the actual research varies so much from project to project and specific suggestions are usually made by faculty advisors, the section on research is, of necessity, very general. Because the process of preparing the report is generally similar from project to project—and because the instructions given are often sketchy—the discussion of preparing the report is comparatively detailed. In the second part of the book, the content and organization of the thesis itself are discussed in some detail. Generally acceptable practices in documentation and in the use of equations, figures, and tables are described and illustrated. The appendix contains sample pages taken from several master of science theses to illustrate typical form and presentation of the content.

No other person and no book can carry out your thesis project and write the report for you; that is your job. But this book should help you to eliminate some of the potential wasted motion.

# Selecting a Topic and Getting Started

In the course of determining what your project will be, you must select a general problem area, find an advisor to guide your research, and define and limit the problem to be investigated. The project must be accepted by the school as a suitable thesis project—sometimes acceptance by the advisor is sufficient, and sometimes other approval is necessary. Careful consideration of each of these steps is critical to the success of the project and may well determine whether or not it will be completed in reasonable time or, indeed, at all. Too early commitment to a project that is ill defined or poorly thought out can make completion difficult if not impossible.

You should begin thinking about thesis possibilities early in your program. As you progress through your course work, you should note general areas that interest you as possible research fields and find out which faculty members work in them. You should take available courses in those areas and begin any extra background reading that may be suggested. It is not at all out of place to undertake preliminary discussions with faculty members who work in areas of interest well before the start of a thesis project. In fact, faculty advisors often feel that students tend to wait too long to discuss potential projects and that the delay adds to the time required for preparation and getting started once the selection is made. An early start usually generates a good attitude toward the work and can give the student a psychological boost. At the very latest, you should be discussing possible projects with potential advisors at the beginning of the quarter prior to the one in which you hope to begin your research. And this doesn't leave much room for slippage or missed bases.

## SELECTING THE TOPIC

When a student develops an interest in a particular subject area, he should approach faculty members who specialize in it to discuss possible thesis projects. Most thesis projects are suggested to students by others, and faculty members actively engaged in research are the people most likely to be aware of suitable potential research projects in their own areas. They are in a position to judge which projects are of sufficient depth to merit a thesis project and at the same time can be handled without undue difficulty, within a reasonable time, and with the resources available. Often, thesis projects are developed as parts of larger research projects being carried out by the advisor. Such projects can be ideal for the student because the advisor is already familiar with many details of the immediate problem and possible approaches to the solution (and he has a special interest in finding the solution). If discussion with a faculty member suggests an interesting project, be certain to ask specific questions about background courses, specialty courses, mathematics courses, and computer courses required or recommended for work on the project, and schedule them as soon as possible. It may not be possible to complete the project without them.

In your advanced technical courses, you may learn about specific potential projects or more general topic areas when the limits of current knowledge of the subject matter are discussed. Further, sponsoring departments often publish lists of potential topics, some maintain files of potential topics with greater or lesser degrees of descriptive discussion, and some require attendance at seminars in which possible topics are suggested and discussed.

Students often suggest their own topics—and there certainly is nothing wrong with this. If a student has developed a particular interest in a given problem, he may derive a special satisfaction from working it through to find a solution. But in such cases, special care must be taken to assure that a faculty advisor qualified to guide the research is available, that adequate research facilities are available, and that the problem is carefully defined and limited early in the project. Faculty members are understandably reluctant to act as advisors on projects that are peripheral to their own primary specialties, and students occasionally propose wholly impossible projects.

Although they may seem obvious, the following considerations should not be overlooked as you select your topic:

1. You will be spending a substantial amount of your time for a good many months on the project. Choose something that will sustain your interest and with which you will be comfortable. If you feel uneasy about a topic, maybe it isn't a good one. If it seems entirely nebulous, maybe it is. Select a different topic.
2. Choose a topic that involves doing the sort of thing that you like to do and that you can do, or would like to learn to do—whether it is design and testing, theoretical development, experimentation, or something else. If you are "all thumbs" with tools and can't drive a nail, you probably shouldn't do an experimental thesis. If you couldn't debug a simple computer program after the thirty-seventh try in your FORTRAN course, you probably shouldn't do a computer simulation.
3. If another student is working on a project similar to one you are considering, or if yours is to be a continuation of someone else's, go

and see him and get his ideas about your proposal. You might even help him for a day or two to become familiar with the kinds of problems he has encountered and to get the "feel" of the project. He will probably be the best person to answer your questions about both the project and the advisor.

4. As far as possible, you should choose a project on which you can do most of the work yourself without much help from other people. Technicians, lab assistants, computer operators, and clerical personnel work prescribed hours, take vacations, and occasionally get sick. You will probably want to work evenings and on weekends when support personnel are not available, and during their regular working hours they will have many other things to do in addition to helping you. The more you are dependent upon them, the more likely your work is to be held up at very inconvenient times.

5. Make certain that any necessary major equipment, tools, and materials are available and operable. Go and see them, touch them, turn motors on, and make sure that they work before you commit yourself to a project that cannot be done without them.

6. If the project will require supplies or materials that are not on hand, find out whether suppliers are readily available, whether funds are available to buy what is needed, and the approximate time between order and delivery. Even when funds are available, extended delivery times can delay a project for months.

## THESIS ADVISOR

Your thesis advisor is responsible for guiding your research efforts and evaluating the result. While there may be one or more additional members on your committee, your advisor has primary responsibility, and he is the one with whom you will work most closely. It is very important that your advisor be someone with whom you are compatible and in whom you have confidence.

The selection of a research topic usually determines who the advisor will be. He is the faculty member best qualified to guide research in the area concerned and with the time and interest to do it. If you select a topic from suggestions made by the department, he is probably the one who made the suggestion (the names of the potential advisors are usually indicated on the lists of suggested topics). If you develop and propose the topic yourself, you will probably be sent to him to discuss it.

If you do not already know the potential advisor, you should have enough preliminary discussion with him to judge whether you would be comfortable working with him and to ensure that you are in general agreement on the problem to be handled. Once a commitment is made, you will be working with your advisor for six months or more, so it is wise to get to know him a bit first.

Here are a few general considerations to keep in mind:

1. Get someone who is really interested in the proposed project. This is almost more important than what the project is. A reluctant or uninterested advisor can be worse than none at all.

2. If he does not have time to discuss the project with you before you agree to it, he is not likely to have time to provide much guidance later on. Avoid advisors who are so busy with other things that they don't have time to advise students.

3. If it is at all possible, talk to students who are working with the potential advisor and get their comments on his effectiveness. If he has been helpful to them, he is likely to be helpful to you. It is sad but true that some people who do excellent research are not good advisors. You want a good advisor—whether he is the most brilliant man in his field or not. But look at unusually unfavorable reports with a slightly jaundiced eye—students who do not do good research often blame someone else, and the advisor is usually the most convenient candidate for blame.

4. Faculty members usually have one quarter (not necessarily summer) off during the year, they sometimes have sabbatical years (years in which they are relieved of regular duties), and they sometimes leave the campus for extended periods of research or consulting. If you need help while your advisor is away, you could lose quite a bit of time waiting for his return. Most potential advisors will not take on new thesis projects when they think such an absence might be in the offing, and arrangements can sometimes be made for substitutes. But an advisor may forget to mention a potential absence, so ask about this. It may save you considerable lost time in your project.

## SHAPING THE PROBLEM

When general agreement has been reached between the student and advisor about the research topic, the advisor is usually appointed officially by the department concerned. One or more additional faculty members may be appointed at this time to serve on the advisory committee. Procedures vary from place to place, but the student is often required to submit a prospectus—a brief written description of the research proposed—before the advisor is officially appointed.

Ideally, the prospectus is an exact statement of the problem to be handled and the proposed plan of attack—a detailed thesis proposal as described in the next section of this chapter. If the student has selected his topic early enough and done the necessary background reading, this is sometimes possible. More often, though, the prospectus is a less specific identification of the general problem area to be considered and a discussion of whatever initial ideas the student may have about the approach to be used. Detail is often sparse. Sometimes the problem is so advanced that only initial work can be described, and sometimes the topic is so new to the student that he has not yet done the background reading and analysis necessary for making a detailed problem analysis.

After your advisor has been officially appointed, you will probably discuss the research problem with him several times before the specifics of the exact problem to be investigated and the research method are determined. (In these early discussions, be certain that you understand the advisor's general philosophy about thesis projects, as well as his expectations.) Your advisor will probably make suggestions about materials to be read and factors to be considered in defining the problem, and you will begin a full bibliographic search (discussed in Chapter 3) to locate and read pertinent published material. This may include information on the theory involved, appropriate research methods, equipment and apparatus, or research studies similar to the one proposed.

As you become more familiar with the problem area and the relevant publications, discussions with your advisor will center upon exact delineation of the problem to be handled and the methods to be used in solving it. Often the problem stated in the prospectus is too broad and general for a thesis project, and it must be limited to something that can be handled within a reasonable time and with the resources available. Several more limited parts of the problem may be considered, narrowed, and analyzed, and several possible general approaches may be outlined before a commitment is made.

Occasionally a student may feel that he is wasting valuable time at the outset in narrowing the problem and determining specifically what he will do. But students are almost universally too optimistic about the amount that can be done in the time available. During the narrowing process, your advisor may "grill" you about your proposed problem and approach. He may appear to quibble about small points—but that's his function. He must be sure that you have a solid understanding of what is involved in the problem and what must be done to solve it. And he must be certain that you undertake something that is of sufficient depth to merit a master of science thesis project, without being too difficult to accomplish. You are supposed to complete a sound research project and earn the degree, and your advisor wants you to succeed. In fact, he may be more than a little bit outraged when a student who could succeed does not. Once a student begins to talk in terms of reduced dimensions and concentrates on specifics, advisors generally feel that he is ready to proceed with the research.

## THESIS PROPOSAL

At this point, a complete thesis proposal is often written. Some advisors and some departments may not require it, and some may require something else, but it is in the student's interest to write one even if it is not required. In preparing it, the student is, in effect, engineering the entire project. The proposal—or something like it—should normally be made early in the first research quarter. If it is allowed to slip beyond this, much of the value can be lost as the door is opened to misunderstandings and unnecessary waste of the student's time.

A thesis proposal (also known as a problem analysis, a statement of work, and by a variety of other names) is an exact statement of the problem a student wants to investigate and the approach he proposes to use in solving it—or, at least, it is as complete and accurate as reasonably possible. It is prepared by the student (usually after considerable discussion with his advisor) and submitted to the advisor (and sometimes to others) for review and approval. When approved, it becomes the enabling document—the official permission to go ahead with the thesis project. Sometimes the advisor or a review committee suggests modifications of the original proposal, and sometimes it is necessary to rewrite and resubmit it before approval is given to proceed with the project.

Your proposal should acquaint the reader with the particular problem chosen, show its significance (that it is a problem of sufficient importance and complexity to warrant a thesis project), and demonstrate that you have a sensible approach to the solution and a good chance of success. Above all, you should show that you have thought about the problem carefully, that you have the background in the field to undertake the project, and that you know what you are talking about.

Clearly, if you can't state exactly what your problem is, you can't very well solve it. And conversely, once you have a clear grasp of what the problem really is and what is involved, you're usually well on the way to solving it. While your primary reason for writing the proposal is to obtain approval to undertake the project, a major benefit is that it forces you to think analytically about the problem. This helps you to understand what you must do in solving the problem and how to do it. Fuzziness or ambiguity in the proposal may occasionally slip by a review committee, but it is likely to cause a great deal of trouble *for you* later as differences arise as to just what was intended and approved. The approved proposal is not an inviolable contract—objectives or methods may change as the research develops—but it is a point-of-departure agreement on what will be done on the project unless something develops to alter the original plan.

You will have to make something like a thesis proposal time and time again throughout your professional life, so learn how to write an effective one now. Sometimes full formal proposals will be required, and sometimes more informal proposals will suffice. But whether you work in industry, government, or the academic world, when you seek authorization for a research project or almost any other major project, you will have to get approval before you can spend time and someone else's money on it. You will have to demonstrate that a problem exists, that something should be done about it, that you have a good idea about how to solve it, and that you have a good chance for success in doing it. Budgets are made and money is allocated on the basis of what needs to be done, the likelihood of success in doing it, and the benefit that will result. Your proposals will often be judged against competing proposals, and your projects against competing projects. You will have to convince the people with the power of decision that your project is necessary and that your particular approach is best. Nobody is going to authorize funds to keep you sitting around and thinking about problems that might arise five years from now when the same money is needed to pay for machine tools necessary to keep the production line moving next month.

The content of a thesis proposal depends, of course, both on the particular problem to be investigated and on local preferences. The following list indicates typical content. Not all items are necessarily appropriate for all thesis proposals, and some proposals may contain information not listed here. As in other communication situations, the information included and its ordering depend upon the individual situation.

1. *Background.* Supply enough background to enable the reader to understand what led up to the problem and its significance. You should describe the general situation sufficiently for the reader to appreciate the problem, but don't trace the history of environmental pollution since the earth was formed. Provide just enough background so that the reader can see that the problem should be solved and appreciate the benefit that will result from solving it. If the problem was sugggested by the advisor, the background will show him that you understand its significance (he already does because he suggested it). If the proposal is to be approved or commented upon by others, the background will help to orient them.

2. *Problem.* State the exact problem that you want to investigate. Do not include any verbal embroidery. Just state flatly what you want to do—for example, "determine what effect a nonuniform electric field has on a fluid-flowing system" or "determine whether effective thrust vectoring can be achieved through the use of a translating plug in a convergent exhaust nozzle." This statement should be set off by itself, not buried in a long paragraph of theoretical discussion. It should be given its own heading so that is cannot be missed and can easily be found again. Your reader will probably want to come back to it several times after his first reading. Make it easy for him to do so.

3. *Scope.* The scope defines the limits of the proposed study: what *will* and what *will not* be covered. Most thesis projects are concerned with parts of larger problems. Usually, only one or two of many parameters are varied, one of many tests applied, two or three of dozens of alloys or compounds tested, or a few of many possible flow rates used. Tell the reader just how much of the area you propose to cover.

4. *Assumptions.* Assumptions are the facts, ideas, or opinions assumed to be true at the outset without further proof—much as certain postulates were assumed without further proof in Euclidian geometry. Such assumptions are usually made to simplify a problem—to cut it down to something that can be handled within the present state of the art and with the equipment or theory now available—or where approximate solutions are adequate. They define the point of departure

from which you will work. For example, you may assume that a satellite may be approximated by a point mass, that the elements of a circuit are linear, that a computer program accurately simulates a given set of actual conditions, that a given system is 99.9 percent reliable, or that someone else's research results are valid. Any such assumptions should be identified and justified (they may simply be the assumptions commonly accepted in the particular kind of study you propose). If they are not identified, you may be attacked for not recognizing them as assumptions. But if you show that you recognize your assumptions and that they are reasonable within the context of your study, the burden of proof is on anyone who disagrees.

5. *Summary of Current Knowledge.* Provide a brief statement of what (if anything) is already known about the immediate problem area. This summary helps to distinguish between what is known and what you are going to try to find out. It clarifies why you may intend to do some things but not others (they have already been done). If, for example, you intend to take measurements between 475° C and 650° C, you may indicate here that reports on studies of the areas above and below this temperature range have already been published. Your study will provide information which will fill the gap between them. Such a summary of current knowledge also indicates to the reader that you have done your homework; you are familiar with important related studies and have the background in your immediate area to undertake the proposed study.

6. *Standards.* Explain and justify criteria to be applied in measurement and analysis. Some of these may not yet be known at the time the proposal is written, but identify any that are. If you are going to make test runs at 20-degree increments between 400° C and 500° C, how closely will you hold the temperature? Will a run at 419° C be considered a good run? 418° C? 417° C? What accuracy will be held in measuring weights? Times? Composition of alloys? Gases? This will give the reader a feeling for both the potential validity of your results on the one hand and unrealistically restrictive limits on the other.

7. *Approach.* Explain how you intend to go about solving the problem. Here you indicate the main sequence (start to finish) of the things to be done or determined in the course of the study. In an experimental project, for example, you might have to do some or all of the following:

> design equipment
> construct equipment
> calibrate equipment
> prepare samples
> make test runs
> write and debug computer program
> run computations
> analyze data
> develop conclusions

The more specific you can be here about how you plan to do what you propose to do, the better. You will demonstrate that you have thought out your general sequence carefully and at the same time provide your reader with a basis for evaluating your understanding of what is involved and your likelihood of success. Nobody wants you to waste your time (and money) on an approach that won't work. If your approach is completely new or markedly different from those previously used in your field, you should justify it—explain why it should be used rather than others.

In all probability, you will not be able to tell exactly how you will do everything—or, perhaps, much of anything. What you do at one stage of the project will depend on the results of the previous stage, and nobody really expects you to know results ahead of time. It may be necessary to modify your approach as you proceed with the project. The final result may, in fact, bear little similarity to your original intent. But you must demonstrate at the outset that you have a sensible approach and that you understand what must be done to solve the problem by the means you propose.

8. *Materials and Equipment.* Indicate what you will need in order to carry out the project and where you think you can get it. If you will use only materials and equipment available in departmental laboratories, say so and name them. If you have made arrangements to obtain something from a cooperating business or industry, say so. If you have determined that what you need will be available at the time you need it, say so.

Don't try to gloss over or obscure the fact that you need something for which you don't yet have a source. Your readers may be able to suggest where you can obtain it. Many a thesis project has been delayed for months or abandoned completely because necessary materials or equipment just couldn't be found. It's far better to modify a proposal or to develop a new one than to waste your time on one you won't be able to carry out.

9. *Other Support.* Identify any laboratory assistance, technical help, clerical help, or other support that may or will be needed in the course of the project. Approximate the amounts as nearly as possible and, if you know that the support is available, say so.

After reading your proposal, your advisor and any other reviewers should have a good idea of what you want to do, what is involved, and where any difficulty is likely to arise. They should be in a position to evaluate the significance of the project, judge your likelihood of success, and perhaps make suggestions. All of the items listed above may not be necessary in your proposal, and much of what is covered will already have been discussed with your thesis advisor. Tentative agreements may already have been reached on many points. But write it all down anyway. Your project may be one of six or eight with which your advisor is involved in one way or another. And advisors are sometimes changed as one leaves unexpectedly for a year off campus and another replaces him. So make the proposal as complete as you can and when you submit it, keep a copy of the approved proposal. A sample thesis proposal is included at the end of this chapter and others are in the appendix as Examples 9 and 10. (Each of the projects described was successfully completed on time.)

The format to be used in the proposal may be suggested by your advisor, or there may be a standard departmental or university form. Generally, it is helpful if you make generous use of headings and lists. By using headings, you identify the blocks of information presented and their arrangement, you make it easy to flip through the proposal and locate a particular piece of information, and you almost force yourself to keep information that belongs together in the same place. If you have a section called "Assumptions," you are less likely to sprinkle unidentified assumptions through the proposal than if you do not. And by using numbered lists you make it much easier for a reader to check individual items and sequences than if you group them in paragraph form. The format used in the example at the end of this chapter should be generally acceptable where no specific format is prescribed.

With the major problem clearly identified and placed in perspective, an orderly sequence of action determined, acceptable standards established, and necessary materials and equipment identified and arranged for, the execution of the plan should follow without undue uncertainty. It takes a certain amount of effort to write a good proposal, and analysis does not mean solution of the problem. But a good analysis is certainly a very healthy head start. And as was noted earlier, if you can't state your problem or how you want to go about solving it, the odds against success are pretty heavy.

## SCHEDULE

Some advisors require that the student prepare a schedule for the completion of the project, and some do not. The schedule may even be a part of the thesis proposal or attached to it and considered in conjunction with it. The thesis proposal describes *what* must be done in the course of the project, and the schedule indicates *when* it will be done and how long each step should take. Certainly you cannot plan months in advance just what you will be doing day by day on a research project—and you shouldn't try to. But even on projects for which close scheduling is clearly impossible (such as those primarily concerned with theoretical development) the approximate time to be allotted to each major phase should be estimated, and a real effort should be made to stay on schedule.

Like the thesis proposal, the schedule has to be tentative—you cannot know what will come up in the course of the research to cause changes in sequence or timing. As the research progresses and the original approach is modified, the schedule may have to be modified. (Some advisors require that they be kept current with copies of modified schedules.) But there should be some sort of plan at the outset by which to allocate time to do all of the things that must be done in the sequence in which they must be done if you are going to complete the project, meet departmental and university deadlines, and graduate as planned.

When the thesis proposal has been written, it shouldn't take more than about a half-hour to prepare a carefully thought out schedule. If it takes any longer, the odds are strong that the approach described in the proposal was not complete and that it should be revised to include any steps or portions of steps that were omitted. On the other hand, development of a schedule may reveal that the proposed project should be further limited—there just will not be time available to accomplish all that must be done to complete the project.

In addition to forcing you to set up a reasonable time frame for accomplishing what needs to be done, the schedule can be a very convenient scale against which to measure progress as you work on the project. It can provide perspective later on when you are immersed in the detail of your work. Students often place copies of their schedules above their desks, in their lab notebooks, or in other places where they will be seen regularly—and where they will act as a prod if the student is falling behind. Used in this way, the schedule can help reduce the sensation of sheer panic that often accompanies the approach of due dates for the drafts of the report.

Here are a few tips about making schedules:

1. Remember to include time at the end for writing the first draft, receiving an evaluation of the draft, incorporating revisions, getting the final draft typed, adding necessary illustrative material, and adding any forms required by your department or university. All of this must be done, and you are the person who must do most of it. *It takes time.*

2. Students tend to be too optimistic about how quickly they can accomplish things. (One experienced advisor says that he normally multiplies the time required in some steps by three!) Things often (and unavoidably) go wrong on research projects. Computer programs need debugging, samples get lost in the mail, equipment breaks down, lab personnel get sick, and there just isn't any way to predict these things or prevent them from happening. Be prepared for the fact that not everything will go smoothly.

3. Where possible, build enough flexibility into your schedule that an unavoidable delay in one step will not completely stop you. Have other things that you can work on while the problem is being straightened out.

4. Leave "water" in your schedule toward the end—uncommitted time to take care of slippage in the schedule. Project planners do this regularly. You can't know what will happen to throw your schedule off, but it's probable that something will. No one is likely to be displeased if you complete your work a week early, but if you're a week late you may miss your scheduled graduation.

If making a simple schedule seems unnecessarily involved, remember that a good one can save you considerable uncertainty and frustration. It shouldn't take long to make one, and most schedules will fit easily on a piece of 8½-by-11-inch paper. Make a schedule even if your advisor doesn't require it. And if someone suggests that a schedule will discourage creativity in your research, make one anyway. You are carrying out a thesis project, not a life-time assignment. Few half-hours will be better spent in the course of the project than the time you spend making your schedule.

Like it or not, you will be working to meet schedule dates throughout your professional life, and your ability to meet deadlines will be of critical importance. Failure to meet schedule dates can result in both financial penalties to your employer and damage to your career—you cannot be trusted to deliver the goods as promised. Being on schedule, or even a little bit ahead of schedule, is often a mark of good planning and sound research effort.

THESIS PROPOSAL

STUDY OF MNOS MEMORY TRANSITION
QUASI-STATIC CAPACITANCE-VOLTAGE
CHARACTERISTICS

Background

The metal-nitride-oxide-silicon (semi-conductor), or MNOS, memory device offers both potential cost savings and functional advantages over many present memory systems. As it is nonvolatile and radiation resistant, the MNOS memory device has specific advantages over conventional solid-state flip-flop memory systems in some applications. Although much slower in information access time, the MNOS memory array structures are capable of presenting large-scale-integration (LSI) technology with bit packing densities up to $10^6$ bits per square inch and costs estimated at one-half cent per bit. However, present MNOS memories are failing to maintain distinguishable binary states as the units approach a range of $10^6$ to $10^9$ write/clear cycles. Consequently, the Avionics Laboratory (AFAL), Memory Technology Branch, is presently sponsoring development and evaluation of MNOS memories to resolve or minimize memory degradation problems.

Problem

The basic problem facing the AFAL is, generally, how to evaluate MNOS memory array products and, specifically, what methods to apply in evaluating degradation trends. This study will investigate the use of low-frequency (quasi-static) capacitance-voltage (C-V) measurements of MNOS devices to characterize patterns relating to the devices' memory degradation. Although the quasi-static measurement technique is well founded in current literature, specific work in the description of the MNOS characteristics has not been published to date. Hence, this study should have direct application in understanding the MNOS device more fully.

Scope

This study will be concerned only with description of quasi-static C-V characteristics as a function of write/clear pulse parameters (pulse width, height, and rise time), number of write/clear cycles, and thermal bias stressing. No attempt will be made to explain why the device degrades.

Approach

From a single batch of discrete MNOS devices supplied by a contractor, a total of six devices will be separated into three test groups of two devices each. Initially, each test group will be subjected to a prescribed set of quasi-static C-V measurements consisting of several incremental ramp-voltage limits and rate changes. The data will be recorded on an x-y plotter and on paper tape via an analog-digital converter. The first test group will then be subjected to a write/clear exerciser using high-rise-time pulses of approximately 50ns for a continuous period of 24 hours. The prescribed set of C-V measurements will be repeated, and the test group will then be subjected to the exerciser for another 24 hours.

EXAMPLE 1.    THESIS PROPOSAL   *Experimental Project*

This procedure will continue for at least seven days or until a significant change in the C-V curves appears.

The second test group will also be subjected to the write/clear exerciser but only the rise-time will be lowered to approximately 200ns. Again, a combination of 24-hour exercise periods and C-V tests will follow for at least seven days.

The third test group will be subjected to the same C-V tests while each device is under heat-soaked conditions. The thermal steps will be from 300°K to 425°K in steps of 25°K.

Theoretical mathematical relationships will also be derived and then compared to the digital C-V data for each test group. Deviations from the expected and observed characteristics, if any, will then form the basis for observing degradation effects on an accelerated basis and forming test criteria for future product evaluations.

Equipment/Support

The electronic equipment necessary for the quasi-static C-V tests will include a Kiethly 602 solid-state electrometer, a triangle-wave generator, a standard scope, an x-y plotter, and an analog-digital converter with a paper tape output unit. Presently, all equipment is available from laboratory resources; however, acquisition of a lower frequency wave generator (to replace the present Wavetek wave generator) on a temporary loan basis from TEA-4 is planned. The clear/write exerciser will be available and will not require modification for this project. Only coordination with the laboratory chief will be necessary for use of the exerciser and the analog-digital, paper-punch unit.

A Hewlett-Packard 9200 minicomputer and appropriate peripheral units (paper tape reader, cassette memory tape, and plotter) will be required for data analysis. This is available, and permission for its use has been obtained. No other equipment or support beyond normal equipment maintenance will be necessary.

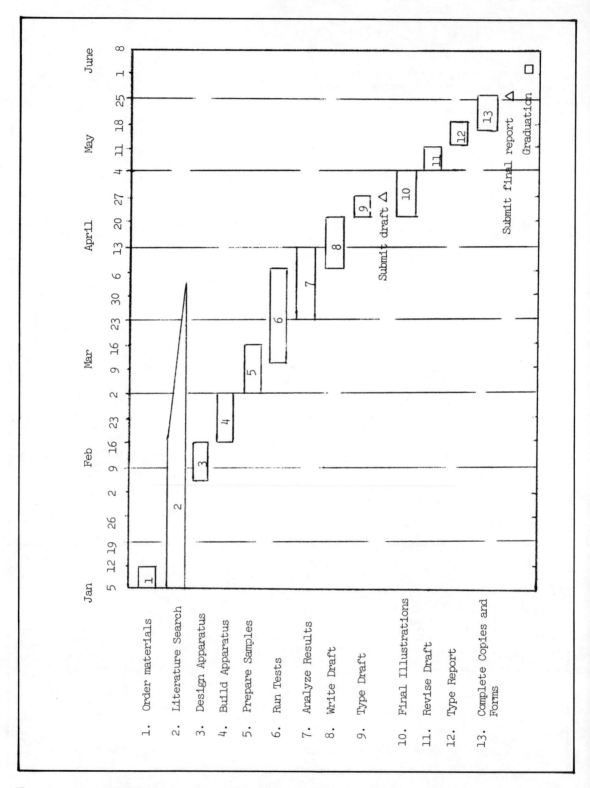

EXAMPLE 2.    PROJECT SCHEDULE    *Note: Bars may be filled in to indicate progress made.*

# 3

# Doing the Research

Every project is different from every other project, and some of the things that are done on one are different from the things that are done on another. But certain steps apply to almost any project, and these are discussed in this chapter. While an attempt has been made to put them in sensible sequence, they cannot be discussed in the order in which they are done because there is no such order: most of them are in progress throughout the research. Some (such as the discussion of working in a laboratory) do not apply to some research projects, but most are applicable to all.

At the outset, keep firmly in mind that you are supposed to be carrying out an independent research effort and that your thesis advisor is supposed to be just that—an advisor. It is your project. In carrying it out you are supposed to demonstrate that you are able to analyze problems, determine and evaluate possible courses of action, select the most suitable ones, and then implement them. Your advisor should be shown that you have initiative and that you are capable of independent thinking. If you go to him for advice on every move you make or ask him to bail you out every time you hit a snag, you may learn to be a second-rate technician, but you will not learn to carry out independent research.

When you are unable to determine what should be done or when you contemplate changing a course of action previously agreed upon, you should, of course, go to your advisor for advice. And when he makes a suggestion, it is generally a good idea to follow it. He may not always be right, but he has probably had a good deal of experience in the general problem area and he has certainly thought the whole project through. If you insist, he may sometimes let you go a few steps along a path that he does not consider fruitful, but few advisors will knowingly let a student waste much time on a method or procedure that is known to be ineffective or unworkable. Having developed your plan and having gotten your advisor's advice, do your own research and carry out the project yourself.

Sometimes niceties can be bypassed, corners can be cut, and details can be let go by the boards. But you should keep your overall schedule (however informal it may be) handy and try to stay on it throughout the project. Usually, there is nothing magic about any of the dates on it except the due date for the final report. Other dates may, in fact, be adjusted as the project progresses—particularly if the scope is broadened or narrowed because the research moves faster or slower than expected. But most of us have a natural tendency to let dates slip (especially, early in a project) without too much concern—it always seems that there will be plenty of time later to get back on schedule. Then, as the project develops, it can become almost impossible to make up a week lost at the beginning. The more dates you let slip, the less likely you are to complete the project as planned and have a respectable report ready in time for your intended graduation date.

## WORKING WITH YOUR ADVISOR

Your advisor's job is to monitor your activity as you progress through the project and to provide guidance as problems (technical, economic, or "political") arise. To do this effectively, he must be kept current on your progress and informed of the problems you have encountered. Meetings with your advisor may be regularly scheduled or they may be unscheduled—depending on the nature of the project, the stage of progress, the initiative you have shown, and your advisor's preference. After the problem and approach are firmly established and the research is well underway, meetings may become shorter and, sometimes, less frequent. Although some projects require less consultation than others, many advisors make it a practice to visit laboratories and other work areas regularly—especially at critical stages of the research. Short contacts often increase toward the end of the project as loose ends are being tied up.

### Preparing for a Meeting

No matter how casual your advisor may be about meetings, always take a few minutes to prepare yourself before going to see him. You know what he needs to know—the progress you have made, the problems you have encountered, and what you expect to do next. If there is much to be covered, prepare a list of the topics you want to discuss ahead of time to make sure that you get things in the right order and that you do not forget to mention important points. Then during the meeting you can check off items as they are discussed. If you leave space between items on your list, you will have room to jot down your advisor's comments as he makes them. This can be very helpful later, especially if many items were discussed and there was substantial comment on some of them. It is often a good idea to give your advisor a copy of the list at the beginning of the meeting. This will give him a rough idea of the points to be discussed and enable him to gauge his comments accordingly. This can save time for both of you.

Your advisor may suggest that you give him a brief written summary of the points covered in the meeting within a day or two after it is held. This can be helpful to both of you, and you should keep a copy for yourself. A summary helps to avoid misunderstanding about what was said and is useful as a record of ideas proposed and suggestions made in the course of the project. (Some advisors review these summaries carefully when making the final evaluation of the project.)

## Meeting with Your Advisor

Although the pattern of the discussion is normally set by the advisor, once the student is well into his research, meetings will usually cover the topics indicated in the previous section. The advisor wants to know what you have done, what significant problems (if any) you have encountered, and what you intend to do next. Don't just walk in and drop a six-inch stack of computer output on your advisor's desk and proudly announce that this is what you have done since the last meeting. Rather, you should summarize what has been accomplished and outline how you propose to proceed. And it is usually a good idea to solicit the advisor's comments and suggestions. If you have made little or no progress since the previous meeting, say so. Your advisor should not be forced to waste time in a lengthy probe to find out what has and what has not been done. This just makes it more difficult for him to advise effectively, and it is unpleasant for both of you. Further, if you try to bluff your way through, you are likely to lose the advisor's confidence.

You should describe any problem areas you have encountered and whatever corrective action (if any) you can suggest. Often, of course, you will not be in a position to suggest the best remedy. So draw upon your advisor's knowledge and experience as problems arise. On some kinds of questions, he may give direct answers. But on others, he may not. As the project concerns a research problem for which the answer is not known—you are breaking new ground and adding something to knowledge in the field—the advisor simply may not know the answers to all questions that might be asked. He will usually suggest factors to be considered, articles to be read, or other possible avenues to the answer. Sometimes he may send you to another faculty member for consultation if a specific problem is outside his primary area. But whatever the source, guidance is usually intended to help you to find the needed information or to prevent you from spending too much time on an unproductive effort. Your advisor hopes to catch small problems before they become big ones which waste your time. But he cannot, of course, do this unless you tell him what you have encountered.

## Scheduled Meetings

If your advisor schedules regular meeting times, be certain to be at the appointed place on time. If you cannot be there, you should inform him well in advance. Advisors usually have a good many other things to do, and missed appointments are a gross waste of their time. In addition to infuriating the advisor, they adversely affect his evaluation of the student's professionalism and his general competence.

Even though your advisor schedules meetings, you should not hesitate to contact him if you need his advice at other times. It's foolish to delay a project for several days while awaiting a scheduled meeting with your advisor.

## Unscheduled Meetings

Sometimes an advisor does not schedule regular meetings but prefers to be contacted as the student feels the need to see him. He may simply ask that the student come in from time to time with a progress report and that he drop in to discuss any substantial problems as they arise. If the student does not keep him current, the advisor may contact the student.

If your advisor prefers to work in this way, you are not relieved of the responsibility of keeping him informed or of seeking his advice when it is needed. He probably decided not to set regular meeting dates in order to insure that you would feel free to contact him as problems arise. He may feel that this greater flexibility allows you to better demonstrate initiative while still permitting him to monitor your progress adequately. So keep him informed about your progress, and contact him when you have a problem.

## Committee Meetings

Your advisor may schedule a meeting with the full thesis committee from time to time (perhaps once per quarter). One meeting may be scheduled soon after the problem has been closely defined, and one or more others later when you are well into the research. In these meetings, you will usually be expected to explain the exact problem (and any changes in scope since the last committee meeting), the approach, the progress to date, and any major problems encountered since the last meeting. Your advisor will already be familiar with most of the material to be covered and will set the ground rules for the meeting. For the convenience of the committee members, you may be expected to provide them with an outline of the topics to be discussed. This kind of meeting is not usually handled as an oral examination—you are not "grilled"—but as an exchange of information in which you bring the committee members up to date on the status of the project. They can then ask questions or make suggestions. Because their specializations usually differ somewhat from the advisor's, committee members are sometimes able to suggest relevant research studies that have been missed in the bibliographic search, provide comments that help to solve problems, or even suggest key ideas that may open new doors in the overall research effort. Although these meetings may last only half an hour, they can be very helpful in clarifying your overall perspective of what you are doing and what you should do.

## Generalizations

Here are a few points to keep in mind about working with your advisor:

1. Your advisor wants to do his job effectively, and he wants you to be successful.

2. Don't bother your advisor with trivia; you are supposed to demonstrate that you can make decisions and carry out the project. You are not supposed to be his technician.

3. When a real problem does arise, discuss it with your advisor. Describe the problem and (if you are in a position to do so) any ideas you may have about possible courses of action.

4. Even if your advisor does not schedule meetings, it is your responsibility to keep him informed. Students who get into difficulty and waste time are usually the ones who do not keep in contact with their advisors. Don't disappear into the laboratory for a month at a time. COMMUNICATE with your advisor about your project; that's what he's for!

5. When your advisor makes a comment or a suggestion, *pay attention to what he says!* While he may not have a Nobel Prize, he is competent in his field; that is why he is an advisor. And while you may some day win a Nobel Prize, you are still learning to be competent in your field.

6. Finally, if you insist upon being a "loner"—good luck. You'll need it. You are the one who will be in jeopardy—not your advisor.

## REVIEWING THE LITERATURE

Usually, a bibliographic search has been made and a review of the literature is well under way (if not almost complete) by the time the thesis proposal is written. Background reading in the general problem area has been done, and reports and articles describing any studies generally similar to the one proposed have been read. If you have not reviewed the relevant literature before writing your proposal, you cannot define the problem with the certainty that it has not already been handled, and you may be unaware of research methods found to be effective in solving problems similar to your own.

Researchers in science and engineering are often accused of being too anxious to get into the laboratory to start working on their problems and unwilling to spend enough time at the outset to find out whether the work needs to be done in the first place. Stories of overlapping or duplicated research abound. More than one student has been well into his research before discovering that the problem he is working on has already been solved. When this happens, valuable time is lost as the problem is altered or a completely new one chosen and researched. If the duplication is not caught until after the project is completed, it can be very embarrassing for all concerned (the wheel has been reinvented for the forty-seventh time). A full discussion of how a bibliographic search is made is beyond the scope of this book. The subject is usually considered at some length in courses in research methods, in thesis seminars, and sometimes in courses in technical writing. If such courses are available to you, it would be well to take them. Because the materials available in different libraries vary substantially, only a general approach to bibliographic research can be presented here.

You have probably done considerable library research in some of your previous course work, and you should be familiar with the basic research tools—card catalogs, lists of periodicals, and indexes—and their locations. If you haven't done so recently, review the general arrangement of the library and the location of the materials you are most likely to be using. Most libraries publish simple brochures describing the arrangement of the holdings and research tools, and many libraries schedule tours at regular intervals. Using such aids can save you a great deal of time later on, and you may discover some very convenient sources that you would otherwise miss.

In early discussions, your faculty advisor will probably suggest several point-of-departure readings to provide general background on your problem area. You should read and discuss these and other materials before making a commitment to a problem area. Your advisor may suggest particular journals or indexes as likely sources of pertinent information. If he does not, ask both your advisor and the other members of your thesis committee to suggest specific readings as well as journals and indexes to be searched. You might also look over the library's list of periodical holdings as well as its indexes for other periodicals that might be helpful. But be certain to take ten minutes to read the prefatory material describing the use of an index before using it in your search. The publishers usually explain just what materials are covered, how the materials are arranged, and how a listing is to be read. If a given index does not cover the publications in your field, put it back on the shelf and find one or more that do. Regrettably, people have been known to spend hours of diligent effort searching through the wrong indexes.

Because so much research in science and technology is either carried out or funded by the government, indexes of government research reports should not be overlooked; the indexes of the National Technical Information Service, the Defense Documentation Center, the National Aeronautics and Space Administration, and other government agencies may prove to be prime sources of information about recent research (reports are often issued long before articles describing the research can be published). Conference proceedings of meetings of the major professional societies are another excellent source of early reports of research in progress or just completed. These often include scores or hundreds of papers describing recent research results; many of these will not be published elsewhere, and it may be a year or more after the meeting before any of them appear in the professional journals. *Dissertation Abstracts International* is, of course, the prime source for information about doctoral dissertations in all fields and for some master's theses.

You may be able to arrange access to automated searches of one or more major data bases—there are many of these (DDC, CA/C, TOXLINE, NTIS, and others) and both their coverage and number are increasing steadily. Ask your faculty advisor and the librarian about them. There is usually a charge for the search, but it can save hours of thumbing through indexes, and you may well discover materials that would otherwise be missed. If your project is part of one that is funded by an outside agency, the cost of the search will probably be absorbed as part of the project funding.

When you have followed up the leads provided by your faculty advisor, committee, and others, and you have searched through the appropriate indexes, you may discover that you have found little that is directly pertinent to your specific research problem. On the other hand, you may have developed an almost overwhelming list of books, articles, theses, conference papers, technical reports, and other materials bearing on a relatively restricted problem area. As you read some of them, you will probably find that most contain bibliographies citing ten, twenty, or a hundred other sources. So some judgment is often called for in deciding which material to locate and read, as you won't be able to read and absorb everything. After you have done some reading, you'll get a feeling for what has been done, how it was done, and which studies are of most interest to your research. Coverage may become repetitive, so you may decide to restrict the breadth of your reading and focus only on those materials that hold particular promise of direct applicability to your exact problem and the methods you will use in your research. (At this point you will strongly appreciate the value of well-written abstracts that give the reader exact statements of material covered.) Your faculty advisor can be of considerable help in narrowing the reading.

As you read the items selected and take appropriate notes, remember to record full bibliographic information. If you don't, you may have to locate the items again when the time comes to write your thesis and cite your sources. This can cause a needless waste of several hours at a time when you have a good many other things to do. The form and content of bibliographic information are discussed in Chapter 13.

After you have made the primary search, your reading will probably continue throughout the project, but at a much reduced rate. You will review current issues of the most fruitful journals as they appear, scan conference proceedings, and perhaps find and read items that could not be located before. And your advisor may suggest additional readings as problems are encountered.

A search of the literature takes time, and most of us do not enjoy spending hours searching through indexes or looking for pertinent articles, reports, or other publications. But the importance of a thorough bibliographic search cannot be overstated. Advisors often feel that students just do not use libraries and librarians effectively. Some students almost seem to believe that if they don't trip over a pile of reports relating directly to their subject, there aren't any. Remember, the purpose of the search is not only to find out whether the exact problem has been investigated but also to find out whether anything at all like it has been done. In addition to building background in the overall subject area, you should develop ideas about research methods, factors to be considered, and methods of analysis from the material you read.

## OTHER PREPARATIONS

It is usually a good idea to take stock of the whole situation before you plunge in and begin doing research. If any time at all has passed since your proposal and schedule were prepared, review them to make sure that you have the full sequence in mind. Make certain that the overall procedure is broken down into smaller steps that can be accomplished in the planned sequence. Psychologists suggest that it is better to attempt a lengthy or complicated project one chunk at a time than to approach it as a single undifferentiated whole. There is a sense of accomplishment as intermediate goals are met—this builds confidence and adds to drive—and difficulty with a single step is isolated so it doesn't seem quite so overwhelming. Besides, any further analysis that is done usually results in better planning and less difficulty along the way.

If you will be working in a laboratory or with a computer, make certain that you introduce yourself to the people in charge and that you make whatever arrangements may be necessary for access, work space, charging out tools and materials, and the like. Familiarize yourself with the laboratory rules; more will be said about this shortly. Walk through the area and become familiar with the facilities available to you. If you are to work with equipment, make sure that it is available and operable—do this even if only a month has passed since you checked it on a preliminary survey.

If you need materials or equipment that are not on hand, order them or make certain that they are ordered. If possible, order somewhat more materials than you think you will need. It's usually better to order enough material to make one more sample than you need than to take a chance on having only enough to make one less than you need. Follow up on all orders regularly to make sure that purchase orders have actually been written and to determine promised dates of delivery. Your advisor's experience and that of laboratory personnel can be invaluable here. If the general procedure and the analysis of required materials and equipment were well worked out in the thesis proposal, you can—and should—order everything that will be needed from outside sources as soon as the project is approved. If necessary orders are not written early in the project or if delivery is slow (procurement often takes three months or more), it may be necessary to alter your schedule—you can't very well run tests on samples that have not arrived. Some waiting time may be used to advantage on other parts of the research, in making drawings, or writing parts of the report. But if it becomes apparent that procurement times will be unusually long and cannot be shortened, it will do no good to mark time while grinding your teeth and praying for a miracle. Try to modify your project so that you will not need the item concerned (remember to cancel the order) or, if this is not possible, pick a new project. This may be hard to do, but it's better than waiting month after frustrating month for something that has not arrived and may never arrive.

## WORKING IN A LABORATORY

If you are working in a laboratory, you should obtain a copy of the laboratory operating rules at the outset, acquaint yourself with them, and follow them whenever you work there. A good many projects may be in process at the same time, and without compliance to common ground rules it would be impossible for them all to progress safely and efficiently. Specific local rules differ, but the following general principles usually apply:

1. In some laboratories you may be allowed to work only during specified hours, while in others you may be issued a key and allowed to work at any time that does not conflict with scheduled demonstrations. In either case, your work should always be conducted in such a manner that it does not interfere with others. If you are issued a key, you are, of course, expected to make sure that the laboratory is locked when you leave after regular laboratory hours.

2. Maintain your assigned work area in a neat and orderly manner. In addition to eliminating possible safety hazards to yourself and others, this is simply good laboratory practice. Janitorial service is often limited or nonexistent. Janitors, quite properly, are reluctant to touch any equipment or apparatus with which they are not familiar and which may be delicate or dangerous. Anyway, you probably wouldn't want anyone making uneducated guesses about how far they should go in cleaning your area or what would or would not affect your apparatus. So it's up to you to keep your own area and equipment clean.

3. The fact that your laboratory has a given piece of equipment does not guarantee that it will be available and working when you need it. Other students may be working on projects that require some of the apparatus you will be using—air supply, shock tube, wind tunnel, or one-of-a-kind items. Make a serious effort to find out whether this is the case, and work out a schedule that will accommodate everyone's needs. Laboratory technicians can be a great help in ensuring that what you need is available and operable when you need it.

4. Follow established patterns in checking out tools, equipment, and materials. Use them only for the purposes for which they were intended, and return them when you are through with them. Do not hoard things you are not using—this may deprive someone else of something he needs. Do not take tools or materials from someone else's work area without his permission or that of the responsible laboratory technician. NEVER remove tools or equipment from the laboratory without the specific permission of the persons responsible for them.

5. Be certain that you are familiar with the proper handling of delicate, dangerous, or complicated equipment before attempting to set it up or operate it. Be especially careful in handling meters, oscilloscopes, recorders, optical glassware, transducers, balances, cameras, and other delicate items. If you are at all uncertain about a piece of equipment, ask the laboratory technician—not another student who may not know any more about it than you do.

6. Inform the responsible laboratory technician whenever you will be working with hazardous material of any kind. Do not work with such materials unless someone else is present near your work area through-

out the time concerned. It is common sense to follow this practice whether or not it is required.

7. Laboratory technicians are usually very helpful in providing information about the use of equipment, and they may help assemble and check apparatus. They should not be asked to clean up your work area or to return tools or equipment to their proper locations. That is *your* job and no one else's. So do it.

It may seem almost insulting to list these points for anyone qualified to work on a thesis project, but no apology is offered. The way in which you carry out your work in the laboratory reflects upon you and the quality of your project. People who continually violate laboratory rules are sometimes banned from the laboratory—as indeed they should be. They are a nuisance as well as being a hazard to themselves and to others around them, and they have no business attempting to do laboratory research.

## RECORDS

Most research workers—like others experienced in working on almost any kind of substantial project—maintain written records of progress as it occurs. On large projects, such as building a dam or a nuclear reactor, these records provide the basis for the many necessary justifications, evaluations, and progress reports as the project develops. On most thesis projects, it is a good idea to keep a running record of what is done and why it is done at the time that it is done. This can make writing the report much easier and may make the report more complete and accurate. It's not easy to remember in April just which of the December test runs were made at 475° C and which at 500° C, or whether it was after the twentieth or the twenty-second run that the shock tube was modified. Further, a good record can be used to preserve insights and ideas about the project—and about other possible projects—as they occur. If these are not written down immediately, they are likely to be forgotten in the press of completing the research and writing the report.

The form of the record and the way it is maintained may vary, but it is usually a good idea to keep it all in one place—even if this means only that all papers relating to the project are put in the same desk drawer. Some advisors suggest (and some require) that a complete laboratory notebook be maintained with regular dated entries, and they may want to see it from time to time as the project progresses. (This is probably more common in design or experimental projects than in programming or theoretical projects.) The student may even be issued a laboratory notebook (some sort of bound book—not loose leaf) and required to return it with his report at the completion of the project. When a follow-on study is to be done, this can be invaluable.

Because so many projects involve the use of computers, and computers can generate so much material so quickly, two comments on records relating to them must be made. First, be certain to mark your card decks (both program and data) at the time you use them and annotate your computer output at the time it is generated. Record the date, test number, program number, and any other identifying information on both the decks and the output. Review the output and comment directly on it at the time it is generated. A week (or a month) later you will have forgotten these details, and it may take considerable time and effort to reconstruct just which input deck and which data produced which output. You may need to verify or to repeat a calculation, and you will certainly have to identify your results exactly in the report. Five minutes spent marking decks and output when you use (or generate) them can save hours of your time and a great deal of wasted motion later.

Second, while it is generally a good practice to save everything generated in the project, some judgment must be applied concerning computer output (unless your family happens to own a large warehouse). Usually, for example, it is not necessary to save the output from all debugging runs. If you do, your desk and work area will become hopelessly cluttered. But the output that you do save should be annotated and filed (stacked) in some readily findable manner.

Whatever the form of the records maintained, they should contain the detail of everything that is done. Advisors often observe that students just do not keep adequate records and that this is one thing that they *must* learn to do. The records are the basis for the analysis to be done and the conclusions to be drawn. The importance of records to the report to be written cannot be overemphasized. The records might include wiring diagrams, circuit analyses, schematics, photographs, justification of assumptions made or reasons for using given procedures, calibration procedures, results of test runs, ideas about the validity of data or other data that might be developed, computer programs, references, outlines of material read, copies of requisitions for materials, calculations, records of telephone calls, summaries of discussions with the advisor, or anything else generated in the course of the project. Sketches or rough drawings of possible illustrations for use in the report are often made as the ideas occur so that they will not be forgotten later in the rush to get the report written. Some advisors even suggest that the student should write down everything he thinks about the project. In the end, the records may very well be thicker than the thesis report itself. But it doesn't take much longer to glue, clip, or note everything in one place or to put it in a desk drawer than it does to toss it in a wastebasket. And when the time comes to write the report, it's much easier to skip over unneeded material in a laboratory notebook than it is to redevelop calculations that were not preserved or to search out a calibration procedure that did not seem important at the time it was followed. So save everything (with the exception of the computer output specifically noted above). Anything you don't need can be disposed of later.

## SNARES TO BE AVOIDED

Once you get into your research, keep at it. The project should be something you work on just about every day. An occasional day away from it can be good for your perspective, but a weekend camping trip here and a few days at the beach there can soon add up to quite a bit of time in which nothing is accomplished. So even when there are other things that must be done, try to spend a little time on the project every day. When you come to a difficult part of the project, don't procrastinate—don't kid yourself into believing that you are analyzing your approach or reviewing your theory when actually you are avoiding a decision or just plain loafing. Keep on schedule. No elves are going to come in the night to complete your apparatus or debug your computer program.

There is, of course, no "right" path for everyone to follow in doing their research. But there are typical missteps and general areas in which time is often wasted or misspent. The following are a few of the most common. Try to avoid them:

1. *Spending too much time attempting to plan perfect procedures, designs, or apparatus or making close theoretical analyses of insignificant details.* While analysis and planning are necessary, you will reach a point of diminishing returns. Then you should quit thinking about it and do something. Jump in and try a calculation or a test run. If it doesn't work, at least you'll have hard information about that one and something to improve on. For example, you could spend years reading about turbulence, boundary layers, lift factors, and associated matters. But you can never be certain how well a radical new airfoil design will work until you test one in a wind tunnel. And when you do, you may discover things that would not have been found if you'd spent another year reading and theorizing. So make one and test it. If it doesn't work as you hope, you have a solid starting point for the next one.

   The converse of this, of course, is failure to take any time at all to analyze factors affecting a problem and the likely possible results of actions that could be taken—failure to figure out what should be done. Some students seem reluctant even to pull out their slide rules or hand calculators and compute a few approximations. This, of course, wastes time and effort (and sometimes materials) and can be very discouraging as test after test fails.

   The middle ground that everyone seeks is to analyze the problem, decide upon the proper course of action, and then follow it. Most people think that they are on the middle ground most of the time. But when you are close to the situation, it can be hard to tell. Your faculty advisor, with his greater experience, should be helpful here as he is farther from the immediate problem and should have a broader perspective.

2. *Failing to check or calibrate instrumentation before using it.* If data runs are made, parameters are changed, or an apparatus altered, butchered, or dismantled before you discover that one instrument was not working properly, you won't know whether any of the data are valid. The entire procedure will have to be repeated, and this may cost you weeks or even months. Check out instrumentation each time

you use it. With some instrumentation, it is important to calibrate both before and after taking data. If the calibration has changed during use, the data are suspect.

3. *Failing to check the data before all of it has been collected.* It is often a good idea to reduce and analyze some of the data early in the collection process. Correction to procedures may be in order before the time and effort are spent in collecting the full complement. If data collected is vastly different from what was expected, don't fudge it. You may have made an error somewhere along the line, so recheck your original calculations, your computer program, your instrumentation, or whatever else may be involved. If you cannot find an error, set your material aside and then recheck it again the next day. If you still don't find an error, you may have discovered something new. But when data do not fit the basic laws, something is usually wrong. If you put ten bananas into one end of a system, ten bananas-worth of output should come out the other end. If only nine come out, there is probably a leak in the system. If eleven come out, your counter may not be working properly. Or, of course, there is the odd chance that you may actually have discovered how to turn ten bananas into eleven.

4. *Spending too much time on the first concrete thing to be done on the project.* During some of your research, you may feel a little uneasy about what you are doing—may not be certain that you are doing the right thing in just the right way. So when the time comes to do something that seems solid, that you are sure is right, and that you do well, you may overdo it—spend more time on it (polishing samples, calibrating equipment, making trivial improvements to apparatus, formating computer output, perfecting drawings) than is warranted. This is a comfortable activity, and you may not want to return to the uneasiness of the next step—so you keep at it. This is like digging the excavation for a building much larger than it needs to be because you like to dig but you don't like laying the foundation or building the walls or the roof. But the walls and the roof have to be built, so get on with it. You'll never complete the project if you don't proceed to the next step.

5. *Refusing to broaden, alter, or further limit the project once you start the research.* The thesis proposal was made on the basis of what you thought would happen in the project and how much you thought you could accomplish. Once you get into the research, it may become evident that some of the factors bearing upon the problem were not apparent at the outset, or wholly unexpected difficulties may be encountered. So it may be necessary to further limit the scope of the research or to alter the approach as you progress. There is no point in wasting your time attempting to solve a problem that cannot be solved in the time available or with the facilities open to you. On the other hand, the research may move more rapidly than anticipated, and you may be able to broaden the scope of the project. Don't squan-

der available research time by making additional tests or running additional calculations to prove something that you have already proven. In any case, don't hesitate to discuss possible revision of the original objectives with your advisor or to modify them if it seems warranted.

Because so many thesis projects involve the use of computers, a few of the common snares concerning their use should be noted:

1. *Not taking necessary course work in programming.* Don't count on figuring out how to write a program when the time comes to do it. No matter how bright you are, this just doesn't work. Take the course work and save yourself considerable humiliation and lost time.

2. *Failing to allow enough time for writing and debugging a program.* Almost invariably, this takes longer than it seems it should. On even a simple program, ten or fifteen passes may be necessary in the debugging process. And the computer is not always available and running.

3. *Not including enough debugging statements when developing a program.* This can be a little tedious, and a debugging statement may seem to be an admission of possible error. But it can save time in the end. With provision for optional intermediate output spaced through the program, it is easy to recognize gross errors and locate and correct their causes. The debugging statements can be removed later if it is necessary (usually it isn't).

4. *Relying too much on the ability of the computer to generate quantities of numbers; not putting enough planning into designing the program or selecting the conditions or cases to be tested.* The huge quantities of numbers that can easily be generated will not substitute for quality in planning—the thinking time spent before using the computer is the most valuable. It may be faster and results may be more significant if three possible critical orbits of a satellite are simulated than if thirty-eight others chosen for convenience are used. Don't just generate piles of output; test the right things about the proper cases.

5. *Taking computer output at face value without even a cursory check.* Ask yourself whether the results make sense. If possible, run through a simple problem with a known solution and see what the program gives you.

6. *Spending too much time refining the format of the output.* Usually, nobody but you will see it, anyway. The simplest way is generally the best way.

7. *Becoming enamored of the computer—computer worship.* Some students become a real burden to everyone by tying up the system. Computer time is not free, and it is not a sin if you don't use all of the authorized time. It is very easy to spend so much time playing with the possibilities of reams of output, plots, and peripheral information that can be generated that everything else on the project falls

behind schedule and the due dates are not met. If this seems to be happening, stay away from the computer for a few days or you'll be hooked beyond recovery—a confirmed dataholic.

## ENDING THE RESEARCH

The approach of thesis due dates is often accompanied by certainty that fate is intervening to prevent proper completion of the project. As time runs out, work may become hurried and quality may suffer. Few people are really satisfied that they have done all they could or should do on their projects, and there is a natural tendency to want to run just one more correlation or to try just one more compound. The schedule may have slipped because of delays in receiving of materials, problems in the theoretical development, difficulties in the computer simulation, balky equipment, approaches that just did not produce usable results, or for any of a dozen other reasons. Often the information generated will not answer the problem originally addressed in the thesis proposal, or, at any rate, not all of it. But at some point you have to stop the research, complete the analysis, and write the report. Remember, the final draft must be accepted by the date specified by your university or the degree will not be granted until the next graduation. It takes time just to write the report, let alone put it into acceptable final form and meet other requirements. The less time you have to do this, the sloppier the first draft becomes and the more likely it is that you will not be able to complete an acceptable final draft on time. Further, the more hurried you are in your writing, the less likely it is that your report will reflect the value of your work. So when you have done as much as you can in the time available and your advisor suggests that it is sufficient, the time has come to write your report.

# 4

# Preparing the Report

Few people really enjoy writing theses or other technical reports, but when research has been completed, a report must usually be written. If you have never written a substantial report before, it may seem like a pretty monumental task, and it does take planning and effort. But if you think it out first and then go about the job in an organized manner, it shouldn't be too difficult to produce an acceptable report in reasonable time. And although one writer will work differently from another, the suggestions in this chapter should provide perspective on the overall job of preparing the report.

## THE DRAFTS

Usually, two complete drafts of the report are written. Where exceptional difficulties are encountered and a major rewriting is required, a third may be necessary. The names given the drafts vary from place to place, but here they will be called the first draft (given to the advisor and committee for comment) and the final draft (given to the school to meet the degree requirements). Normally, the first draft is submitted to the advisor about three weeks or a month before the due date for the final draft. Usually, the advisor and the other members of the thesis committee read and comment on the draft, which is then returned to the student. If the comments are lengthy or a substantial revision of the draft seems in order, the advisor usually discusses the suggestions with the student in some detail. The student then incorporates the suggestions and prepares the final draft for submission to the advisor by the date on which it is due.

Because practice varies from department to department and sometimes even from advisor to advisor, be certain that you understand which draft is to be evaluated or whether both are to be considered. Some advisors take the position that the first draft should represent the student's best effort

34

and should be the copy evaluated because the changes incorporated in the final draft are essentially suggestions by the advisor and other committee members. Others prefer to accept a less perfect first draft and base their evaluation of the report wholly (or almost wholly) on the final product. Still others consider both. So it is important that you know the local ground rules, as you will probably have to make a good many small compromises between time and quality as your due dates approach. But it should be recognized that the better the first draft is written, the easier it is to prepare the final draft.

## EARLY WRITING

Almost universally, advisors say that students do not start writing soon enough. It takes time to write a technical report on a research project, and editing, typing, and producing a reasonably decent draft takes more time. If you try to cram all of this into a few days at the end of the project, the coverage is apt to be uneven, the organization weak, and the expression faulty. The job of rewriting to produce an acceptable final draft in time to meet the due dates may be impossible. So there simply is no substitute for writing as much as you can as soon as you can, and few other things can contribute more to producing a well-written report or to reducing panic as due dates approach.

An additional (if unwelcome) benefit sometimes results from beginning the writing early in the project. Weaknesses in theoretical development, testing, data taken, analysis, or other parts of the research are sometimes exposed when the attempt is made to describe them exactly. If you begin writing early enough, time may be available for further testing, analysis, or whatever other action may be necessary to correct any deficiencies you discover.

Much of the first draft can be written in rough form as the research is performed—and this is usually the best time to do it. When you make your theoretical analysis and develop your basic equations, you will write the essentials down anyway—so if you expand the development just a bit (you have the intricate details and logical sequences in mind at the time), you will have written the full theoretical development. When you finally get your apparatus together and working, write the description and include any necessary drawings, diagrams, and photographs (it is good practice to include a few more than you think you will need). You have the apparatus before you then, and you have just solved any tricky problems in the design, assembly, and calibration—so this is the time that it will be easiest to write in full detail. It is fresh in your mind and all notes are at hand; nothing has been lost, and the equipment has not been butchered or damaged. When you decide upon the parameters to be varied in your computer program and the values to be used, write the description down. This is the time that you have the exact definitions well in mind, and writing them down will probably supply a needed check on the overall logic anyway—just as a good problem analysis is an effective check on the approach to the project as a whole—and the writing may turn up modifications that should be made. On many problems, half or two-thirds of the draft can easily be written before the research is complete. Experimental procedures, equipment and apparatus, theoretical development, or basic assumptions will not be changed by the analysis of data, so they can very well be written before the analysis has been completed.

You cannot, of course, be certain just how individual pieces written far in advance will fit together when the first draft is prepared. Some may have to be shortened, some may be joined with other material in writing full sections of the report, some may be placed in appendices, and some may not be used at all. It will be necessary to add introductions, transitional material, and further explanations. But if you get substantial parts of the main body of the discussion down on paper while the details are fresh in your mind, the job of tailoring the parts to make your first draft is comparatively easy. It doesn't take long to write a description of test runs made during the week just past, and the more such "chunks" you have, the easier it is to produce your first draft when the time comes.

As the "chunks" are produced, they may be placed in your laboratory notebook for safekeeping, or a "dummy" report may be started. A dummy is a collection of the parts of a report thus far completed, and it is usually kept in a loose leaf notebook—this facilitates adding to and rearranging the content and the substitution of new material when a given part is rewritten. If a dummy is started, a tentative outline of the thesis is often placed in it, and individual sections and subsections are checked off as they are written. As the dummy grows, blank pages may be placed in the appropriate places to identify sections, illustrative material, or appendixes not yet written. Thus, by looking at the outline and leafing through the material, you are always aware of what is yet to be written and what illustrative material is yet to be prepared. Further, as you work with the dummy, faults in organization, content, and expression become obvious, and they can be modified with comparative ease before the first draft is put together and submitted.

## PLANNING THE REPORT

As your research progresses, you will inevitably give some thought to the report that you will write: What information is necessary? What is unnecessary? How should the information be arranged and presented? You will probably develop some solid ideas about the main sections needed, their sequence, and their coverage. It's a good idea to jot these ideas down (perhaps in rough outline form) as they occur.

The most common patterns of organization and content are described in Chapters 9 through 12 of this book, and these patterns should be helpful in developing a tentative outline. If you didn't do so during your search of the literature, you should certainly review the organization of several theses reporting on projects of the same general kind as your own. A number of these should be available both in your departmental and university libraries.

Your advisor may ask to see a rough outline of the intended organization of the report (indicating at least the sequence of main sections and appendixes and the general content of each) or, perhaps, a more detailed outline at about the end of the quarter prior to the one in which the degree is expected. He may discuss the outline with you at some length to make sure that the report will represent the project effectively. If your advisor does not ask to see an outline, it will probably be to your advantage to make one and discuss it with him anyway to make sure that your plan for developing the report is not completely at variance with his own ideas about the general strategy of organization. In effect, if your advisor agrees with the sequence and coverage of the outline, he approves the basic engineering of the report that will result. While you can't anticipate all details of your development, you will be able to proceed with the knowledge that the intended approach appears to be generally acceptable. But the outline should not be regarded as an inviolable plan. You may decide to revise it as the sections are written and you see how they fit together.

All advisors will agree that the main development of the research should be described in the text and that supporting detail that would interrupt the flow of the text or that would be of interest to only a few readers should be placed in appendixes. But opinions may differ on the specifics of what should be in the text and what in the appendixes of a particular thesis. There may be disagreement about where the cutoff point should be and just which information is part of the main development and which is supporting detail. Considerable rewriting and rearrangement of material can be avoided if you can gauge your advisor's preferences before going too far in putting your rough draft together. In addition to showing him an outline, you might ask him to suggest two or three well-written theses describing projects more or less like your own and, perhaps, two or three that he considers not to be well-written. In glancing through them you will get a good impression of his preferences about arranging the material, as well as other points that you might not have thought to inquire about.

Further, both major and minor revisions to the first draft may be reduced if you write the main development sections of the report first and your advisor comments on them as they are written. Many advisors are willing to review and comment upon some or all parts of the report as they are written—some will even insist upon it. This can be a great help to both the student and the advisor. The student is provided with feedback on the general acceptability of his organization and expression, he is able to take this into account in writing succeeding sections, and he has more time than would otherwise be available to modify his material in accordance with the comments. The advisor is alerted to any possible problems in the writing and is relieved of the necessity of commenting fully on the whole report in a very short time when the rough draft is received. Further, fewer comments should be necessary on the later sections, as they will have been written in the light of comments previously made. This does not mean that the advisor dictates the report to the student, who merely acts as a secretary. The student retains responsibility for the end product. But advisors often maintain that the student who does not submit at least a few sections for review as they are produced is the one who has to do the most rewriting later.

Some advisors prefer not to receive parts of the thesis as they are written. In some cases (particularly on projects which are parts of larger "open-ended projects"—projects that may never be completed but on which a series of students make progress), somewhat less can be written ahead of time, and the advisor may feel that comment on those portions would not be of substantial help to the student. Or the advisor may feel that he cannot comment with assurance on a part of a complex report until he sees the whole; suggestions concerning one section may be affected by the way in which others are organized and presented. Comment on individual sections is virtually impossible for the advisor when the student has not shown him a complete outline or when there has been no discussion of the content and development of the report. It is difficult enough for the advisor to provide helpful comment on an individual section; when he is not sure how or where the section will fit into the report or what explanatory material will precede it, it is almost impossible.

## WRITING THE FIRST DRAFT

The sections of the first draft are not necessarily written in the order in which they will appear in the complete report. Usually, it is easier and more efficient to write parts of the main development and some of the appendixes first—perhaps even before the exact content and sequencing of information in all other sections have been firmly established. It has been pointed out that the description of procedures used, theoretical development, review of the literature, and other parts of the report should be "roughed out" as these things are accomplished, and that this is usually well before the research is completed or the final outline determined. When much of the writing is done in advance, there may be no readily identifiable point at which the preparation of the first draft begins—the research simply diminishes and ends as the writing progresses. One blends into the other. When all of the parts have been put into draft form and necessary tailoring has been done to ensure that each is properly introduced and that the transitions between parts are effective, the first draft is ready for editing and typing.

As you begin writing, it is a good idea to have departmental and university deadlines well in mind, and you should obtain and read carefully whatever specifications there may be for the final report (paper, typing, binding, illustrations, and other matters of format and presentation). If anything in the specifications is not clear to you, inquire about it in your department or at the graduate school. If you understand the specifications and have them readily available from the beginning, you can follow the accepted practices as you write and perhaps eliminate the necessity of modifying the entire text later.

## Outlining

When you are ready to write a section, be certain that you know what you want to cover and the sequence in which you want to cover it before you start writing. If you haven't already made a fairly detailed outline of the section to be written, you should make one. If you made a detailed outline earlier, go over it to make sure that the coverage is complete and that the sequence is effective. Your ideas may have changed since you made the outline.

An outline is simply a list of the topics to be covered in the order in which they will be discussed. It is a tool used in writing, a guide to be followed—nothing more. If you were going to build an airplane (or a lawnmower or a nuclear reactor or almost anything else) you wouldn't just order a few tons of material and start cutting, bending, machining, welding, and riveting. Among other things, you would develop a design first and make detailed drawings specifying the parts needed, how they should be made, and how they should be assembled. If the design was faulty, the parts wouldn't fit together properly, some would probably be forgotten, and the airplane wouldn't fly. In making an outline you are, in effect, engineering the writing—determining in detail just what topics will be covered, the order in which they will be organized, and the information that will be presented about each in the attempt to communicate your subject matter effectively to your reader. It doesn't take long to make and check an outline, and the outline should help you in the following ways:

1. *Ensure complete coverage.* It is much easier and faster to spot possible omissions by running your eye down a topic list several times than it is to catch them by reading and rereading ten or fifteen pages of text. And if an omission is found, it is much easier to pencil new topics into a list than it is to rewrite the text concerned.
2. *Ensure effective order.* Again, it is easier to check sequence from a list than from several pages of text. And it is much easier to change the sequence of items on a list than to move blocks of material around after the section has been written.
3. *Produce a smoother result.* When much material is added or moved by arrows, paste-ons, or inserts, the door is opened to ineffective transition and faulty references. If material is moved from page 3 to page 9, you may forget at the time that some of the material formerly on page 3 was drawn upon on pages 5 and 7. This adds to the editing and rewriting necessary in later drafts as these slips are noticed and corrected. Once material has been moved, it may be difficult to find all of the spots that need touching up and smoothing out.
4. *Save time and effort.* When you write from an outline, you can usually move much faster. You have already determined your sequence and coverage, so it isn't necessary to continually stop to think about them as you write. Further, all of the changes mentioned in the three items above add to both writing time and editing time—and this can really mount up if there are many of them.

5. *Lessen typing difficulties.* If you hand your typist a manuscript full of arrows, paste-ons, and material written on the backs of sheets, you are just making the job more difficult and increasing the likelihood of retyping.

The amount of detail needed in the outline varies with the author and the section to be written. A relatively simple list of main topics may be enough if the section is to describe simple experimental procedures, while a more fully detailed list with subtopics and sub-subtopics may be needed to write a well-organized section reviewing the published literature on a given subject or one presenting a complicated theoretical development. But whatever the case, if you try to write with no outline at all, it is almost certain that the writing will take longer than it should, that it will be badly organized, and that it will require substantial revision. So determine what you want to write before trying to write it.

An outline is not a magic wand, and using one will not eliminate all potential difficulties in the writing, but it should enable you to come a lot closer to effective organization, complete coverage, and good flow of expression on your first writing. If you don't know how to make an outline, see any good book on technical writing. Doubtful students who try using an outline on a section or two often become their most ardent advocates. Professional technical writers almost always use outlines of one kind or another.

## Writing

Having planned the organization and coverage of the material to be written, you are ready to do the actual writing—this is when you actually sit down and "knock it out." Often, this is also when you wish you'd kept a more complete laboratory notebook! It's usually a good idea to do most of your writing in one place—a quiet place with pencils, paper, a dictionary, your laboratory notebook and all other records, and your dummy and any other material previously written readily at hand. You shouldn't have to stop and look for these things when you need them. Try to have at least an hour (preferably longer) available for work each time you sit down to write. (You wouldn't go to the lab and set up equipment to run an experiment if you had only fifteen minutes to work.) If you try to write for only fifteen or twenty minutes at a time, you will probably waste much of the time getting started and produce bits and pieces that do not blend together smoothly without substantial reworking.

If portions of a section were written as the things described were done, or if a dummy was compiled as the research progressed, the writing of a given section may move very quickly. You simply put the various parts in the proper order, write missing subsections, and add introductory and transitional sentences. The section may, in fact, require little more than editing and polishing. If parts were not written in advance, you will have to do the entire job from scratch.

When you start to write, write! Don't just sit at your desk and think about it. If the first sentence of the introductory paragraph does not come easily, skip it and start with the main content of the section. This is usually easier to write anyway, and you can come back and write the introductory material later. Try to write rapidly, to get as much down on paper as you can as quickly as you can. Don't stop to polish your sentences, to review mechanics, or to smooth out transitions as you write. These can be cleaned up later. Generally, if you stop to polish and edit as you go, you will progress very slowly, you will tend to lose perspective on what you are writing (and have to reorient yourself continually), and balance and clarity of expression are likely to suffer.

As the writing develops, there may be spots in which it seems desirable to depart somewhat from the outline. Details may have been omitted when the outline was made or the actual writing of one subsection may suggest a more effective grouping or sequence for some of what is to follow. Fine! Depart from the outline. It is a tool to be used in the writing, not a holy writ that cannot be violated. But if a major departure is to be made, you should make the change on the outline and review its effect on overall balance and sequence before proceeding. Sometimes a convenient regrouping in one place can necessitate a very inconvenient or ineffective regrouping of later material.

If you write for much more than an hour at a time, it will probably be good for your perspective (and for your anatomy) to take a ten-minute break: get up and walk around, have a sandwich or whatever appeals. But don't start watching a ballgame, begin painting a room, or get into a political discussion with a neighbor. Take your ten minutes and then get back to the writing.

When a section has been completed, read it over and add any necessary introductions, transitions, or blocks of material that may have been skipped in the writing. Pieces that seemed difficult at the beginning are usually much easier to write after the bulk of a section has been completed. General expression may be smoothed out and clarified, and obvious mechanical and grammatical slips attended to. Then set the section aside and do something else.

## Revising and Editing

Most writers allow days or weeks to pass before revising and editing their material. This enables them to approach it with a fresh viewpoint and a little more objectivity than would be possible immediately after it was written. You have probably had the experience of rereading something that you wrote a year or more earlier and discovering that it was not at all as well organized or as clearly expressed as you remembered it. You may even have thought something like, "How could I have written that?" This has happened to most of us. The passage of time allows a more critical scrutiny of our own writing —we are able to see faults that were missed earlier. So let each section of your draft age for at least a few days before you return to it for revision and editing. The intervening time can be used to complete research, to work on other sections of the report, to complete illustrations, or to do any of a dozen other things that will have to be done.

When you do reread and edit, be thorough. It is usually desirable to work on at least a whole section at a time so that you can judge the effectiveness of overall organization and note any weakness in coverage that might not be evident if smaller parts were read separately. In reviewing, do not read a section through expecting to catch everything that needs correction in a single pass. This just won't work. Instead, go through the section several times looking for specific things each time. To the extent that it is possible, it is probably most efficient to find and correct faults that require substantial rewriting first and then look for smaller faults on succeeding readings. Just how many times a given section is reread may depend on what it is, how much you find to correct, and how rushed you are.

On the first reading, you might consider the overall organization and content of the section and make any necessary major additions, deletions, or alterations. It would probably be best to reread the entire report at once to check organization, but that is not usually possible at this stage—it hasn't all been written. So work with as much of it at a time as you can. If your outline was carefully made, there should be few major changes—but the passage of time sometimes brings new insights. Keep in mind that the report should be comprehensible to a reader who has no prior knowledge of the project— even though your advisor and committee members are obviously quite familiar with it. The stage must be properly set for the reader to understand both the report as a whole and the individual topics presented. Pay particular attention to sectional introductions (often very weak) and to transitions between subjects within the section (often lacking). With the section complete, it should be easier to spot gaps between ideas which—however sound the sequence— may cause the reader to wonder why one topic follows another. Fill them in with transitional phrases, sentences, or paragraphs to lead the reader smoothly from one subject to another. Lack of transition is one of the most common faults in first drafts.

On the next reading, you might check the accuracy of all facts and make sure that all equations are correct and all assertions supported. On the third reading, you could give attention to the writing itself: Make sure that the style is consistent, that individual sentences are direct and clear, that they actually say what you intend, and that the expression flows well. On yet another reading, you could concentrate on catching errors in spelling (a red flag to some readers), punctuation, and mechanics. A final reading might be made just to make sure that all corrections have been made and that the overall effect is as you want it. While you may not actually reread each section as often as suggested here, remember that sometime in the future a reader who is totally unfamiliar with the project will be able to read only what you have actually put on paper, not what you meant to say or what you thought you said.

If you are unsure about some of your expression, try reading it aloud. Your ear will sometimes catch faults that your eye misses. And it can be *very* helpful to have someone else read what you have written. Even if he is not familiar with your technical field, another reader will often spot cumbersome or faulty phrasing and simple mechanical errors that you have missed. If someone does read your draft for you and tells you that a passage should be reworked, don't argue with him. You asked him to read it to spot just such problems!

Because the quality of your final report will reflect in some measure upon your faculty advisor, he wants it to be a creditable job. Although his main comments on the draft will be concerned with the technical content and presentation, he will probably also mark patches of vague or confused expression and instances of faulty spelling, mechanics, or punctuation for correction (his acceptance of them would reflect badly upon him). Don't force him to spend his time editing bad writing or proofreading careless typing. He is a professional in his field, not a high school English teacher, and he is likely to react very unfavorably to a report that has been sloppily prepared—however well the research itself may have been done. In fact, if the writing is unusually poor, he may simply give the draft back to you and tell you to clean it up before he will read it.

When you have thoroughly reviewed a section and have made all of the changes you consider necessary, look over the manuscript before giving it to your typist. If some of the pages are unusually cluttered with crossouts, interlineations, arrows, and inserts, copy them over to make the typist's job easier and to eliminate possible causes of error in the typing. This can save you time and money in the end because these are just the pages on which you are likely to find spots of patching that have not been worked smoothly into the text. The more you catch before the draft is typed, the less there will be to correct later.

## WORKING WITH A TYPIST

A good typist can easily make the difference between a neat report comfortably submitted on time and a sloppy report that misses the due date. As a rule, you shouldn't plan on typing your own thesis because you'll have plenty of other things to do. And you shouldn't ask your wife or a personal friend to type it either. You can't demand quite the same perfection from your wife or from a friend that you can from someone who is being paid to do the job. It is important that you locate a good typist early, make your arrangements with her well before you need her services, and then carry out your end of the bargain. A good typist is a skilled professional who can eliminate many potential trouble spots—she may not even tell you how many obvious spelling errors, skipped words, or blunders in format she corrects. Search high and low for a good one, and then treat her with consideration. You need her more than she needs you.

Departmental secretaries often type theses during their off-duty hours, and they can be ideal for the job if they are available. They are usually familiar with university and departmental requirements, they are often experienced in typing theses, they are already familiar with much of the technical language involved, and they know the importance of meeting due dates. When questions come up on small points—they always do—departmental secretaries can often find the answers without waiting to ask the student about them. But if you do arrange to have a departmental secretary type for you, be very careful about taking up her time during her normal working day. Lengthy conversations about your thesis at times when she should be working on departmental business can make you very unpopular with both the secretary and the faculty.

Departments sometimes maintain lists of thesis typists, and the departmental secretaries can often tell you something about the experience and competence of the people listed. Departmental or college bulletin boards are another convenient source of names, but information about the experience of the people listed is not always readily available. Fellow students who are in the process of having their own theses typed may be an ideal source of information, as they can provide first-hand accounts of the competence of their typists. But bear in mind that some students make unreasonable demands of their typists, so unfavorable reports may be grossly exaggerated.

Be sure to consider the following questions when selecting your typist:

1. Does she have all of the symbols you need? If your department requires that all equations be fully typed and your typist does not have some of the symbols you need, you may have difficulty locating the additional symbols (and roughly matching the type style).
2. Is she experienced in typing theses? While experience is not essential, it can save small errors in format which may require retyping.
3. Does she live near you and is she generally accessible? This can be quite important as the final draft is being completed and you have many small odds and ends to correct or complete.

When you have selected a typist, be sure that she knows approximately how long your thesis will be (for her own scheduling purposes) and when she will get the copy. If you don't yet know, make your best guess. Be clear about whether she is to type both the first and final drafts or just one or the other. Most typists charge by the page (whether the page is filled or not), and most charge somewhat more for pages containing typed formulas and equations than for those containing only text. Further, there is usually an additional charge for placing page numbers on substantial numbers of drawings or pages of computer output. So be sure that you understand the basis for computing the cost of the typing and whether this includes any necessary corrections.

The following suggestions can save you time and misunderstandings when the typing is done:

1. Write legibly so that the typist can read what you give her. She has probably never seen your handwriting before and may not be familiar with the technical language in your field. Illegible handwriting is probably the greatest single cause of lost time (and corrections) in the course of having theses typed. Use ink or a pencil

with soft (dark) lead. Be especially careful in writing foreign names and equations. The spacing of equations, the placement of subscripts (keep them down) and superscripts (keep them up), and possible confusion between some Roman and Greek letters (as lowercase "p" and "rho") are major causes of error. Be certain that you use discernible capital letters where you want capital letters and lowercase letters where you want lowercase letters. What you write is usually exactly what you'll get.

2. Be consistent in format—especially in using headings. Don't make the typist guess which are supposed to be main headings, subheadings, or sub-subheadings.

3. Deliver your material to her when you say you will. If she has set aside a week for your thesis and you deliver it two weeks late, you can't expect her to put someone else's work aside to do yours. If you know that yours will be late, call her and let her know. She may be able to shift her schedule.

4. Unless the report is unusually long, try to give the entire draft to the typist at once. This makes it easier for her to put in continuous effort in her available time (she may type faster than you think she can). Remember that you may need to check pages in one section while editing another. If the typist has the pages you need, you will lose time.

5. Take the time to explain the job when you deliver it. Go over anything unusual with her to be certain that she knows what you want. The less guessing she has to do, the less likely she is to guess incorrectly.

6. If she doesn't already have them, give her copies of any departmental or university specifications that may apply to the format she should follow.

7. Allow her adequate time to produce good work. Don't call her every hour to find out how many pages she has typed; you'll just irritate her.

8. Be sure she knows how to reach you in case she has questions. Give her your telephone number and, if you are not always available, tell her when it would be most convenient for her to call.

9. If it is at all possible, keep a copy of the draft while she is preparing the typed copy. This makes it easier to answer questions by telephone. Further, if one of the two is lost or damaged (this occasionally happens), you don't have to rewrite the whole report.

## ILLUSTRATIONS

It takes time to prepare illustrations, and making them can become a real problem—especially if there are many of them or if you have not started writing soon enough. Illustrations should be planned before they are made and, like everything else, the sooner you start, the better. You can have your photographs taken, make rough sketches or layouts, and obtain copies of illustrations to be altered well before you write the text that they will illustrate. And it's a good idea to put them in your lab notebook or your dummy. Rough illustrations should be prepared in detail sufficient to show the size of the illustration, what will be in it, and how it will be labeled. In this way, you won't forget what you intend, and your advisor can judge its effectiveness. But time should not be taken at this stage to make exact drawings—approximate representations are all that are needed. Whenever you write a part of the material in rough form before preparing the first draft, you should also make rough layouts of any illustrations that will accompany that part of the text. As these passages are expanded and other material is added to form the first draft, the copy should be reviewed and any additional sketches placed where they are needed.

Just when the rough sketches should be turned into finished illustrations varies from project to project. But whatever the case, *large or complicated illustrations for which revision or complete replacement would be expensive or time-consuming should be shown to your advisor for comment before being put into final form,* and anything unusual about the form or style to be used in them should be discussed. If your advisor reviews parts of the thesis before the first draft is submitted to him, illustrations for these parts may safely be put into final form as soon as he returns them with his comment. When the first draft is the copy that is evaluated, it may be necessary to have the finished illustrations in time to include them in it. But if there are many illustrations, the advisor does not usually require the finished form in the first draft. You should find out what is expected and plan accordingly. If a professional illustrator is to make some or all of the final illustrations, time must be allowed for him to do his job. And the typist must be told how much space to leave in the text and where to leave it for each illustration. The most common kinds of illustrations used in theses and some of the applicable conventions are discussed in Chapter 15.


## PREPARING THE DRAFTS

As indicated earlier in this chapter, two drafts of the thesis are usually necessary. For the purposes of the following discussion, it will be assumed that the report will be evaluated primarily on the basis of the first draft and that any necessary alterations suggested by the advisor and committee will then be incorporated to produce the final draft. While this practice is not universal, it is the most common. If the procedure in your department is different, you should adjust the suggestions below accordingly.

### First Draft

The first draft should present the full development exactly as you propose to have it in the final report. All illustrations should be in place, equations should be in proper form, pages should be numbered, and departmental and university specifications for format should be followed. Minor inked corrections are usually allowed in this draft, and rough sketches may be permitted if there are to be many illustrations. But copies (*not originals!*) of the actual finished illustrations should be used if it is at all possible; they produce a much better impression than sketches, and the advisor is in a much better position to evaluate their effectiveness and accuracy.

All copy received from the typist, however good she may be, should be proofread carefully. Particular attention should be paid to formulas and equations and to entries in tables (errors in tables can easily go undetected). If possible, get someone to proofread the tables with you—one of you should read aloud from the typed copy while the other checks the handwritten original. Don't expect your faculty advisor to function as a proofreader.

If inked changes are not permitted, any pages on which corrections are necessary should be returned to the typist as soon as possible. It can save time for both of you if you put *light* pencil marks next to any material that is to be corrected and attach a piece of paper with the correction on it to the page concerned. Then give the typist only those pages on which there are to be corrections. Ask her to correct the typed copy but to leave the pencil marks on the pages. In this way, it will be very easy for you to review the material when it is returned, make sure that all corrections have been made, and then erase the pencil marks. If you give the typist the entire report (both the pages needing corrections and those that are perfect), and if she erases your pencil marks and removes your attachments, you may have to read the entire report again to find the spots that needed correction—and you are likely to miss some. You may want to keep a list of the pages that you give to the typist so that you can check them off as they are returned to you. This reduces the possibility of losing any as they are passed back and forth between you and the typist.

When you have proofed and corrected all of the pages and inserted all illustrations in their proper places, take the time to leaf through the entire report from front to back just once more to make certain that everything is there and in order. This may save excuses and the late delivery of missing pages. Then deliver the draft (with any necessary copies) to your advisor for evaluation. While he is reviewing it, you can attend to any remaining odds and ends (such as completing the last few illustrations, filling out required forms, or preparing for the oral presentation).

## Final Draft

The advisor and other members of the thesis committee usually take about a week—perhaps a little longer—to review and evaluate the draft. If major revision is to be suggested, they may discuss it among themselves before returning the draft. The advisor may collect all copies and return them, but it is probably more common for the student to collect them himself from the individual committee members. In either case, suggested changes (other than minor typographical or grammatical corrections) are usually discussed—perhaps at some length—as the copies are returned, and you should be certain that you understand all comments before attempting to revise the report. If portions of the draft were shown to your advisor as they were written, they should require very little revision. But if the text was not shown to the advisor in advance, there may be quite a number of small changes in wording or passages in which detail must be added, deleted, or rearranged. The first draft may be commented upon quite heavily. But don't fight City Hall; do what is suggested. While you are now the expert on your exact topic, your advisor is more familiar with the general field and applicable conventions. He has probably written and reviewed a good many more reports than you suspect.

When the suggestions have been incorporated into the draft, it should be put through the sequence of typing, proofing, and correction just described. When an illustration or other material is to be attached to a page, all typing on both the page and the piece to be added should be completed *before* the cementing is done (use rubber cement; do not use glue). Otherwise, the page may be torn or permanently wrinkled when it is placed in the typewriter for additional typing. Special care must, of course, be taken in proofreading the copy to be certain that it is perfect; usually, all corrections must be almost undetectable. It may be an unpleasant surprise to discover how much careful effort it takes to have the numbers and titles typed on all figures, to have minor corrections made in all copies, to make sure that all pages are numbered in proper order (sometimes page numbers are not added until all other typing is done), to make sure that added material has been cemented in its proper place in all copies, and to prepare the required number of copies in acceptable form. If you don't do this, nobody else will. So don't plan any weekend trips just before the final draft is due.

It is sometimes possible to avoid a complete retyping of the report, but the extra planning and coordination involved may require more effort than is warranted by the possible savings in typing costs. If page numbers are not typed on the first draft but are added later to reproduced copies, usable pages of the first draft may be numbered and inserted into the final draft. Any addition or deletion of material early in a section, though, necessitates retyping all subsequent pages within the section as the rest of the copy is shifted upward or downward on the page. Further, the advisor and other committee members must feel perfectly free to write on all pages of the first draft and to suggest whatever changes—major or minor—seem appropriate. They share responsibility for the quality of the report, since it will reflect upon themselves, the department, and the university. So it is usually best *not* to plan on reusing any pages from the first draft in the final draft, with the possible exception of data tables and similar appendix material.

When all copies are complete and in the prescribed final form, they are usually given to the faculty advisor for review and evaluation (any omissions or errors may require minor retyping). Signatures of all committee members on an approval page are sometimes necessary, additional submission and record forms may be required, and usually the thesis must be reviewed and approved by the graduate school. Procedures vary widely; it may or may not be your responsibility to attend to these matters. But you should be certain that you know what is expected of you and that you accomplish it without delay.

# 5

# Oral Presentation

An oral presentation is usually the last hurdle to be cleared on the way to a master's degree. But while preparation for it is necessary, the presentation should not be regarded with undue trepidation. With the thesis problem resolved and the rush to get the report into acceptable form over, it may, in fact, be almost pleasant to speak about what you have accomplished to a group of people who are knowledgeable in your field. As a rule, you will be expected to present an organized oral discussion of the project in which you demonstrate your competence in the subject area and your ability to answer questions about it—much as is done in the presentation of a paper to a professional society. Sometimes the atmosphere is formal and sometimes rather informal, but seldom is the student "grilled" (no bright lights and rubber hoses). You have to know what you are talking about, but then, after having worked on the project for a good many months, you ought to.

The presentation is usually made after the final draft has been submitted to the advisor. The time and place are normally determined by the advisor with consideration given to the convenience of the student. Sometimes the advisor, the other committee members, and the student are the only ones present. On the other hand, some departments coordinate the thesis presentations and publish departmental schedules so that invited guests, interested faculty, and other students may attend those presentations that interest them. Students are, in fact, sometimes required to attend a given number of thesis presentations (among other things, it's a good way to get ideas about possible thesis topics) as a departmental requirement.

When only the committee and the student are present, the procedure may be quite informal, with the student describing what he did and the committee asking questions. They may even interrupt the student as he progresses in his discussion. When there is a larger audience, the procedure is apt to be a little more formal. Occasionally, a department may schedule a series of four or five presentations in succession on a single afternoon, with each student moderating one presentation (introducing the speaker and handling the question period) as well as making his own. In any event, the student is told well ahead of time just when his presentation is to be made and how long it should be so that he can prepare for it effectively. Usually he is allowed something between fifteen and fifty minutes for the basic presentation and this is followed by a ten to thirty minute question period.

Just exactly what must be done in preparing for an oral presentation depends on local practice, but the following suggestions should be helpful in most cases. They describe preparation for the more complete "formal" presentation, so some may not apply when only the committee meets with the student on an informal basis. But it's better to be overprepared than to be underprepared.

## PREPARATION

1. Look over departmental thesis instructions. There may be some ground rules concerning the oral presentation. If there are, be sure to follow them.
2. Get your advisor's suggestions. He will probably control the arrangements and procedure, so find out how he intends to handle them and what his preferences are. He will probably be your best ally.
3. Review the entire project. Pay special attention to basic assumptions and background reading done early in the project. You may have forgotten significant details, and someone is likely to ask about them.
4. Select the information to be used in the presentation and put it into logical sequence. Keep it simple—your time will be limited so you can cover only essential details. Usually, something like an oral abstract of the thesis (with some amplification) is expected. The problem should be identified exactly and its significance shown. The method used should be described in sufficient detail for a listener to understand what was done and how it was done (any unusual apparatus should be described). Results relevant to the main conclusions should be summarized and the way in which they were analyzed and interpreted should be described. Major conclusions and recommendations should be well defined and clearly supported by the results presented. Examples or typical cases are often helpful in describing procedures, significance, and applications. Usually there is not time to derive equations in detail—derivations, computer programs, and other time-consuming developments should be summarized. Anyone who wants detail on a given point can ask about it during the question period. Unless you are directed to do otherwise, set the presentation at the technical level suitable for a professional in your field who is unfamiliar with your research project.
5. Prepare any necessary visual aids or other supporting materials. Slides, flip charts, overhead projectors, opaque projectors, blackboards, and reproduced handouts are the most common means of presenting pre-

pared materials, but anything that is available to you and effective for your purpose can be used. But don't get too fancy. You are describing a research project, not making an advertising display. Keep visuals simple, clear, and readable. Make them large enough to be seen and read easily from the back of the room or your intended point may be lost. And do not use too many of them or the mechanics of their use may become cumbersome and detract from your presentation. Graphs, tables, and other illustrations in the report often contain information about topics not covered in the oral presentation. They should be redrawn to eliminate extraneous information—include only that which is to be discussed. Supplementary visuals may be prepared for use in case of questions about other detail.

6. Prepare a topic outline. Generally, it is better (and much easier) to speak from a topic outline than from a fully developed text—the impact is better, and there is less chance of getting lost.

7. Practice the presentation several times. You should probably have a minimum of three dry runs. The delivery time should be noted on each dry run, and detail added or deleted to meet the suggested time limit. If you plan to use visual aids in the presentation, use them on the dry runs to assure that the mechanics of presentation go smoothly and that their use is included in the timing. If it is at all possible, get someone (preferably someone with some knowledge of your technical field) to listen to your practice runs and criticize your presentation. Then, if the listener tells you that you seem to belabor a minor point or that another point was not clearly explained, don't argue with him. You asked him to listen for just such faults. Once you have verbalized your presentation a few times, you should have little difficulty searching for the right words or expressions in the actual presentation. Nothing improves the flow and expression more than practice.

## PRESENTATION

1. Check the room shortly before the time scheduled for the presentation to make sure that everything is in order. If a projector is to be used, plug it in and turn it on (bulbs sometimes burn out—you might even want to have an extra one on hand). Make sure that all slides are numbered and stacked in proper sequence, handouts are ready, and chalk is available. Some of this may be the custodian's normal responsibility, but you, not he, will be the one standing before the group and making excuses if you are unable to present your data or show a drawing of your apparatus.

2. Deliver the presentation in a straightforward manner. If you have practiced it a few times, it should come easily. Be confident and professional but not overbearing. Avoid the temptation to speak quickly and to add detail that was not used in the dry runs—you

will seem more professional and more competent if you speak slowly and clearly. You should seem interested in what you are saying and enthusiastic about your project. Try to get a little variation into your delivery—don't drone on and on monotonously and put everyone to sleep. On the other hand, don't try to be too witty. Few things detract more from the overall effectiveness of a technical presentation than unsuccessful attempts at humor.

3. If possible, display a drawing, schematic, or other representation of your apparatus, test model, analytical model, test plot, or other major item *early in the presentation.* No amount of talking can orient your audience as quickly and effectively.

4. Make sure that you understand each question asked and that you know what you are going to say before replying. It is perfectly acceptable to pause a few seconds before answering. If more than six or seven people are present, it is usually a good idea to repeat each question before answering it. This will ensure that everyone has heard the question and that you have understood it properly (and it will give you a few seconds more to frame your answer). Don't guess or try to bluff your way through answers—the person who asks a question often knows the answer. If you do not, say so.

## EVALUATION

Performance in the oral presentation usually enters into the final evaluation on the thesis project. While it may represent a relatively small portion of the overall assessment, it may well raise or lower the evaluation. Any gross misconceptions or areas of complete ignorance revealed in answers given to questions can certainly cause reevaluation of the whole. Performance is usually judged by the committee members, but other faculty members present sometimes participate in the evaluation. Although specific factors identified for consideration vary, the overall sum is essentially the same. You are supposed to prepare a concise description of the project (problem—method—results—conclusions), present it in an organized and professional manner, and answer questions about what you have done. To the extent that you do this effectively, you have done what was asked. A typical evaluation form is shown in Example 3, and something like it is often used. But whether or not such a form is used, the topics indicated on the sample are probably considered in the evaluation of most presentations.

Oral Presentation of a Thesis

Audience Evaluation

Speaker's Name _____    Evaluator's Name _____

|  | Excellent | Good | Fair | Poor |
|---|---|---|---|---|

1.  Organization: Did the speaker
    organize his material so that
    it was forceful and interesting
    to you? Did he explain his
    problem, method, results, and
    conclusions clearly? Did con-
    clusions appear to be valid and
    based upon evidence?

2.  Bearing: Was the speaker at ease?
    Did posture, gestures, or manner-
    isms detract from the overall
    effect of the presentation?

3.  Expression: Was his expression
    exact and concise with proper
    choice of words and in acceptable
    English?

4.  Diction: Did he speak clearly
    with correct pronunciation?

5.  Delivery: Did he speak fluently
    with proper force and emphasis
    and without hesitation and
    pauses? Loud enough?

6.  Illustrations: Did he use graphic
    or other illustrative materials
    effectively? Could they be seen?
    Were they pertinent and easy to
    understand?

7.  Time: Did he present a balanced
    development within the time
    available?

8.  Questions: Did he handle ques-
    tions clearly and with confidence?

EXAMPLE 3.    EVALUATION FORM FOR ORAL PRESENTATIONS

# 6

# Evaluation of the Project

Occasionally, the overall evaluation of the thesis project is made by the advisor alone, but more often all members of the thesis committee participate. If there is no formal committee, two or more qualified faculty members ("readers") may be appointed to read the thesis, attend the oral presentation, and evaluate the student's performance on the project. In any case, the advisor's opinion is normally weighted more heavily than the others, perhaps accounting for 50 or 60 percent of the final evaluation. The advisor, of course, has been closely associated with the project since its inception and can draw upon personal knowledge of the way in which the problem was developed and defined. He knows the amount of time and effort spent on the project and the effectiveness with which they were applied throughout, as well as the imagination, initiative, and resourcefulness demonstrated by the student in solving problems. Although committee members may have attended progress-reporting sessions and, perhaps, have been called upon for advice on specific problems in their own areas, they must rely more heavily on the information contained in the report and presented at the oral presentation in evaluating the student's success in handling the research. Readers, of course, must base their judgments almost entirely on the report and the oral presentation.

While the report is the end result of the project—perhaps the only tangible result—the evaluation is based on the student's handling of the entire project, not the report alone. He may carry out excellent research without solving all or even most of the problem defined at the outset. Unanticipated circumstances or unavoidable snags may prevent the solution, or the problem may simply be "open-ended." Logical approaches do not always produce results, equipment fails, and theory does not always hold up in practice. If the problem selected was a good one, and if the student defined and limited it well, developed a logical approach, used sound procedures, and worked diligently, this is usually sufficient, even though he was not able to arrive at the solution. Everyone hopes to produce the final beautiful solution to his problem, but demonstration that a particular approach will not work or that a particular procedure is faulty under a given set of conditions sometimes contributes as much to knowledge in the field as does a demonstration that another approach will produce the desired results. So a project in which the problem was not solved may be judged to be excellent research, while conversely, one in which the problem actually was solved by blind luck, through sloppy procedures, and with minimum effort may be unacceptable.

The specific factors identified for consideration in the evaluation vary, but, like those used in evaluating oral presentations, the sum is much the same from department to department and from university to university. The factors considered in most evaluations are discussed briefly in the following paragraphs. An evaluation sheet something like the one shown in Example 3 may be used in rating the overall project.

BACKGROUND STUDY. The breadth and thoroughness of the search of published literature, the depth of understanding gained of the topic area, and the effectiveness with which the information found was used in the research and reflected in the report are all considered and evaluated: they are the foundation upon which the study was based.

PROBLEM. The understanding and precision with which the problem was defined, limited (or expanded), and analyzed, and the overall grasp shown of the problem and its implications are, of course, critical. The relative difficulty of the problem (its complexity, the techniques required, the amount and kind of analysis, mathematical development, or experimentation necessary) is usually taken into account. A complete solution of a simple problem may not be evaluated as highly as significant progress or a partial solution to a more difficult problem.

RESEARCH. Assumptions made must be appropriate and valid, and they must be clearly identified and justified in the report. Procedures used throughout the research should be logical, reliable, and suitable to the study. Originality and thoroughness should have been shown in attacking the problem. Resourcefulness should have been displayed in surmounting difficulties as they arose. Results should be accurate and applicable to the solution of the problem.

INTERPRETATION. This concerns the effectiveness with which results are presented, appropriate comparisons made, and necessary explanations developed. Sound judgment should be evident in the evaluation, analysis, and interpretation of results used to develop conclusions and recommendations.

REPORT. Information should be selected, organized, and presented to reflect clearly the things that were done and their significance. Necessary information should be in the text, appendixes should be used where they are appropriate, and illustrative material should supplement and support the text. Expression should be clear and exact, the style appropriate, and the whole presented in acceptable English. Format must be consistent and in accordance with local specifications.

ORAL PRESENTATION. The evaluation of the oral presentation, discussed in Chapter 5, is usually considered.

CONDUCT OF THE PROJECT. This is a very important but rather intangible group of judgments. In effect, it reflects the degree of organization, professionalism, and general good sense with which the project was carried out. Planning and scheduling throughout the project are weighted heavily, as are the budgeting of time and the degree and consistency of effort shown throughout the project. The student's promptness in keeping appointments, his initiative, the understanding of technical matters he demonstrated in discussions with the advisor, and the effectiveness with which he applied the advisor's suggestions will affect the advisor's evaluation of overall conduct of the project. General understanding of alternatives and the ability to select a reasonable course and implement it efficiently to produce reliable results (without frequent errors) are important. The advisor forms impressions of all of these things throughout the project, and all of them are considered in evaluating it as an independent study. Sudden bursts of effort and concern on the day before the oral presentation are not likely to affect his evaluation of the overall handling of the project.

# 7

# The Report: General Information

A thesis is a full technical report on a research project. It must present sufficient description of the problem, the research, the results, and the outcome that a qualified reader can understand what was attempted, what was done, what resulted, and what it all means. Because the thesis project is an academic effort in which the student must demonstrate his competence to carry out research and report the results, the report often contains more complete development of the ideas presented and more thorough explanation and justification of the research than might be found in some other technical reports. Like most other reports, it contains three essentially different general classes of material: prefatory material, text, and supplementary material.

1. *Prefatory Material.* The prefatory material (sometimes called "front matter") is contained on the opening pages of the report. It identifies the report, tells the reader what is in it, tells him where it is, and tells him anything else that the author thinks he should know about the project (such as how it developed and who provided help). The prefatory material usually includes most or all of the following: a flyleaf; a title page; a preface; a table of contents; lists of illustrations, tables, and symbols; and an abstract. These identify the report for the reader and help him to find his way around in it.

2. *Text.* The text is the main body of the report. Here, the problem is defined, the research is described, and conclusions and recommendations are developed. The text should not normally be a chronological description of everything done on the project (much of which is often irrelevant to the research presented); nor should it include detail that does not contribute directly to an understanding of the main development of the research (if necessary, this detail can be placed in an appendix). Although the material presented may be complicated, the text should lead the reader clearly, with a minimum of distraction, from the statement of the problem, through the research, to

the report's conclusions and recommendations. The text usually includes an introduction, several developing sections, and one or more
concluding sections.

3. *Supplementary Material.* The supplementary material is the "back-up"
material—the interesting and valuable detail which is not included in
the text but which supports, explains, and underlies material presented
in the development of the text. It includes the bibliography, any
necessary appendixes, and sometimes a vita (brief biography of the
author).

Of course, the relative proportions of text and appendixes vary considerably among theses, both because of differences among projects and because of the individual preferences of students and advisors. In one thesis
there may be twice as many pages of appendixes as there are of text (this
makes it easy to convert the text into an article for submission to a professional
journal), while in another the text may be longer and there may be virtually
no appendix material at all. As indicated in Chapter 4, considerable rewriting
and rearrangement of material can often be avoided if general agreement on
the placement of detail can be reached before the first draft is written.

## STYLE

The report should be written so that someone with a master's degree in the
professional field concerned can understand it without undue difficulty. The
reader's competence and intelligence should not be insulted—he does not need
a basic course in differential calculus or a complete description of how an
oscilloscope works. But the intended reader has no more familiarity with the
immediate problem or the theory and procedures involved in the research
than you had when you undertook the project, so he must be oriented and
the development must be explained. Do not assume that he has your thesis
advisor's knowledge and experience or the background that you have developed in the course of working on the project. And don't force him to look up
the meanings of highly specialized technical terms or to locate and read a
dozen journal articles in order to puzzle out the meaning of each section of
the report. Write the report so that he can understand it.

Expression should be in the formal style usually found in technical
reports and in technical and scientific journals. This is sometimes called technical style and sometimes called by other names; but whatever the name, the
object is to communicate the subject matter to the reader as clearly and as
exactly as possible and in the form that will be easiest to understand. The
style should be as unobtrusive as possible so that the reader can proceed
without undue conscious attention to the expression itself. If the reader is to
be pleased by the writing, it should be because of its directness and clarity
and the ease with which he can read and understand the material—not be-

cause of any verbal trickery or literary embellishments. The thesis is a report on a substantial research project, not a philosophical discourse on the meaning of life.

Although full discussion of formal technical style will not be presented, here are a few of its most important characteristics. They are illustrated in the sample thesis pages included in the appendix. More complete discussion can be found in any good book on technical writing.

1. Sentences should be grammatically correct, and standard practices should be followed in usage, punctuation, mechanics, and spelling (save your originality for the research itself). If you can't write a sentence properly after using the language daily for twenty years or more, why should anyone believe that you can design a workable laser after only six months of study?

2. The first person singular may be used in the preface, but the rest of the report is usually written entirely in the third person. Two exceptions to this are:
    a. The first person plural is sometimes allowed in mathematical developments. Thus, "Substituting Eq 5 into Eq 14, we obtain . . ." may be allowed in place of "Substitution of Eq 5 into Eq 14 produces . . ."
    b. The second person is sometimes permitted in describing routine mechanical procedures (such as calibration of equipment) in an appendix or in describing an algorithm. "Place the sample on Tray 2 and turn the primary (red) knob slowly clockwise until the indicator points to 0."

3. Expression should flow as smoothly as the technical nature of the material will permit. Don't sacrifice precision, but be careful not to cram too much detailed modification into a single sentence—break it up for easier reading. Be especially careful of piling up five or six modifiers before a noun. This makes for a very heavy style that may bring the reader to a halt: "The River Edge production model SBT airframe weight error percentage was 2."

4. Wherever possible, sentence structure should be simple and direct, and familiar concrete words should be used. Avoid complicated syntax and long, wandering sentences. Do not try to impress the reader with your vocabulary. He will probably have enough trouble with the necessary technical vocabulary (include definitions where it seems desirable) and the complex concepts without having to look up the meanings of words or to puzzle through complicated sentence structures. Remember that your purpose is to communicate the subject matter. If the reader is impressed at all, it should be with your work and the clarity of your discussion.

5. The tone should be objective and unemotional as you present the facts. The reader may begin to wonder about the objectivity of the rest of your study if you write a sentence like the following: "This

beautifully designed apparatus certainly would have worked perfectly had it not been for the gross carelessness and wholly irresponsible attitude of an inferior laboratory technician."

6. Contractions (can't, don't, won't, shouldn't) should not be used. They have been used in this book, but the book is not a technical report on a research project.

7. Evaluative terms (big, little, heavy, light, cheap, expensive) should not be used without a reference frame, and be careful in using modifiers that appear to limit but do not (considerably, mainly, several, rather, very). How large is a large variation? And if you were told that a parachute was usually quite dependable, would you jump with it?

8. Technical jargon and shop talk should be used only where they are necessary. They are often useful in reducing repetitious wording, and sometimes they are almost indispensable. But overuse can cause whole generations of misunderstanding (the terms are often local usages) as well as reducing precision and degrading the professional tone of your writing.

Overall, expression should be kept as simple and concise as possible. Paragraphs should be fully developed, but don't use a long-winded paragraph to say what would be better expressed in a short sentence or two. Consider the following:

> Manifestly, therefore, it is incumbent upon you to propitiously inaugurate and vigorously sustain all appropriate viable measures to assure assiduous eschewance of such dysfunctionally counter-productive, ignoble, dissilatory dribblings, turgidly banal inanities, pompous vacuousness, and amorphously acrid circumlocutions as may, whether adventitiously or resultant of unconscionable malific misdirection, pose gelid interdictions to those crystalline essences of clarity traditionally characterized in response-balanced incremental programming of verbal structures in the integrated systematization of concept transmission.

That sentence in fact tells us to say what we have to say as clearly and directly as possible.

## SPECIAL NOTE

Because thesis projects are carefully controlled research projects addressing actual problems, the results are sometimes publishable in professional journals in the fields concerned. Departmental and university requirements are usually flexible on many points, so it may be possible to write the final draft of the thesis in such a way that it is relatively easy to modify or extract the text for submission to a journal. If your results warrant it, you may want to obtain a copy of the style sheet of the major professional society in your field and a copy of the instructions for authors for the journal(s) concerned (these are usually published in each issue). Then, to the extent possible, you can follow the conventions suggested (as in numbering equations, preparing figures, citation and bibliographic form, and similar matters). If you do this, special care must be taken to be *very certain* that the final draft will meet departmental and university requirements. Talk to your advisor before undertaking something that may not be either warranted or acceptable. Be certain that he understands what you intend and that he (and the university) agree to any variant forms to be used. Otherwise, even if you succeed in your secondary purpose (easy modification for submission to a journal) you may fail in your primary purpose (acceptance by the university) and be forced to recast and retype the entire report.

# 8

# Prefatory Material

Prefatory material is the material at the front of the report preceding the actual text. It presents any necessary information about the project reported in the text and tells the reader what is in the text and where to find it. The format and sequence of this material are often exactly prescribed in university specifications for the thesis. If they are, the specifications should be closely followed. Where there are no such specifications, the following format should be generally acceptable.

## FLYLEAF

A flyleaf is commonly included in theses bound in cardboard covers when there is a cutout or window in the front cover. The information on the fly-leaf—usually only the title of the report, the name of the author, and the year—is placed so that it is visible through the cutout. This page is not usually included in reports with other kinds of covers.

## TITLE PAGE

The title page identifies the report—tells the reader what the report is and where it came from. Although the arrangement of the material varies, typically it includes:

1. The title of the report—this should identify the research project as exactly as possible.
2. An identification of the report as a thesis and the name of the degree for which it is submitted.

3. The author's name and degree(s) (not including the degree for which the thesis is written).
4. The university, college, and department in which the thesis is written.
5. The year (and sometimes the month) of submission.

## PREFACE

The preface is a statement from the author to the reader about the thesis project and the resulting report. It is the only place in the report in which you can write directly to the reader in the first person. What you say in the preface is up to you, but avoid making it a list of trivia; it should mention only significant matters. A typical preface might include:

1. Personal reasons for selecting the particular thesis project.
2. Explanation of modifications to the original project, including any limitations imposed after the project was begun and their effects upon the scope of the research or its validity.
3. Acknowledgment of indebtedness to major works not directly cited in the report or of a special debt to one of the works cited.
4. Acknowledgment of help received from your advisor, laboratory personnel, librarians, typists, and any others who aided you in the course of the project.

NOTE: Do not use your preface to complain about the shortcomings of others, or as an alibi sheet to gloss over your own.

## TABLE OF CONTENTS

The table of contents shows the reader what is in the report and where it is. It is customary to list the following in the sequence in which they appear in the report:

1. Each item of prefatory material except the flyleaf, title page, and table of contents itself.
2. Each main section of the report (usually identified by consecutive Roman numerals). Local practice differs on the listing of subsections. But unless sections are very short and the full content is obvious from the sectional title, it is customary to list subsections (and sometimes sub-subsections) in indented lists following the larger sections of which they are parts.
3. Each item of supplementary material. In listing appendixes, be certain to include the title of each appendix as well as the appendix letter or other designation. A reader seeing Appendix B listed without a title would have no way of knowing what it contained without turning to it to find out.

## ADDITIONAL LISTS

Most theses require additional prefatory lists to help the reader find and identify things in the report. The most common lists are described here in the sequence in which they usually occur in the report. A given report may include all of them, some of them, or none of them.

### List of Figures

If a report contains three or more figures (illustrations), it is customary to include a list of figures, although local practice may vary. All graphic aids (photographs, drawings, maps, diagrams, graphs, and the like) *except tables* are given descriptive titles and assigned figure numbers (usually Arabic numerals) in a single consecutive series in the order in which they appear in the report. Figures contained in appendixes are included in this series. Several variations of this system are described in Chapter 15. All figures with their titles and page numbers are listed in sequence in the list of figures.

### List of Tables

All tables in the report, including those in appendixes, are given descriptive titles and assigned numbers (usually uppercase Roman numerals) in a single consecutive series in the order in which they appear in the report. If there are three or more tables in the report, it is customary to provide a list of tables similar to the list of figures described above. If the list of tables is short and will easily fit on the same page as the list of figures or on the last page of that list, it may be put there. But don't crowd the lists. Several variations of this system are described in Chapter 15.

### List of Symbols (or Notation)

If many symbols are used in the report or if the first and later uses of symbols are separated by many pages, a list of symbols should be included. Thus the reader will know where to look to find the meaning of a particular symbol as he progresses through the report or when he returns to it. He won't be forced to leaf backwards through the report to find the meanings of symbols previously defined. If a list of symbols is included, the symbols should be arranged in an order that will seem logical to the reader and that will make it easy for him to find the one he is looking for when he needs it. For example, all Roman alphabet symbols might be listed first in consecutive order, then all Greek symbols in consecutive order, then others.

NOTE: Don't forget to include units of measure where they are called for!

### Glossary of Terms (or Definitions)

If the report contains many terms that are not widely known in your field, or if some terms are used in a different (specialized or more limited) way than they are normally used in the field, it will be helpful to the reader if you gather them together and define them all in a single place. Such a list may be placed in the prefatory material. If, however, the list is longer than two or three pages, it should probably be placed at the back of the report as an appendix.

## ABSTRACT

An abstract is a short condensation of the report—a thumbnail sketch of the whole. As in a small photograph of a large painting, the tone and proportion remain, but the details fade. In a thesis, as in most kinds of technical reports, the abstract is usually the last item in the prefatory material. Additional copies of the abstract are often published apart from the report in indexes of abstracts. A potential reader usually reads the abstract to determine whether the report contains information of sufficient interest to warrant his obtaining it or, if he has it in hand, reading it. If you do an excellent piece of research and develop important conclusions but do not reflect the worth of the study in your abstract, your information may well lie undiscovered for years. No one will search out the report or read it because they will have no way of knowing that it contains information that would be of interest. Unfortunately, the abstract is often the worst-written part of the report. There is no way of knowing how much excellent research may, in effect, be lost because of poor abstracting.

Your abstract should identify your exact problem (with any important limitations), tell how you went about trying to solve it (the general method or procedure—theory applied, tests made, measures used, variables evaluated), indicate the most important of your specific results, and present your main conclusions. Occasionally, important recommendations, and sometimes other items of information essential to understanding what was done, are included. From this, someone in your field should be able to determine whether he wants to obtain and read the report.

Don't just name the main sections of the report or list the general topics discussed in them. Rather, to the extent that it is possible within the limits of the abstract, you should summarize the information presented. If you just name the topics, the reader will learn little or nothing about the research. The following, for example, could apply to almost any report on an experimental project, but it tells the reader nothing about what was done or what resulted. Although the example is fictitious, it is not too different from some actual thesis abstracts (or, at least, their first drafts).

> The problem is exactly defined and placed in perspective. After a review of pertinent studies, the test equipment is explained, procedures are described, and all tests are discussed. Results are presented and suitable statistical measures are applied. Comparison is made to existing theory, and appropriate conclusions are drawn from the information generated. Several recommendations for further study are made.

To be of any value to the reader, the abstract must identify the problem, name the equipment, describe the procedures, name the tests, indicate the nature of the results (numbers or ranges), identify the statistical measures, and state the main conclusions and recommendations. These provide the reader with at least a rough idea of what was done and a basis for deciding whether or not the report is likely to be of interest.

Because most thesis abstracts are about a page long (some universities prescribe word limits—often in the range of 250–600 words), the phrasing must be compact. There is no room for much detail or for verbal embroidery. Because you have spent a good part of your time for a number of months on your project, it may seem impossible to condense it to meet a word limit. But do it anyway. Everyone who ever wrote a thesis has had the same problem.

## General Guidelines

1. Make the abstract a self-contained unit. It should *not* refer to particular sections of the report or to other sources, and the reader should not have to look elsewhere in the report to understand the abstract.
2. Write in complete sentences (not telegram style) and keep the tone and emphasis consistent with that in the text. Make the expression as smooth and easy to read as possible.
3. Where possible, avoid highly technical language known only to research workers in one small corner of your academic field. Otherwise some potential readers might not realize that the report is of interest because they simply cannot understand what it is about.
4. Do not include graphs, tables, examples, footnotes, derivations, nonstandard abbreviations, or nonstandard symbols. Keep equations to the *absolute minimum* (preferably there should be none at all).

Certainly it is difficult, and sometimes downright painful, to cut the abstract of a 100- or 200-page report down to a single page or a page and a half, but readers don't expect detail in the abstract. If it tells them what the study is about, and if they are interested, they know that they'll get detail in the text. So chop away and get the abstract down to the bare minimum that will tell the reader what he needs to know in order to decide whether he wants to read the report. As you read other people's abstracts, you will see the value of brief factual abstracts. If you have to review a hundred or so abstracts to find reports and articles pertinent to your thesis problem, you will probably bless the authors who kept to the minimum essentials.

# 9

# Introduction

The introduction to a thesis, like the introductions to most other kinds of reports, should tell the reader what the report is about. If he has seen the abstract, the reader has a general idea of what the problem was, how you went about solving it, and how it came out. But the abstract, because it is an abstract, contains little or no detail. The introduction supplies details about the problem itself and what you undertook to do.

You have probably had the experience of reading well into a report before discovering that it didn't cover the kind of experiment or discussion that you thought it did. If so, you were probably misled by the introduction into expecting something different from the actual content of the report, and you may have wasted time and effort on something that was not of interest. The introduction to your thesis should prevent this from happening to your readers. It should clearly identify and limit the problem concerned, indicate roughly how you went about trying to solve it, and tell the reader the order in which the information is presented. If a reader is interested, he can then proceed to read the report with a minimum of uncertainty.

Much of the information contained in the introduction is the same as that presented in the thesis proposal, though the discussion of some topics may be expanded. In fact, if the thesis proposal was complete and the project was carried out without modification of the original intention, it should be possible to use much of the proposal in the introduction with little or no change. There is nothing shady or unprofessional about doing this. In the proposal, the problem to be investigated was identified and limited. In the introduction to the thesis, the problem which has been investigated is identified and limited. If the information was precisely stated in the proposal, there is no particular reason to change the phrasing in the report.

## INFORMATION USUALLY INCLUDED

The introduction is sometimes the most difficult section to write effectively, and it is often one of the last sections to be put into draft form. The topics usually covered include background, problem statement, scope, assumptions, general approach, and sequence of presentation.

## Background

There should be enough background discussion to enable a competent reader in your general technical field to understand your problem and its significance—to understand why the problem investigated really is a problem. As was indicated earlier, you should include only the minimum background necessary to understand the exact problem and the benefit that may result from solving it. Don't trace the theory of combustion from the time primitive man first rubbed two sticks together to produce fire. And don't burden the reader with a lengthy narrative description of what Enrico Fermi did in 1936. If a substantial historical development is included in the report, it should be placed in a section following the introduction (if it would actually be necessary for most readers) or in an appendix (if it would be of interest to only a few readers—the more likely case). In rare circumstances, the historical development forms a separate main section preceding the rest of the introductory material, which then becomes Section II. But this is seldom justified.

## Problem

This is an exact statement of the specific problem you undertook—whether you solved it or not. It is the thing you tried to do. As in the thesis proposal, it should be a flat statement without extraneous verbiage, and it is usually placed in a separate paragraph with a heading for easy identification. (Readers often come back to the statement of the problem while reading the text.) It should not be buried in the middle of a lengthy paragraph of background material or literature review. While the statement of the problem can often be taken directly from the thesis proposal, sometimes this is not possible. If your problem is modified, broadened, or limited in any way (as is often the case) after the research project is approved, the statement of the problem must obviously be revised to reflect the research actually reported in the thesis. It can be pretty embarrassing if you state a given problem in your introduction and then describe research dealing with either an expanded or narrowed version of it in the body of your text.

## Scope

This is a description of the limits of the study actually reported in the thesis. It indicates to the reader something of the breadth and depth of the research so that he will know what to expect in the report. As most theses are concerned with limited parts of larger problems, you should name the parameters varied, the ranges over which they were varied, the tests applied, the particular shapes or alloys tested, or the temperatures used. These may vary from the scope suggested in the thesis proposal; you may have done more, fewer, or different things than you originally intended. But the reader is not usually concerned with your original intention; he wants to know what you are actually reporting on.

The scope is closely tied to the statement of the problem and often—especially if the description of the scope is relatively short—the two are presented in a single subsection headed "Problem and Scope."

## Assumptions

This presents the ideas or opinions assumed to be true and accepted without further proof at the outset of the research. As indicated in the discussion of the thesis proposal, such assumptions are usually made to simplify a problem —to cut it down to something that can be handled within the present state of the art and with the equipment or theory available—or where approximate solutions are adequate. The assumptions which underlie either the statement of the problem itself or the general approach to the research as a whole should be stated and justified in the introduction. They are a part of the point of departure from which you worked, and if they are not identified and justified (even if they are commonly accepted in the kind of research you are reporting), you may be attacked for failure to recognize them. Assumptions bearing only upon a limited portion of the study—such as a particular procedure or manipulation—should be indicated in the text where the matter to which they apply is presented.

## General Approach

This is a brief description of the main sequence you followed (from start to finish) in the research reported in the text. It gives the reader a general idea of what you did in the course of trying to solve the problem—an overall view of the research effort as a whole. Do not include detail here; that will be presented in the text and appendixes. And do not include missteps that contributed nothing to your results. Just describe the main steps followed in developing the information which led to the conclusions and recommendations at the end of the text.

## Sequence of Presentation

This is a simple statement of the order in which the main sections of the report follow—a road map of where the reader is going and how he is going to get there. While this is indicated in the table of contents, it is usually a convenience for the reader to be told the sequence in which he will find the material after he has read the detailed description of the problem and the general approach to its solution. Where the sequence of presentation exactly parallels the main steps in the approach, the two are often combined in a single subsection ("Approach and Presentation"). The appropriate section number in the report is indicated with each main step in the approach as it is described.

## INFORMATION OFTEN INCLUDED

While they are not quite as common as the six topics just described, three other general topics are often discussed in the introduction. They are theory, review of the literature, and major definitions.

### Theory

Theoretical development in the introduction should usually be limited to that which is essential to understanding the problem or that which underlies the general approach to its solution. If the full theoretical development is lengthy, it should not be placed in the introduction but in a main section following it. If it would be of interest to only a fraction of the potential readers, it should be placed in an appendix or left out of the report entirely. In some projects, of course, the primary objective is substantial theoretical development. In reports on such projects, several sections of theory may comprise the main body of the text. These will be discussed in the following chapter.

### Review of the Literature

This is a brief discussion of the published studies bearing directly upon the problem to be investigated. It establishes your point of departure for the reader—the state of knowledge on the topic at the time the project was undertaken. Further, it demonstrates that you are familiar with the material reviewed and its significance to your project. Usually, each study is discussed in chronological sequence; the author's name(s) is mentioned (with appropriate reference to your bibliography) and the findings pertinent to your study are indicated. Where studies on two or three distinctly different topics are reviewed, those on each topic may, of course, be presented separately in chronological sequence within topics. Only those studies directly contributing to your own point of departure should be mentioned, though significant studies which substantiate or contradict others may be indicated. Limitations in the scope or the procedures used in the studies discussed that affect the applicability of their results to your own study should be highlighted.

This sounds like an easy thing to do, but if there has been much research in your area it may require considerable careful analysis and judicious selection (as well as familiarity with the pertinent literature) to do it effectively. Detail explained in the studies reviewed must be eliminated (your reader can get it in the originals if he is not already familiar with them), and only the findings directly pertinent to your own study should be mentioned as you bring your reader to date. While it may almost seem that you are asked to write the history of mankind on the head of a pin, the review should be kept brief—a page or less should be sufficient in most cases. If the review requires more than two or three pages, it should probably be placed in a section following the introduction. In those rare instances in which a major purpose of the thesis is a review and evaluation of the work in a given area, the review may, of course, fill several main sections following the introduction.

## Major Definitions

These are definitions of concepts critical to an exact understanding of the problem or of your approach to its solution. They are basic to your point of departure and the development of your research, and some may require a paragraph or more of discussion and amplification. It may be necessary to describe specific limitations—ways in which your own usage differs from general usage or that in other technical fields. These definitions may be based upon terms or results developed in research studies which are not widely known or accepted in your field or they may be derived from them with necessary modifications to fit your purposes. They are not simply definitions of technical terms used in your research. As indicated in Chapter 8, such terms should be presented in a glossary located either in the prefatory material or in an appendix. The use of highly specialized terms before they are defined is a fault found in the first drafts of many introductions.

## GENERAL COMMENT

This chapter covers the types of information most commonly found in introductions, but no two problems are exactly alike. If there is other information that a reader will need at the outset in order to understand what the report is about, by all means include it. But resist the temptation to try to tell the reader everything at once. If your introduction gets much longer than four or five pages, you may well be including detail that belongs in a later section or an appendix. The introduction should tell the reader what the report is about; it should not begin presenting the main information itself.

# 10

# Developing Sections

In the introduction of the report, the problem to be investigated is defined, the general approach to the solution is stated, and the sequence of presentation within the report is indicated. In the concluding sections, the solution to the problem (insofar as one has been developed) is presented, any recommendations are made, and the research is summarized. Between the introduction and the concluding sections are the developing sections of the report. These are the sections in which the main body of information developed in the course of the project is presented. In them, the experiment is explained, the theory is derived, or the design is developed. The primary steps in the research are presented in detail. A reader's judgment of the validity of the conclusions, the workability of the design, or the significance of the summary which follows will rest upon the completeness, accuracy, and relevance of the information presented in the developing sections: what was done, why it was done, how it was done, what was not done and why it was not done, the results obtained, the manipulation of the data, the development of equations and formulas, the analysis of controlling variables—all significant information developed in the course of the study and leading to the final outcome presented in the concluding sections. Whatever the project, the reader is likely to be looking for holes in the explanation, and the author must try not to leave any.

There may be only two or three developing sections, or there may be many more. Just how many are used depends on the project and the student's judgment of the best way to present the information. The object should be to organize and present information in the way that will be clearest to the reader, who should be led through the technical development to the concluding sections with a minimum of confusion and distraction. He should be given the information necessary to understand the procedures used, the derivation of equations, or the theoretical development, but he should not be encumbered by irrelevant material. He should be given the information necessary to understand the research and to support the conclusions, recommendations, or discussion in the concluding sections, but he should not be forced to wade through a minutely detailed chronological description of everything done on the project (a fault in many first drafts). Ideally, when a reader has read the thesis, he should feel that he was given just the right information and that the author has presented it in the "inevitable sequence"—that no other sequence would have been as effective.

In the pages that follow, the general organization of individual sections of the report will be discussed briefly, and then several common patterns of developing sections often found in thesis reports will be described.

## ORGANIZATION OF INDIVIDUAL SECTIONS

In each section, of course, the object should be to present the necessary information on the topic concerned to enable the reader to understand the discussion as easily as possible. The derivations and concepts presented may be complex and highly technical, and they may require the very careful attention of the reader even when presented as clearly as possible. The reader should not be given the additional burden of trying to figure out what the section is all about and where it is leading him. So the simpler and less cluttered the organization, the better.

Often there is a brief introductory paragraph (or paragraphs) identifying the topic to be covered and indicating the order in which it will be presented. This sectional introduction might contain the following:

1. *Background.* Provide just enough to show that the topic should be discussed and that this is the place in the report for it.
2. *Topic.* Give an exact statement of the topic to be covered, even if it is only an expansion of the sectional heading.
3. *Scope.* This is occasionally explained if it differs significantly from what might be expected. (Detailed derivation of equations is necessary because of differences between your research and other studies in the area. Use of a given computer program for simulation studies will not be fully discussed because it has been justified at length in an earlier study.)
4. *Order of presentation.* Describe the sequence in which main divisions of the section will be presented. (Elrod's second hypothesis will be discussed first, then Wright's extension to three-dimensional flow, and finally Hitchcock's experimental verification.) Like the statement of sequence at the end of the introduction, this lets the reader know where he is going and how he's going to get there.

Given this information, the reader knows what the section is about, what is covered, and how it will be presented. If other orienting information seems desirable for the topic concerned, it can certainly be included. But if the additional description becomes long or complex, it should probably be placed in a subsection following the introductory paragraph. Like the introduction to anything else, the sectional introduction should just tell the reader what the section is about; it should not present parts of the discussion itself.

Following the introductory paragraph(s), the main body of the discussion is presented in the order indicated in the introduction. Development within topics should be complete, transition between ideas should be smooth, and the sequence should seem logical to the reader; he should be given the necessary information in the order that will be easiest for him to follow and in the detail appropriate for the subject under discussion. Subheadings, sub-subheadings, sequence signals, lists, and transitional statements between ideas are all helpful in keeping the reader oriented. They should not, however, be used to the extent that they become obtrusive and hold up the flow of material. Overuse of organizational aids can become artificial—just when they cease to be helpful in leading a reader through a complex topic and start to become unnecessary gimmickry is largely a matter of personal judgment, but everyone can probably agree upon extremes of overuse and underuse. The latter is probably the more common.

Sectional summaries are sometimes used when the material in a section is diverse or when the section is long and it seems appropriate to restate the main points of the development or to summarize the results derived. Usually, though, summaries are not necessary. If a theoretical development has been explained, or if equipment or a procedure has been described, there is not usually much need for a summary.

Generally, the longer the section and the more diverse the content, the nearer the section's organization approaches that of a short independent report. The shorter the section and the more restricted the coverage, the less need there is for organizational devices. In a two-page section describing a simple procedure, the section headings and the topic sentences of the paragraphs may be all that are necessary.

## EXPERIMENTAL PROJECTS

In an experimental project, the experimenter does something to find out what will happen as a result. Sometimes the thing is done simply to find out what the result will be; at other times, the thing to be done is carefully selected and limited in an attempt to attain a desired result. In either case, the developing sections of the report should tell the reader what was done, how it was done, and what resulted, so that he can understand the basis for conclusions drawn or recommendations made at the end of the text. The "experimental ideal" is to include enough information on these topics to permit a reader to duplicate the experiment if he should want to. The sequence of developing sections in a typical experimental report might be the following:

> Theory
> Equipment
> Procedure
> Results

## Theory

Here the theoretical basis underlying the experiment is explained so that the reader will understand how the experimental approach taken applies to the problem stated in the introduction. The author should demonstrate that current theory pertinent to the study and previous experimental work have been taken into account in developing the approach used. He should also show how existing concepts have been applied in developing the experiment.

## Equipment

Equipment and apparatus used should be exactly identified. If any special equipment was designed and built for use in the experiment or if a special setup was made, it should be explained in sufficient detail for a reader to understand what it was and how it worked—so that he can judge its adequacy for the use to which it was put and the validity of the data generated. It is not necessary to include an extensive description of standard equipment. Simply identify oscilloscopes, meters, manometers, balances, and other common devices as they are known to people in the technical fields in which they are used. But anything developed especially for the project and any modifications made to standard equipment should be described in detail. Procedures used in calibration and operation of new or altered equipment should also be included—there is nowhere else that the reader can look to find them. With standard equipment it is sufficient to state that the recommended or accepted calibration and operating procedures were used. (If there are several different accepted procedures, the one used should be identified.)

Drawings, wiring diagrams, flow charts, and any other materials necessary to explain the equipment or apparatus and how it worked should be included. If the description becomes excessively long, simplified descriptions with partial drawings or schematics showing critical shapes and clearances may be placed in the text, with the full detail presented in an appendix for any reader who may wish to refer to it.

## Procedure

The full procedure followed in carrying out the experiment should be described in sufficient detail for the reader to understand what was done and how it was done in developing the data or results. This description will be the basis for the reader's judgment of the validity and applicability of the results and, ultimately, of the conclusions based on them.

Procedures that are well known in the technical field concerned (the operation of common equipment) need not be described in detail. Relatively new or uncommon procedures available in the open literature are usually described briefly, and references are made to the sources in which they are presented in complete detail. But when a completely new procedure is developed and used in the experiment, it should be described fully and justified so that the reader will understand exactly what was done and be in a position to evaluate it. Similarly, any modification of a familiar procedure should be explained. When a new procedure is not described, the reader is justified in dismissing the results as unreliable—if you won't tell how you got your results, there must be something wrong with your method.

When a particular approach or procedure used proved fruitless—it would not work or would not produce usable results in the immediate experimental situation—it is usually described in an appendix. If the procedure seemed logical to you, it may well seem logical to your reader. And if you don't describe what you did and, if possible, why it didn't work, your reader may well wonder why you didn't try it. He may then waste his time and effort attempting something that you have already found useless. This has happened more than once. Knowing that something will not work is often as important as knowing that something else will—as can be attested by thousands of do-it-yourselfers who have ruined their television sets, their plumbing, or their automobile engines.

Generally, then, those procedures which led to the results contained in the report are presented in the text so that the reader can proceed without distraction through the main development of the experiment and directly to the results and conclusions. Procedures which were used but did not produce results are reported in an appendix. Two exceptions to this general rule should be noted. First, calibration procedures (if they are not described, someone else may never be able to duplicate your results) and long or detailed descriptions of equipment operation (which would slow the reader) are usually reported in appendixes. Second, if none of the procedures was successful and the problem was not solved, the procedures are usually reported in the text. When there are no significant results to analyze and no conclusions to draw (beyond the fact that the procedures did not work), the procedures can form the bulk of the developing sections.

## Results

The results section usually presents the data generated (or some of it), any processing of the data, the results of the processing, and, sometimes, discussion of the results. For many readers, especially professionals in the field, this is the most important information in the report.

If the data developed is voluminous, samples may be presented in the text, but most (or all) of it is usually presented in appendixes. In following the development of the experiment, the reader will not usually stop and analyze all of the data; he should not be forced to wade through pages and pages of data tables, photographs of samples taken after testing, or oscilloscope traces in the body of the text. But he may choose to review the data or check particular computations after he has followed the experiment through, and the author has an obligation to include enough information to allow him to do this. So unless the quantity is prohibitive, the raw data is usually included in appendixes for the reader's perusal.

Any processing performed on the data should be described and justified. If a standard method is used, it should be identified. If the procedure is relatively new or unusual, it should be described and the source cited. If the method is developed to suit the needs of the experiment, it must, of course, be described in detail. In any case, unless it is unusually simple or self-evident, the method should be justified, any assumptions involved should be stated and justified, and sample calculations should be included (usually in an appendix).

The processed data resulting from the procedures described is usually presented on consolidated tables or in graphs. These can often be presented comfortably in the text. But if they are so numerous that inclusion in the text would impede the reader, samples may be placed in the text and the remainder put in appendixes.

To the extent that it is necessary, discussion of the significance of the processed data is usually placed in the text, and any conclusions developed from it are sometimes developed and justified as it is presented. Although conclusions are gathered in a later section, specific development at the point at which the underlying results are presented is sometimes necessary to show the reader just which data lead to a given conclusion and how.

## THEORETICAL PROJECTS

In theoretical projects, the emphasis is on a theoretical development of some kind. It may be focused either upon explaining an observed phenomenon or upon developing theoretical predictions of what might happen in circumstances that have not yet been observed. The general pattern of development usually moves from the known to the unknown, and the sequence of developing sections in a typical theoretical report might be as follows:

Existing Theory
New Theory
Application

### Existing Theory

Here, any existing theory bearing upon the problem and underlying the theory to be developed is presented and discussed. This is usually done through a sequential discussion of material in the open literature with appropriate citation of the sources discussed and evaluation of their worth and pertinence to the problem dealt with in the thesis project. If several separate lines of development are to be drawn together in the theory presented later in the report, they may be traced and evaluated in separate main sections or subsections, depending upon the length and complexity of the comment necessary to each.

If the theory developed in the project is at variance with one or more existing theories, the existing theories are usually described and evaluated. In such cases, particular care must be taken to ensure that the competing theory is fully described (unless it is very well known) and fairly presented. While the author may be certain that his own development is superior and more applicable to the problem under consideration, if he seems to "load the dice" against the existing theory, he will lose the confidence of his reader.

The level of familiarity that the reader may have with existing theory often presents a problem. If the theory is complex and drawn from scattered sources, full explanation comprehensible to a reader totally unfamiliar with it may become very long. Explanation may be unnecessary for other readers in the immediate field who are already familiar with much of it (of course, they can skip the explanation and move on to the actual development of new theory). But if the underlying theory is not presented fully, many readers may not be able to follow it without locating and reading the sources cited. A qualified reader should not be forced to find and read something else in order to understand the report—the development must be complete enough that a reader familiar with the major current work in the general field can follow it. If some aspects are based upon material with which a substantial proportion of potential readers would not be familiar or upon obscure or generally inaccessible materials, it may be necessary to include more complete development of that material (perhaps in an appendix) than of the rest of the discussion.

## New Theory

This is the theory developed in the project, so there should be no problem in assessing the reader's familiarity with the subject matter—it is new to him. Therefore, the development must be complete or the reader will not be able to follow it. Original concepts must be explained fully, and specific terms defined exactly—there is no place else to look them up! Where equations are derived, symbols must be identified and intermediate material should be sufficiently complete for the reader to follow derivations without undue mental gymnastics. Although the reader's intelligence should not be insulted, when he is told that "simple manipulation" leads from one equation to another, it should not be necessary for him to work it out for himself with a pencil and paper. As all students know, an additional equation or two in a series could often save the reader a frustrating hour of "simple manipulation."

While the complexity of the theory developed—and the number of sections needed to present it—varies from project to project, complete and orderly presentation should always be the goal. And because the very nature of the material can open the door to confusion, special care must be taken to present the development in the sequence that will be easiest for the reader to understand, to make the sequence evident to him at the outset (in the sectional introduction), to use headings and other organizational aids to guide him through it, and to explain each phase of the development fully as it is presented.

## Application

There is usually a section in which the newly developed theory is applied to a specific problem and the results obtained evaluated, perhaps by comparing them to those obtained by other means. A fully developed application of the theory is not always possible, but at least a limited test is usually attempted to validate the development and provide a basis for evaluating the result of the study. This may involve computer simulation, empirical testing, analytical comparison, or other measures of the soundness and applicability of the theory derived.

## THEORETICAL-EXPERIMENTAL PROJECTS

In some projects, a substantial theoretical development is produced and then tested experimentally to determine its validity. Such a project is, in effect, both a theoretical and an experimental project. In the report, the theoretical development is usually presented first, and predictions are made about what should happen in an experimental situation according to the theory that has been developed. The experiment is then explained, and the results presented. The predicted and actual results are then compared, and the comparison is the basis for conclusions regarding the validity of the theory developed. Thus, the developing sections of the report usually include both those normally expected in the report of a theoretical study and those expected in the report of an experimental study, and the material within sections is essentially that contained in the corresponding sections of theoretical and experimental reports. A typical report might contain the following developing sections:

> Existing Theory
> Theoretical Development
> Theoretical Predictions
> Equipment
> Procedure
> Results
> Comparison of Predictions and Results

Any additional sections necessary for the full explanation of the project would, of course, be added, and two or more sections might be included on any of the topics listed. Any of the sections listed might be combined with others or eliminated where warranted by the nature of the project itself. But the theoretical sections are usually presented first, and where combinations are made, the theoretical sections are kept separate from the experimental sections.

## DESIGN PROJECTS

In a design project, the problem is to design a new system or subsystem or to design a modification to an existing one. The design may be developed to fill an immediate or projected need (as a piece of test equipment or a special purpose computer) or simply to determine how something might be designed and whether it would be workable (as a high-powered laser or a radically new wing for supersonic aircraft). In some projects, the design alone is developed; in others, a prototype is built and, perhaps, tested. To the extent that something is designed, produced, and operated, design projects are sometimes much like experimental projects involving the development of new equipment, but the emphasis is usually different. In a design project, the equipment itself is the object of the study; in most experimental projects, on the other hand, it is the information generated by the equipment that is sought. To some extent, this is perhaps more a difference in degree than in kind.

As has been indicated, the sequence of developing sections in a thesis often roughly approximates the sequence in which the study is carried out. Thus, the thesis reporting a typical design project might include the following developing sections:

> Detailed Analysis (of the problem)
> Theory
> Design
> Fabrication
> Testing and Evaluation

To simplify the following discussion, the term "equipment" is used in referring to the item designed. But it must be recognized that a design project may be intended to develop electronic currents, master system designs, new components for existing equipment, or almost anything else.

## Detailed Analysis

Although the problem itself is stated in the introduction, a more complete analysis and discussion of the conditions under which the projected equipment would be used and the exact design requirements are usually necessary as a starting point for the development. This might include analysis of similar existing equipment and its performance and limitations, close analysis of the conditions under which the equipment would be used, the required levels of performance, limitations (such as those pertaining to safety, strength, cost, and compatibility with other equipment) imposed upon the design, and explanation and discussion of any other general considerations that will influence the development of the design. Just what may be necessary here will vary, but the information presented should establish the design criteria and equip the reader to understand the basis for decisions made in the actual development of the design. It should orient the reader so that he will not continually wonder why the design is developed as it is in the following sections of the report.

## Theory

Any necessary theoretical development on which the design (or part of it) is based should be presented in detail. In some projects, the theoretical development may be quite substantial, perhaps representing the bulk of the effort on the project. Relevant portions of existing theory may be reviewed, modified, and extended to meet the requirements of the immediate problem. Appropriate studies should be cited and commented upon and necessary formulas and equations derived just as in the theoretical sections of other theses so that the overall theoretical concept against which the design was developed is clear to the reader.

## Design

Here, the actual design—the intended result of the project—is developed. If it is relatively simple, only one main section of the report may be required; but if it is complex, two or more may be necessary. Decisions made in the course of the development should be discussed and justified, and, where appropriate, they should be related to the governing design limitations and theory presented in the earlier sections. Discussion should focus on the critical and significant elements of the design (strength of materials, shapes of airfoils, or composition of circuits) rather than on trivia having little or no effect upon the effectiveness of the design (the sizes of screws and fillets or the colors of enclosures).

Relatively simple drawings and diagrams should be included in the textual discussion as it is developed. But while full detail about the design is necessary (this is the primary product of the study), the reader should not be held up by numerous or complicated drawings as he proceeds through the text. These should be placed in appendixes.

## Fabrication

When a prototype is made, the fabrication is sometimes described in the sections in which the design is described and sometimes it is described in a separate section. If the process of fabrication is relatively straightforward and techniques are generally obvious, the description may be omitted or any portions requiring explanation may simply be included with the discussion of the design as it is developed. If, on the other hand, procedures or sequences are unusual, complex, or critical, they should be described fully in a separate section of the text or, perhaps, in one or more appendixes. Significant procedures should be described in sufficient detail that a reader can understand what was done to produce the prototype and assess the suitability of the procedures (heat treating, extrusion, aligning critical parts, or sealing connections).

## Testing

While it is not always possible to test the prototype developed in a design project, many are tested to determine performance against the criteria established at the outset. In such cases, the testing should be described fully, and the results presented in detail as the basis for conclusions about the effectiveness of the design. If the design is modified on the basis of test results and then retested, the modifications and the results of subsequent testing should be described. Sometimes it is necessary to carry out several iterations of modification and testing in the process of refining the design—all should be described and discussed. In such cases, particular care must be taken to make certain that a full description (including modified drawings, schematics, wiring diagrams, photographs) or the final design is available all in one place. The reader should not be forced to mentally patch together an original design and several partial modifications in order to visualize the complete final design.

## COMPUTER PROJECTS

A computer project is one in which the primary effort is centered upon the development (and, usually, validation) of a computer program or upon the use of computers in developing results. The project problem may be essentially a design problem, a theoretical problem, or even an experimental problem, but a substantial portion of the effort involves the computer. Thus, the difference between computer projects and others is, again, often more a matter of degree than of kind. Although the classification itself may be dubious, the reports of such projects can easily become almost unreadable if they are not carefully organized, so some separate comment is in order.

When the purpose of the project is the development of a program, the developing sections of the report may be generally analogous to those of a design study (the program is the thing to be designed). Thus, the development might include the following:

> Detailed Analysis (of the problem)
> Theoretical Development
> Development of the Program
> Validation

As in design projects, the problem usually requires more complete definition than can comfortably be presented in the introduction, so detailed expansion is provided immediately following it. Existing theory applicable to the problem is then reviewed, necessary extensions are developed, and, perhaps, the basic algorithm presented. Then the program itself is developed—in much the same way as the design is in a design thesis. The focus should be upon the major decisions made in building the program rather than on minor problems with subroutines. Where the sequences may appear to be unnecessarily long or roundabout, they should be explained and justified. Following the description of the program's development, there is usually some sort of validation, often a comparison of results obtained through its use on a given problem with those obtained from other sources (empirical results, test results, results obtained by other computational means).

Because of the mass of detail that may be involved, special care must be taken to be certain that the text flows as smoothly as possible and with a minimum of distraction; masses of data, lengthy derivations, and pages of symbols should be kept in appendixes. If the program itself is the object of the project (as with a test of optimal design or a new method of computation), it is usually sufficient to include simple logic tables in the text and place the program in an appendix.

If the programs developed are incidental to the overall purpose of the project, logic diagrams (with suitable explanation) are often all that is placed in the appendix, though relatively simple programs that are not available elsewhere may well be included. If programs are available elsewhere, only modifications made for use in the study need be included.

In any case, neither the text nor the appendixes should be loaded down with dozens or hundreds of pages of programs, progressive modifications to subroutines, or output that few if any readers will ever actually use. These can be put in a file cabinet and later reproduced and forwarded to anyone who may request them.

## REVIEW OF THE LITERATURE

Occasionally, the purpose of a thesis project is to review the entire open literature in a given area and develop a report which presents and evaluates the current information in the area—sometimes the report is to be used as a text or a supplementary text for a course. This kind of project is not common, and some advisors feel that it does not adequately allow the student to demonstrate his ability to carry out independent research in the sense intended. Others, however, consider such projects to be both appropriate and valuable in areas in which advances have been rapid and no publication has yet effectively compiled, reviewed, and evaluated work in the field. The time and effort required in researching such a topic effectively and analyzing the result may be as great as or greater than that necessary in carrying out other projects. It takes hours of work and may require a seemingly interminable search for obscure publications, so a student who is not at ease in the library certainly should not undertake such a project.

If the work in the field reviewed has generally proceeded along a single line with research and advances building cumulatively upon one another, the sequence of sections is dictated by the sequence of the research. In each section, the studies evaluated chronologically follow those considered in the previous section. It is more common, though, for research to proceed in different directions and by different means at the same time. Therefore, the sequence of sections in the report is usually by topic, with each section considering all studies related to a given topic. Materials discussed in any given section or subsection may be presented roughly in chronological order, but much of the material discussed within any one section may predate much of that in an earlier section and postdate that in a later section. It is the author's concern to analyze the material available, categorize it into general topic areas which seem to be logical divisions of the overall subject, and put the topics into a sequence that will seem sensible to the reader. It is important that the sequence chosen be one that permits the later sections to build easily upon the earlier sections (to assure that the things discussed early in the report do not require excessive explanation that depends upon materials better presented later under another topic).

The research in a given field does not usually fall easily into clear-cut categories; some studies draw upon others that seem logically to belong in different general categories (no matter what general topics are chosen, this still happens). The body of research is completely intertwined. Everything depends on everything else, no block of research can be fully explained without drawing upon the others, and there is no obvious "right" entry point into the mass. So definition and ordering of sections of the report may evolve as a series of compromises. The reviewer's touchstone must be the minimum of confusion and the greatest ease of understanding for the reader who is not familiar with the field. The "inevitable sequence" is not always evident, and the author may make several attempts at categorization and arrangement before settling upon the one to be used. On this kind of project, considerable time and rewriting can be saved if the author makes several alternative outlines before attempting to tailor his sections and fit them together. By doing this, he is more likely to produce an organization that appears clear and direct to the reader than he would otherwise be.

Within each section of a report reviewing the literature in a given field it is important that the coverage of the section be clearly defined and explained at the outset. Main lines of development within the section are usually essentially chronological—studies are described and evaluated in the order in which they appeared—but where logic suggests that studies on a given portion of the topic should be taken out of chronological sequence, this should be done.

If the purpose of the project is to review all of the literature on the topic, *all* of it should be reviewed, but emphasis should, of course, be placed on the most significant studies and those which hold the most promise for future development. If the purpose of the study is to review only the most significant studies, then only these need be commented upon. In either case, each study mentioned should be cited properly, and full bibliographic information on each should be listed in the bibliography.

## VARIATION FROM GENERAL PATTERNS

The general patterns of developing sections that have been described are just that—general patterns. They are sequences that are often followed, but *by no means should these or any other patterns be followed blindly*. The developing sections of a thesis should be chosen and ordered in a sequence that will lead the reader as easily as possible through the research in a logical sequence. No general pattern is any better than the common sense with which departures are made from it, and certainly the sequence that may be effective in describing one project will not necessarily be effective in describing another.

For example, the general pattern of development for describing an experimental project is theory, equipment, procedure, results. The following are some of the common variations:

1. In some experiments, the theory involved is minimal and may easily fit into the introduction. If it would be of interest to only a few readers, it may be put in an appendix. In either case, there would be no separate section on theory. If no theoretical discussion is really necessary to understand the basis for the experiment or its implications, none should be included.

2. If selection and preparation of test samples are complex and critical, a separate section describing the samples may be necessary.

3. If the equipment or apparatus used requires little or no description, it may only be discussed briefly in the section on experimental procedures. Conversely, if the experimental procedures are routine or depend entirely upon special equipment developed for the experiment, they may be described in the section on equipment. On the other hand, if either the equipment or procedures are diverse, two or more sections may be required for either. But don't strain to have separate sections here or elsewhere if they are not really needed.

4. If the processing of data is lengthy and several complicated procedures are used, more than one section describing results may be required.

5. If results are voluminous or the necessary related discussion is substantial, discussion may be presented in a separate section instead of being included in the section presenting results. If portions of the results relate to distinctly different parts of the problem, there may be two or more sections, each presenting results and related discussion bearing upon one part of the problem.

6. If several distinctly different experimental procedures are followed to produce, in effect, two or more "mini-experiments" within the project, several individual sections may each describe one of the mini-experiments. Each section would have subsections on theory, equipment, procedure, and results as required.

Other variations could be listed, and a similar list could be produced for each of the other general types of projects discussed in this chapter. But whatever the names given the sections, the general principle of organization should remain. The sequence usually moves from what was known to what was done, what resulted, and what the reader should make of it. Blocks of information are identified as clearly as possible with headings and subheadings and are grouped and presented in the order that will be easiest for the reader to understand.

# 11

# Concluding Sections

The concluding sections present the answer to the problem stated in the introduction (as well as any secondary answers developed along the way) and whatever suggestions you may have about applications and further research. The problem was stated in the introduction, the developing sections described how you went about solving it and any additional information you developed in the course of doing it, and the concluding sections complete the text by telling the reader what he is to make of it all.

## USUAL CONTENT

The most common kinds of information included in the concluding sections are conclusions, recommendations, and discussion.

### Conclusions

These are inferences based upon evidence (facts or results) developed in the report. They are the answers you were after when you undertook the study. Usually, they should be presented as flat statements without much elaboration. After working on the project for months, there is a natural inclination to want to present solid conclusions—and sometimes a tendency to overestimate their importance or general applicability. But do not present unwarranted conclusions based upon insufficient evidence obtained in a limited study. Don't maintain that all metal plates will fail at 5000 PSI simply because the two you tested did. There is an old saying to the effect that students, like the seven blind men of Hindustan, tend to judge the entire elephant by his tail or his ear or his trunk. But many readers of professional journals are not so sure that it applies to students any more than it does to anyone else.

## Recommendations

These are suggestions for further research or other courses of action that follow as a result of the information developed in the study. Often, they are things you would have done yourself if you had had the time. In the course of the project, you may well have spent more time thinking about the exact problem concerned, the procedures you used and their limitations, and the meaning of your results than anyone else ever has. By the time you finish, you are the expert on the subject. Although possible modifications of procedure, further studies that could be performed, and applications of the information generated may be obvious to you (you have been thinking about them for several months), they will not necessarily be evident to your reader (he has only been reading the report for an hour or so), so tell him what you think might follow. If you have been keeping a close log of ideas as they occurred in the course of your study, you may be surprised to find that you had almost forgotten some of your own ideas already. If they form the basis for possible further studies, put them in the report as recommendations for further study so they won't be lost.

Recommendations need not necessarily be included in every thesis report. Sometimes the immediate problem was solved and further research is not necessary—fluid flow was identified and diagrammed, the effect of a variation in temperature was measured, or a computer program was developed and debugged. If no recommendations seem to be in order, don't strain to contrive trivial recommendations just for the sake of having some in the report.

## Discussion

This is connected discourse in which the results of the study are examined, justified, expanded upon, evaluated, or interpreted. Here, again drawing upon the thinking you have done in the course of the study, you have the opportunity, as perhaps nowhere else in the report, to present your own ideas about the approach, procedures, and equipment used and to comment on the results, conclusions, and recommendations developed and their meaning. Some departments or some advisors may not feel that discussion is appropriate material in a concluding section but may permit it in an earlier section in which results are presented (sometimes there is a section called "Results and Discussion").

## GUIDELINES

No single choice or arrangement of concluding material fits all theses—choose the material necessary to conclude the report on your project and arrange it in a way that will seem logical to the reader. There may be a single section, or there may be separate main sections containing conclusions, recommendations, and discussion. Probably the most common ending in theses in science and engineering is a single section called "Conclusions and Recommendations" with very limited discussion accompanying any conclusions or recommendations requiring it.

A concluding section (or, at least the first one) often begins with a brief introductory statement tying the section to the problem stated in the introduction (whether or not the entire problem was solved). In addition, it is often desirable to include a sentence or two placing such limitations on the conclusions and recommendations as may be called for by the method used or the breadth of the study. Readers sometimes turn directly from the introduction to the conclusions without reading the developing sections, so, to the extent possible, conclusions and recommendations should be written so that they will be comprehensible to someone who has not read the text. In that sense, they should be able to stand alone.

The following guidelines should be used in framing sections containing conclusions, recommendations, or discussion:

1. Use direct positive statements, quantitative where it is appropriate. Try for simple, uncluttered sentence structure that cannot be misunderstood. (This, of course, should be your intention throughout the report.) Specific conclusions are often presented in the past tense (things that were found—a structure failed or a +.87 correlation was found), more general conclusions in the present tense (universals—they continue to be true), and recommendations in the future tense (things that should be done and what will happen if they are).

2. If you have more than one or two conclusions or recommendations, put them in numbered lists for easy identification. Avoid running them together in long paragraphs.

3. Use headings to identify separate blocks of material, such as conclusions, recommendations, and discussion. If items in a headed section are numerous or diverse, use subheadings (General Conclusions, Specific Conclusions, Performance of the Model, Possible Applications in Gas Dynamics, and so forth).

4. If individual conclusions are developed from particular portions of the text, consider using page numbers to key them to the supporting pages.

5. If individual recommendations are derived from individual conclusions, consider presenting them in pairs or keying the recommendations to the conclusions.

6. As a rule, do not include argument in the statement of a conclusion. If argument or justification is necessary, it should be in the preceding text or in accompanying discussion.

7. Do not introduce new material in your concluding sections. All material from which conclusions, recommendations, or discussion are derived should be in the developing sections.

## OTHER CONTENT

Three other kinds of concluding sections sometimes used are Applications, Summary, and Design Summary, though the names used for them may vary.

### Applications

These are suggested uses of the information developed in the study. In some theses, the applications are presented as recommendations. But in others (particularly theoretical studies) where there are no conclusions or recommendations of the sort described previously, a section on applications may effectively conclude the text.

### Summary

A summary of the most important information developed may be used as the concluding section when the thesis is primarily a review of the published literature in a given area. In addition to the summary, the section may include an overall assessment of progress in the area; a general evaluation of developments thus far; a discussion of trends; comment on areas in which further development is needed, likely, or in progress; and, perhaps, a discussion of present and potential applications. If a summary is not appropriate, all or part of the remainder of the coverage listed above may be included in a section with an appropriate title (such as Future Development or General Evaluation).

### Design Summary

A summary and evaluation of the main features of the design that has been developed and of its performance in any testing done may effectively conclude a design project. Recommendations for modification, further testing, and possible applications may be appropriate.

# 12

# Supplementary Material

While the concluding sections bring the actual text of the report to a close, additional material usually follows—this is the supplementary material. Although not a part of the text, the supplementary material provides information of interest to some or most readers, detail that will add to (supplement) their understanding of the information contained in the text itself. The supplementary material commonly found in theses includes a bibliography, one or more appendixes, and sometimes a vita.

## BIBLIOGRAPHY

The bibliography is a list of the sources (published and unpublished) directly drawn upon and cited in the report. The individual items are usually arranged in alphabetical order according to the last names of their authors and numbered in the sequence in which they appear on the list. Sometimes, however, the items are listed in the sequence in which they are cited in the report. The sequence used is entirely a matter of local or personal preference. In either case, it is customary to single-space between lines within an entry and to double-space between successive entries.

Obviously, the number of entries in a bibliography varies widely according to the amount of direct reference to other works necessary in the report. When a primary purpose of the thesis is a complete review of published material on a given topic, the bibliography may be extensive. Usually, though, there is no particular merit in a long bibliography—it may just indicate that the author is unable to distinguish between important and trivial material in his field. The forms for individual entries are described in Chapter 13, and a typical bibliography is included at the end of that chapter. Others are included in the appendix as Examples 38 and 39.

Occasionally a list of works not cited in the report (background reading, further discussion of particular topics, or other material) is included. This list is separate from the bibliography and is usually placed following it. It may be titled "References" or "Suggestions for Further Reading," or given some similar name. Entries on such a list are sometimes annotated—short descriptive or evaluative comment on the work may be included with some or all entries. But such lists are not really justified in most theses (if a work is drawn upon substantially but not cited directly, it can be acknowledged in the preface), and many advisors feel that they should never be used (if a source is not directly cited, there is no reason to list it). If a supplementary list is used, it should be kept short; the report will be read only by people in the technical field concerned, and they will not need introductory readings. Don't pad the list! The more superfluous material you include, the more likely the reader is to feel that you don't know what is common knowledge in your field or what is extraneous to your specific study.

## APPENDIXES

An appendix is a section which follows the text of the report and presents information (usually close detail) which supports or amplifies material in the text. The main development of the text is complete without it, but the appendix material may be essential to the close analysis of equipment and procedures used, data gathered, manipulations performed, or almost any other matter touched upon in the running text.

Most readers will read through the text to understand what was done, how it was done, and what resulted before turning to an appendix for close detail on a particular point of interest. They should be able to follow the theoretical development or the experimental procedure in the text easily, and they should not be forced to struggle through pages and pages of data tables, computer programs, or calibration procedures in the process. These should be in appendixes where the reader can refer to them when (and if) he is interested. Some readers may never read a given appendix—they simply may not be interested in detail on the material covered. Others, particularly people doing research in the same area or by the same general method, may find the appendixes the most valuable part of the report. But if this material were included in the running text, many readers would be less impressed by the thoroughness of the detail than by the lack of judgment shown in interrupting the flow of the text. Some might not read the report because too much time would be required to wade through detail in which they had no interest.

Just what specific material should be placed in an appendix is essentially a matter of personal judgment (your advisor's experience and preferences can be of help here). A particular procedure that one person might consider essential to the development of the text might be considered supplementary by another, so exactly where the line is drawn in a thesis depends to some extent on who is doing the drawing. But the overall aim is to put essential information in the text and supporting or supplementary information in an appendix.

## Content

The specific kinds of material contained in appendixes are immensely varied. No list can be complete, but the following will suggest typical content in scientific and engineering theses:

*Data tables* (*raw or processed data*). Sometimes a sample is put in the text and the rest in an appendix.

*Mathematical derivations of uncommon formulas or developments of secondary interest.*

*Sample calculations.* Include these if they are complex—but don't show your reader how to add 2 and 2.

*Flow diagrams.*

*Computer programs.* Include a logic diagram—your reader may want to modify your program slightly to fit his particular problem, so save him the hours of trying to puzzle yours out. Standard programs readily available elsewhere need not be included, but new ones developed in the project often are. However, even with a new program some advisors recommend inclusion only of a logic diagram.

*Computer output.*

*Background materials.*

*Information about equipment.* Include photos and sketches, calibration procedures (expanded details), operational procedures (expanded details), drawings, wiring diagrams.

*Glossary of terms.* This should be in an appendix only if it is longer than two or three pages. Otherwise, it should be in the prefatory material.

*Supporting documents.* Include full copies if necessary.

*Fold-out illustrations.* Include these only if they are referred to frequently. Wherever possible, avoid using any fold-outs at all.

*Letters.*

*Questionnaires.*

*Maps.*

*Descriptions of blind alleys.* Describe any approaches or procedures that you tried but which did not work. As was indicated earlier, if they seemed logical to you, they will probably seem logical to a reader, who might wonder why you didn't try them. He might even spend considerable time and effort trying them himself, only to find out what you already know—that they don't work. Researchers are sometimes reluctant to admit that they ever do anything that doesn't work, but they shouldn't be. If a given researcher reports nothing but a string of smashing successes without a misstep in complicated experiments, you may well wonder whether he is reporting complete information, and that may lead you to wonder about the completeness and accuracy of the information that he does report. Don't report simple blunders such as time lost because you forgot to turn on a piece of equipment, because you forgot to calibrate it, or because you misplaced a decimal point; but report procedures or approaches which seemed plausible but just didn't work.

*Any other supplementary information that you feel would be helpful to some of your readers in understanding what you did, why you did it, and how you did it.*

## Presentation

A given thesis may have no appendixes, it may have a single appendix, or it may have several appendixes, depending upon the kinds and amounts of information needed to support the text. Some general rules for the presentation of appendixes are indicated below. Style sheets vary from university to university, but these suggestions will be generally acceptable in most places:

1. Refer to each appendix in the text of the report at the point at which the information the appendix supports is presented. If you feel that the information contained in the appendix is necessary to supplement the text, the reader may wonder whether you have included it somewhere, so tell him.

2. If there is only one appendix, simply call it Appendix and give it a descriptive title such as, "Appendix: Sample Calculations of Dose Rate." If there are several appendixes, identify each with a capital letter and a descriptive title. The letters are assigned in the sequence in which the appendixes appear (much like figure numbers) so that a reader will know what kind of information the appendix contains.

   Appendix A: Calibration Procedure for Rheboid
   Appendix B: Computer Program to Calculate Probable Growth
   Rate
   Appendix C: Data Tables

3. List both the appendix letters and titles in the table of contents. If the letters alone are listed, a reader cannot tell from the table of contents just what is in the various appendixes or which is the one that he may be looking for. To find the oscilloscope traces or the data tables, for example, he will simply have to thumb through all of the appendixes until he stumbles on the one he is looking for, and this may take a while if there are many of them. Or, he may simply miss the fact that you have included information that would be of value to him.

4. Start each appendix on a new page and place the identifying letter and title at the top of the page for easy identification. Some specifications require that the first page of each appendix contain only the identifying letter and title of the appendix. Most do not, however, as this may add five or ten essentially blank pages to the report.

5. Limit the coverage in each appendix to a single subject or body of data. If a given appendix contains several diverse kinds of informa-

tion, it is more difficult for the reader to find what he's looking for easily and the function of identifying titles has been somewhat defeated.

6. The sequence of appendixes is entirely up to you. Unless there is reason to do otherwise, they are usually presented in the sequence that the information they support appears in the text.

7. Each appendix should be a complete self-contained unit. Usually a simple paragraph or two of introduction (perhaps containing direct reference to the pages of text supported) is sufficient to identify the material contained and explain what it is. Bear in mind that readers often refer to an appendix for specific details long after reading the text itself. They should not be forced to reread the text in order to understand an appendix.

8. From the beginning of the introduction through the last page of the last appendix, the pages are usually numbered in a single consecutive series. Some universities prefer that the appendix pages be numbered separately with alpha-numerical page numbers (A1, A2, A3, B1, B2, B3 . . .), and if yours does, that is how you should number them. But this system can make it a little harder for the reader to find particular pages when the appendixes are numerous or lengthy.

9. Observe the same rules in the appendixes as you did in the body of the text regarding margins, headings, handling of figures and equations, and other matters of format and presentation.

## An Admonition

An appendix is included to support or amplify the text; it should not be a dumping ground for miscellaneous bits of information that can't be worked in anywhere else. Don't try to include every scrap of information read or generated in the entire course of the thesis project. Include only that which helps to explain what was done, how it was done, why it was done, and the result. Leave out everything else. Very few advisors are impressed by material included only to build a thick report (a tactic familiar to one and all long before you started your project). Most advisors are more likely to be impressed by the common sense with which you recognize and winnow out the chaff, and the conciseness, clarity, and accuracy with which you present the necessary information. We're all concerned about ecology these days, so don't pollute your appendix. Dispose of extraneous information in biodegradable trash cans.

## VITA

A vita, a brief professional biography of the author, is required in the thesis by some schools. In the vita, the author lists the date and place of his birth, his parents' names, the educational institutions he has attended (and degrees earned), and then his experience and anything of significance that he has done in his professional field—teaching experience, other experience in the field, publications, professional activities, papers presented, honors received. The vita should not exceed a single double-spaced page (most are well under this), and it should not be padded out with trivia which adds nothing to the author's qualifications. Listing your high school biology club simply makes you look unprofessional. A vita is usually written in the third person, but some schools permit the first person to be used.

# 13

# Citation and Documentation

Citation and documentation are simply the identification of information and ideas taken from other sources (published or unpublished) and the listing of the sources used—telling whose material helped you in your project or was used in your report. This is done for several reasons; those most commonly discussed are the following:

1. To give credit where credit is due (simple ethics).
2. To make it easy for a reader who questions a borrowed fact or idea to check it at the source. (If you won't tell where you got it, there must be something wrong with it.)
3. To make it easy for the reader to get more detail from the source if he should want to.
4. To lend the authority of a highly regarded source (as the president of the American Chemical Society or a Nobel Prize winner in physiology) to the borrowed material.
5. To meet legal obligations. (If you won't act ethically, you may be made to wish you had.)

Some judgment is required in deciding just when sources should be cited, but the following general rules of thumb should be adequate for most situations:

1. Cite the sources of all direct quotations.
2. Cite the sources of particular facts, ideas, or methods (such as theories, data, formulas, procedures, or other information) directly attributable to a specific individual or source whether or not they are presented by direct quotation.
3. Do not cite the sources of information which is widely known and accepted in your field *and* which is available from many independent sources. Thus, it would generally be unnecessary to cite the original source of $E = Mc^2$ (though in many cases you would probably men-

tion Einstein's name when introducing it), of the atomic weight of oxygen, or of the cosine of 81° 32′.

Wherever possible, it is customary to cite the primary (original) source of the information presented. You never know whether or not a secondary source (one which quotes the original) has presented the information fairly or completely. (Read a few partisan newspapers or listen to a few biased news commentators reporting the same story.) If you build upon misinterpretation, you simply compound the error—and, perhaps, call attention to your own failure to follow good practice. It is not always possible to use primary sources (as with old, obscure, or foreign language publications), but they should be sought out and used wherever possible.

No one will expect you to be the originator of everything you do or every idea you use. All advances in science and engineering are built upon the accumulated knowledge of the past, and you can't very well develop the first workable oscilloscope, table of atomic weights, or theory of the expanding universe for use in your research. These things have already been done. On the contrary, it is very poor practice to fail to take advantage of the best previous work in your field—and to acknowledge the sources drawn upon. When information attributable to a specific source or individual is presented in the thesis without direct quotation, special care must be taken to assure that the source is properly cited. Failure to acknowledge the source is plagiarism, and the fact that the material has been rephrased (is not quoted verbatim) is completely beside the point. Plagiarism is the presentation of someone else's ideas or methods as one's own, and theft is theft whatever the reason given. Recognizable plagiarism will destroy the credibility of the author—*sometimes permanently.*

The overwhelming majority of use made of borrowed material in theses is perfectly legal under the "doctrine of fair use"—the reasonable and expected use of copyrighted material in science and technology which does not lessen the value of the original. Indeed, citing someone else's work may add to his prestige and increase the demand for the original. But special care must be taken when the thesis is to be made available for mass distribution, when direct quotations are used, and when someone else's unpublished materials are used (these are under copyright from the time they are written). If you are not familiar with standard practice, ask your advisor about any local directives concerning the use of copyrighted material, and if there is any doubt, check further with the graduate school. The Copyright Office has published a series of short bulletins discussing specific points in the copyright law, including its application in scholarly work, and the law itself (Title 17 of the U. S. Code, PL 94–553, Oct. 19, 1976) defines fair use. These should be readily available in your library should you want to check any questionable points. The odds are probably a million to one against legal difficulties in any individual case, but this is small consolation to the one who has them.

Formerly, published sources of material cited or quoted were almost universally identified in footnotes at the bottoms of the pages on which the citations or quotations occurred, and the practice is still followed in many fields. In science and engineering, however, simpler numbered reference systems are widely used, both in professional journals and in many kinds of technical reports—including theses. Reference to sources is made by notation directly in the text, and all sources cited or quoted are listed in a bibliography at the end of the report. So footnotes indicating sources are not needed. This reference system makes the preparation of typed copy much easier, generally reduces the clutter at the bottoms of pages, and eliminates the problem of form for footnotes (there are many forms, and some of them are both complicated and unwieldy). And for many purposes, a numbered system is much easier for the reader to use. The names of the authors of important studies are usually mentioned in the text where reference is made, and the reader does not normally stop in the middle of a paragraph to run to the library and locate a referenced work. So usually there is no particular reason to have the full bibliographic information at the bottom of the page.

The general form of the bibliography was described in Chapter 12, and samples are included both at the end of this chapter and in the appendix (Examples 38 and 39). A reference system and the forms for individual bibliographic entries for books, journal articles, other publications, and unpublished sources are described in the following pages.

## REFERENCE NOTE

Reference to sources is made by parenthetical notation in the text itself directing the reader to the sources listed in the bibliography. A form that is commonly used is as follows:

| | |
|---|---|
| (6: 27) | Refers to a single page in a single source (page 27 in the sixth item listed in the bibliography) |
| (6: 27–32) | Refers to several pages in succession |
| (6: 27, 32, 38, 46) | Refers to pages not in succession |
| (6: 27; 8: 36) | Refers to pages in two (or more) sources |
| (6: IV, 27) or | Refers to a source in which the pages in chapters |
| (6: Chapter 4, 27) | or sections are numbered in separate series |

NOTE: Brackets [   ] rather than parentheses (   ) are used to enclose the reference note in most professional journals, but they are not available on all typewriters. Some schools prefer the standard use of parentheses, while others permit the use of either parentheses or brackets.

In some conventions, the word "Reference" or the abbreviation "Ref." is placed inside the parentheses preceding the page numbers. Thus, the complete reference note would be (Reference 6:27) or (Ref. 6:27).

Sometimes only the number of the source is indicated in the reference note, not the page numbers within the source. Thus, the full reference note is simply (6). This form is widely used in technical and professional journals in which the majority of references are to journal articles. Usually there is no difficulty in finding the information cited because the articles are relatively short and the procedure used or the information developed in the entire article is referred to. But when the reference is to information (a particular table or theory or procedure) in a longer work, this form is very ineffective. The reader may be forced to page through 500 pages of text to find the material cited—if he ever does.

Where it seems awkward or superfluous to list page numbers in each citation, a compromise is sometimes made: some citations include page numbers and others do not. When the source cited is long or when a specific piece of information on a specific page is cited, page numbers are included in the reference note. When the source cited is short (a three- or four-page journal article) or when reference to the entire work is intended, only the number of the source is indicated.

## Placement of Reference Note

The reference note is usually placed in the text at the end of the material cited (in the same place that the superscript symbol for a footnote would be placed). If this is at the end of a sentence or other grammatical structure which is followed by punctuation, the punctuation is placed after the reference note. When an entire subsection is based upon a single source, the reference note may be placed after the sectional heading. When the source of a figure or table is cited, the reference note is usually placed immediately below it and flush with its right-hand side; but in some conventions, it is placed immediately after the title of the figure or table. Use of the reference note is illustrated in the sample pages included in the appendix.

## BIBLIOGRAPHIC ENTRIES

The preferred forms for bibliographic entries vary widely both among and within professional fields, but the information contained in individual entries is usually about the same. In most cases the differences are minor—largely matters of sequence, capitalization, abbreviation, and punctuation. If no preferred forms are prescribed by your university or your department, those described on the following pages should be generally acceptable. They indicate how books, articles, and other source materials are often listed, and how several variations from the most common cases may be handled. Where variations not covered by these forms occur, keep in mind that the purpose of any entry is to fully identify the source concerned so that a reader can locate and examine it if he wants to. To do this, he usually needs to know who wrote it, what it is called, and where, when, and by whom it was published. If the material has not been published, he needs to know whom to contact for further information about it. By familiarizing yourself with the forms to be used before you do your background reading, you can be certain to record all necessary identifying information as you take your notes. This can save the time and effort of returning to the sources later to obtain missing dates, publishers, volume numbers, or whatever else may otherwise have been missed.

## Books

The three blocks of information used in listing books are the name of the author(s), identification of the work, and the publishing information. Periods are used to separate these three items, commas and a colon are used between some of the items within them, and a period is placed at the end of the entry.

The generalized form for a bibliographic entry is as follows:

> Author. Title of Book. City of publication: Name of publisher, year of publication.

### 1. *Author*

SINGLE AUTHOR. The surname is listed first, then a comma, then the given name and/or initials, and finally a period (if periods have been used after initials, an additional period is not necessary). The author's full first and middle names, his full first name and middle initial, or initials only may be used. Probably the most common practice is the listing of the author's full first name and middle initial (thumb through the hundreds of cards for Smith, Brown, or Johnson in your library if you feel that this is unnecessary). But wherever possible, the same form should be used throughout the bibliography, although full names or both initials may not always be available.

> D'Azzo, John Joachim
> D'Azzo, John J.
> D'Azzo, J. J.
> D'Azzo, J.

TWO AUTHORS. The names should be listed in the order in which they appear on the title page of the book. The first name listed on the title page is inverted as described above and followed by the word "and." The second author's name should not be inverted; his first name or initials precede his surname. The surname is followed by a period.

> D'Azzo, John J. and Constantine H. Houpis.
> D'Azzo, J.J. and C.H. Houpis.

THREE OR MORE AUTHORS. The form described for two authors is used, and additional names, not inverted, are simply added on the end.

> D'Azzo, John J., Constantine H. Houpis, and James E. Hitchcock.

As this form may become unwieldy, the name of only the first author may be listed and followed by et al. (the Latin abbreviation for "and others").

> D'Azzo, John J., et al.

No Individual Authors. If no individual author is listed on the title page or elsewhere (as in the case of some conference proceedings, committee reports, and similar volumes), the sponsoring committee, section, or society may be listed as the author.

## 2. Identification of the Work

For many books, the title is the only item to be entered. But any of the other items listed should be included (in the sequence indicated) when they apply.

Title. The name of the work is listed and underlined. The first letter of the first word in the title and of all other main words are capitalized (articles, short conjunctions, and short prepositions are not usually capitalized).

Volume Number. If the book is one of a numbered series of volumes, the volume number (underlined) follows the title. If the volumes within the series have separate titles, the title of the volume follows the volume number, is written in the same form as the overall title, and is underlined.

Edition. If the work cited is any edition other than the first edition, the edition number is placed in parentheses and spelled out (Second Edition, Third Edition, Fourth Edition). Because the content of a book and the pages on which information falls are different from edition to edition, this can be important to a reader attempting to find cited information. Whenever an edition number is not listed, it is assumed that the first edition of the book concerned is the one cited.

Editor or Translator. If the work has been compiled, edited, or translated by someone other than the author(s), this should be indicated. The stature and competence of the editor or translator have a significant effect on the worth of the work.

Contributed Foreword. If someone other than the author of the book wrote the foreword, his name may be included. While such forewords are not common, they may be important. Often, the authors of contributed forewords are better known than the authors of the books in which the forewords appear, and their evaluation and comment on the material contained is significant. They may or may not be listed in the bibliographic entry.

## 3. Publication Information

Publisher. The city in which the publisher is located and the name of the publishing company are listed with a colon separating them. If several cities are listed on the title page, the first one is usually the headquarters; if it is not clear which is the headquarters, a librarian or an index of publishers should be consulted. The publisher's headquarters is usually in a major city (New York, Boston, Philadelphia) so the location is well known. If the city is not well known, abbreviation for the state is often listed after the city.

Either the full corporate name of the publisher (St. Martin's Press, Inc.) may be used, or an abbreviated form (St. Martin's). But all listings should be handled in the same way.

DATE. The year of publication of the edition used is the last item in the entry. This should not be taken from the title page but from the copyright notice (usually located on the reverse side of the title page). Where several dates are listed in the copyright notice, the latest date listed is the date to be used.

### 4. An Exception

A section or chapter of a book may be written by someone other than the primary author, or the entire book may be a compilation of materials by many authors. Reference to this material is made by listing the author of the section referred to, its title (in quotation marks), and then the title of the book and the standard publication information.

**Examples:**

Myers, Glenford J. Software Reliability: Principles and Practices. New York: John Wiley and Sons, Inc., 1976.
   [Simple entry.]

D'Azzo, John J. and Constantine H. Houpis. Linear Control System Analysis and Design: Conventional and Modern. New York: McGraw-Hill Book Company, 1975.
   [Book with two authors.]

Blankowitz, Fernando G. et al. Computational Methods in Thermodynamics. Atlanta: Jardin Press, 1978.
   [Book with three or more authors; only the first need be listed.]

Kepler, Harold B. Basic Graphical Kinematics (Second Edition). New York: McGraw-Hill Book Company, 1973.
   [Edition number placed following the title on all but the first edition.]

Stewart, John M. and Janis D. Young. Solid Phase Peptide Analysis. Foreword by R. B. Merrifield. San Francisco: W. H. Freeman and Company, 1969.
   [Author of a signed foreword is listed following the title.]

Wulf, William A. "Language and Structured Programs" in Current Trends in Programming, Volume 1, Software Specifications and Design, edited by Raymond T. Yeh. Englewood Cliffs, N.J.: Prentice-Hall, Inc., 1977.
   [Article in a compilation. The book is one volume in a series. The editor is listed following the title.]

Committee for Energy Development. Nuclear Reactor Analysis, Foreword by Charles J. Bridgeman. London: Laubenthal International Ltd., 1979.
   [Book without an individual author listed.]

## Articles in Periodicals

Periodicals are journals, magazines, newspapers, pamphlets, or other publications which are published at regular or irregular intervals in a series. Although individual issues are usually dated and numbered, all issues appearing in a given period of time (usually a year) are normally grouped and given an identifying volume number. Volume numbers are assigned consecutively and most begin and end with the calendar year. Some begin at other times—a volume of a given periodical might begin with the first issue published on or after July 1 and end with the last issue published on or before the following June 30.

In most periodicals, individual issues begin with page 1, and pages are numbered consecutively throughout the issue. In some, though, the pages are numbered in a single consecutive series which begins with the first issue of a given volume and ends with the last issue of that volume. Thus, the first issue of the volume might contain pages 1 through 120, and the sixth issue of that volume might contain pages 721 through 840.

Just as there are differences in the ways in which volume numbers, issue numbers, and page numbers are assigned in various periodicals, there are also variations in the binding and storing of periodicals by libraries and other depositories. So, it is customary to list the volume number (and sometimes the issue number), page numbers, and the date in the bibliographic entry for an article in a periodical. Not all of this information is always needed to locate each source, but all of it can be helpful at one time or another.

The generalized form for a bibliographic entry is as follows:

Author. "Title of Article," Name of periodical, volume number: page numbers (date).

**AUTHOR.** The form used is the same as that for the author of a book. Wherever possible, the same form should be used throughout the bibliography. An unsigned article is not anonymous; the editor of the journal knows who wrote it. For these, begin the entry with the title of the article and use the first main word of the title for alphabetizing in an alphabetized bibliography.

**TITLE.** The title of the article is placed in quotation marks and followed by a comma, but it is not underlined. Normally, capitalization is handled in the same way as in the titles of books: the first letter of the first word and of all succeeding main words are capitalized; articles, short prepositions, and short conjunctions are not capitalized. If, however, the author appears to have intentionally departed from customary practice to attain a particular effect, the author's practice should be followed.

**JOURNAL.** The name of the periodical in which the article appeared is written out in full, underlined, and followed by a comma. (The names of journals are sometimes abbreviated, but form should be consistent throughout the bibliography.) Capitalization is as in the title of the article. The volume number is then listed and underlined. If the journal is one of a group published by a professional society or by sections of a society (such as the IEEE), any identifying letters, abbreviations, or numbers should be placed after the volume number and underlined. Individual issue numbers are sometimes placed in parentheses (but not underlined) following the volume number. If the issue number is listed for one periodical entry, it should be included for all periodical entries in the bibliography. The last of these items is followed by a colon.

PAGE NUMBERS. In most professional journals, and in many others, the pages on which an article appears are consecutive, so the beginning and ending pages are all that are listed. In some journals, articles are continued on nonconsecutive pages. In such cases, it is sufficient to list only the consecutive pages on which the first part of the article appears (64–72), but the later pages on which it is continued are sometimes indicated (64–72, 79, 83–84) or (64–72+). Entries for newspaper articles should include the section if specially labeled (as A, B, C, and so forth), page number, and column number.

DATE. The month (or quarter) and year of the journal issue concerned are enclosed in parentheses (June 1978) or (Summer 1977). If the periodical is issued at less than monthly intervals, the day of the month is usually included (December 18, 1978).

> **Examples:**
>
> Bregoli, L. J. "The Influence of Platinum Crystallite Size on the Electrochemical Reduction of Oxygen in Phosphoric Acid," Electrochemica Acta, 23: 489–492 (June 1978).
> [Simple entry]
>
> Weichel, Hugo. "The Uncertainty Principle and the Spectral Width of a Laser Beam," American Journal of Physics, 44 (9): 839–40 (September 1976).
> > [Here the issue number is listed immediately after the volume number of the journal. If it is included in one periodical entry, it should be included in all periodical entries in the bibliography.]
>
> Dickel, John R. and Herbert J. Rood. "Integrated Masses of Galaxies," The Astrophysical Journal, 223 (2) Part I: 391–409 (15 July 1978).
> > [Article with two authors. The journal appears in two separately bound parts.]
>
> Magruder, Steven F. "Classical Interactions of 't Hooft Monopoles," Physical Review D: Particles and Fields, 17 (12): 3257 (June 1978).
> > [The journal appears in four separate parts with individual names.]
>
> "Fifty and a Hundred Years Ago Today," Scientific American, 236 (6): 16 (June 1977).
> > [This listing would be placed in an alphabetized bibliography among the "F's"—alphabetized according to the first main word of the title.]
>
> Halloran, Richard. "Gas-Price Bill Faces Renewed Resistance," The New York Times, 127: D-3, Col 1 (August 2, 1978).
> > [The section (if labeled), page, and column are identified in newspaper articles.]

## Reports, Brochures, Manuals, Pamphlets, and Sundry Publications

This large and diverse group includes all publications other than books and periodicals. The documents may be published by universities, industries, businesses, government agencies, professional associations, or any other group (so-cial, professional, political, or anything else), and it would be fruitless to attempt an exhaustive listing of the categories of publications involved (technical reports, sales brochures, test specifications, equipment descriptions, and so forth).

As nearly as possible, the information listed in the bibliographic entries for these items should approximate that for books. But there is no uniformity in the identifying information contained in the documents, and there is no reason to believe that there ever will be—or that there should be. Each is produced to meet the immediate needs of the originating group, so a profusion of sponsoring organizations, contract numbers, project numbers, report numbers, company document numbers, revision numbers, revision dates, company names, division names, agency names, committee names, working group names, and other bits of possible identification information may be indicated on the title page or elsewhere in the publication. On the other hand, there may be virtually no identifying information at all. It would be naive to believe that identification of the "right" information for a bibliographic entry is necessarily clear-cut or obvious. If five bibliographers were given a dozen or so of these documents to list, they would probable produce five different lists.

The bibliographic entry should include enough information to enable a reader to evaluate the worth of the document and to locate and obtain it if he wishes to do so. It is not necessarily redundant to include two or even three identifying numbers (report number, contract number, project number, and so forth) when it is not evident which is primary. Different agencies or depositories may index documents in different ways. While the entry should not ramble on and on, it should include enough information to identify the document fully.

The generalized form for a bibliographic entry is as follows:

Author. Title. Description. Publisher, date.

**AUTHOR.** If the author of the publication is indicated, he is listed in the bibliographic entry in the same manner as the author of a book or article. If no author is indicated, one of two other things is commonly listed in his place in the entry. First, if the publication was produced by an identifiable group within the company or agency that published the document, the name of that group (a committee or department or branch within the larger company or agency) is listed in place of an individual author. Second, if the publication is part of a numbered series (technical notes, technical reports, company manuals), the number and any associated alphabetical prefix or suffix are listed in place of an author. If a number of the documents in such a series are to be listed and individual authors of only a few are known, in the interest of consistency all should be listed according to the prefix and number. The authors that are known can then be listed following the titles of the corresponding items.

**TITLE.** The title is underlined and capitalized in the same manner as the title of a book.

DESCRIPTION. When it is not immediately obvious from the rest of the information in the listing, a brief descriptive identification (usually no more than five or six words) of the source is given (service manual, design study, promotional brochure, president's report to the stockholders). This may contain contract numbers, revision numbers, the names of sponsoring agencies, or any other available information that would aid the reader in identifying and, perhaps, obtaining the item concerned.

PUBLISHER. As nearly as possible, the same form used for books is used here. The originating agency or corporation is the publisher, and the city of publication is usually the city in which the publisher's headquarters is located.

DATE. For most items, the year of publication is sufficient. For items on which dated revisions are issued (such as product descriptions, technical manuals, or technical orders), the full date—including the day of the month—may be necessary to aid in identifying the exact version used.

SECURITY CLASSIFICATION. If the document is a classified government report, the security classification should be clearly indicated following the date.

DOCUMENT NUMBER. If the document is available through a central depository (such as the National Technical Information Service or the Defense Documentation Center), the alphabetical prefix and identifying number assigned by that depository to the document should be listed in parentheses. This is the number used in ordering the document.

### Examples:

Kimbleton, Stephen R. Computer Model Systems: Annual Report. 1 March 1971 to 29 February 1972. PMG-72-1 Report on ISDOS Research Preject. Ann Arbor, Mich.: Performance Modeling Group, University of Michigan, June 1972. (AD 751 618)
[The report is available from the Defense Documentation Center.]

Urasek, Donald C. and Royce D. Moore. Performance of a Single-Stage Transonic Compressor with a Blade-Tip Solidity of 1.3. NASA-TM-X-2645; E-6763. Cleveland, Ohio: Lewis Research Center, NASA, November 1972. (N73 11002)
[The report is available from NASA.]

Klein, Gary A. Software Tool(s) for Evaluating the Effects of Finite Word Length. MS thesis. Wright-Patterson AFB, Ohio: School of Engineering, Air Force Institute of Technology, June 1977. (AD A055 777)
[This thesis is available from the Defense Documentation Center.]

Morris, Mark Douglas. Studies of the Ontogeny and Structure of Phleom in Young Sporopytes of the Tree Ferns. PhD dissertation. Durham, N.C.: Duke University, June 1977. (ON 7810808)
[The dissertation is available from University Microfilms International.]

Alpha Instrumentation Cables. Product catalog No. EC2. Elizabeth, N.J.: Alpha Wire Corporation, 1978.
[No component of the corporation is cited as the source, so the catalog would be placed in the "A's" in an alphabetized bibliography.]

Committee on Conservation. The Case Against Disposable Packaging. Report 43-C2. Washington, D.C.: Department of Transportation, 1978.

Lee, David A. "Regularizors for Observing Diffusion Processes," Modeling and Simulation, Volume 7, Part 1, Proceedings of the Seventh Annual Pittsburgh Conference, edited by William G. Vogt and Marlin H. Mickle. 173–180. Pittsburgh: Instrument Society of America, 1976.

[Paper presented at a professional conference and published in the proceedings.]

## Unpublished Sources

While unpublished sources are not usually as accessible to the reader as others, they should be fully identified if information taken from them is used in the thesis. When source information is provided directly to you (as by a scientist or an executive) to help you in your research, particular care must be taken to ensure that the person providing it is aware of your intent to use it in a thesis and that he gives permission for its use. This is only common courtesy. Further, violation of copyright may be involved if letters, class lecture notes, or similar materials are reproduced without the permission of the author. Unauthorized or premature publication of test results, proprietary information (generated and, in effect, owned by an individual or organization), private opinions, or similar information may cause considerable embarrassment or financial loss to the authors.

The form of entry used for unpublished sources must, of course, vary; but the reader should be given sufficient information to evaluate the worth of the source and to locate it if he wants to. As nearly as possible, he should be given essentially the same information as for published sources. The author, the title (if any), a description of the material, the name and location of the originating organization, and the date of the item concerned should be listed if appropriate (they are not all necessarily appropriate for all unpublished entries). Because the source is not a published work, the position or title of the author is often included to indicate his competence in the subject area.

### Examples:

Maybeck, Peter S., Professor of Electrical Engineering. Lecture materials distributed in EE 7.65, Stochastic Estimation and Control I. School of Engineering, Air Force Institute of Technology, Wright-Patterson AFB, Ohio, 1978.

Corwin, Donald L., President. Personal correspondence. Thermistron Corporation, Audubon, Pa., April 6, 1979.

Davis, Scott M., Vice President–Sales. Personal interview. Thermistron Corporation, Audubon, Pa., April 17, 1979.

Millett, Stephen M., Professor of Biology. Dissonant Zinc Reactions in Microbiology (tentative title). Unpublished text. College of Science, Carter University, Albany, Ohio, 1979.

Grice, Steven O. An Analysis of Decision Factors in Long Range Corporate Financial Planning. Unpublished MS thesis. School of Business Administration, University of Michigan, Ann Arbor, Mich., March 1979.

### Bibliography

1. Aukerman, P. W., et al. "Radiation Effects in GaAs," Journal of Applied Physics, 34: 3590–3599 (December 1963).

2. Barnes, C. E. "Neutron Damage in GaAs Laser Diodes: At and Above Laser Threshold," IEEE Transactions on Nuclear Science, NS-19: 382–385 (December 1972).

3. Bolz, R. E., and G. L. Tuve. Handbook of Tables for Applied Engineering Science, (Second Edition). Cleveland, Ohio: CRC Press, 1973.

4. Campos, M. D., et al. "Cavity Competition in Anomalous Emission Intensity in Double-Heterostructure (DH) Lasers," IEEE Journal of Quantum Electronics, QE-13: 687–691 (August 1977).

5. D'Azzo, J. J. and B. Porter. "Algorithm for the Synthesis of State-feedback Regulators by Entire Eigenstructure Assignment," Electronic Letters, 13: 230–231 (April 1977).

6. Edstrom, C. R. "A Dirichlet Problem," Mathematics Magazine, 45: 204–205 (September 1972).

7. Farrell, O. J. and B. Ross. Solved Problems in Analysis. New York: Dover Publications, Inc., 1971.

8. Friedman, B. Principles and Techniques of Applied Mechanics (Eighth Edition). New York: John Wiley and Sons, 1966.

9. Greenway, M. K. An Investigation of the Relationship Between Takeoff Gross Weight and Mission Requirements for Geometrically Optimized Aircraft. MS thesis. Wright-Patterson AFB, Ohio: School of Engineering, Air Force Institute of Technology, May 1977. (AD A055 882)

10. Hengehold, R. L. and F. S. Pedrotti. "Plasman Excitation Energies in ZnO, CdO and Mgo," Journal of Applied Physics, 47: 287–291 (May 1976).

11. Jones, J. J., Jr. "On the Zeros of Functions with Values in Hilbert Space," Resumes Des Communications, International Congress of Mathematicians, 17: 86 (August 1974).

12. Jones, J. J., Jr., et al. "On Kinematic Similarity of Systems of Differential Equations," Notices of the American Mathematical Society, 24: A-474 (August 1977).

13. Korn, G. A. and T. M. Korn. Mathematical Handbook for Scientists and Engineers (Second Edition). New York: McGraw-Hill Book Company, 1968.

14. Kressel, H., and I. Ladany. "Reliability Aspects and Facet Damage in High-Power Emission from (AlGa)As CW Laser Diodes at Room Temperature," RCA Review, 36: 230–239 (June 1975).

EXAMPLE 4.   ALPHABETIZED BIBLIOGRAPHY   *Authors' initials used. Issue numbers of journals not included.*

15. Lambert, K. P., et al. "A Comparison of the Radiation Damage of Electronic Components Irradiated in Different Rdiation Fields," Nuclear Instruments and Methods, 130: 291-300 (December 1975).

16. Lee, D. A. "Regularizors for Observing Diffusion Processes," Modeling and Simulation, 7: 154-159 (June 1976).

17. Leighton, W. "A Substitute for the Picone Formula," Bulletin of the American Mathematical Society, 55: 325-328 (1949).

18. Luke, T. E. and S. E. Cummins. "Efficient White-Light Reading of Domain Patterns in Bismuth Titanate," Ferroelectrics, 3: 125-130 (July 1973).

19. McCann, R. C. "Lower Bounds for the Zeros of Bessel Functions," Proceedings of the American Mathematical Society, 64: 101-103 (May 1977).

20. Moore, A. H., et al. "A Comparison of Crandall and Crank-Nicholson Methods for Solving a Transient Heat Conduction Problem," International Journal of Numerical Methods in Engineering, 9: 938-943 (September 1975).

21. Relton, F. E. Applied Bessel Functions. London: Blackie and Son Limited, 1946.

22. Shankland, D. G. "Electron-Gas Plasma Oscillations Computed by Means of Wigner Functions," American Physical Society Bulletin, Series 11, 20: 816 (June 1975).

23. Southward, H. D., et al. Fast Neutron Effects on Diffused Gallium Arsenide Lasers. AFWL-TR-73-23. Kirtland Air Force Base, New Mexico: Air Force Weapons Laboratory, 1973. (AD 912532)

24. Vaughan, J. C. et al. Laboratory Tests of an Air Cushion Recovery System for the Jindivik Aircraft. AFFDL-TR-74-64. Wright-Patterson AFB, Ohio: Air Force Flight Dynamics Laboratory, April 1974.

# 14

# Equations and Formulas

Much of the development of your ideas will probably be presented through the manipulation of numbers and symbols in equations and formulas. Practices in handling equations and formulas vary widely, but the suggestions listed here should be acceptable in most theses. To avoid continued repetition, the suggestions have been stated in terms of equations, but for the most part they apply to formulas as well.

## IN-TEXT EQUATIONS

Some equations, usually simple ones not developed in the study, are presented within sentences in normal lines of running text. As they are not displayed—set apart by vertical spacing—they are called in-text equations. The only special rules that apply in their presentation are:

1. Double-space before and after an equation within the line in which it appears, as for example:

    thus setting $\Delta = 0$ and assuming constant flow . . .

2. If punctuation immediately follows the equation, space once before the punctuation and twice after it:

    by setting $\Delta = 0$ , then the assumption of constant flow . . .

Sometimes this practice is followed only when the in-text equation involves three or four terms, but not when it is a simple equivalence of two terms (as $\Delta = 0$).

## DISPLAYED EQUATIONS

Longer, more complicated equations, and equations that are referred to in further development of the text, should be set apart from the text and presented as described in the following paragraphs. This makes them easier to work with, makes it easier for the reader to follow the development, and makes a much better-looking typewritten page.

## Spacing

Displayed equations should be spaced as follows:

1. Double- (or preferably triple-) space vertically before and after an equation and between equations in a series. This sets them off from the text and makes it easier to follow development.
2. Center an equation or series of equations horizontally on the page.
3. If it is convenient to do so, align a series of equations on their equal signs.
4. If an equation is too long to fit on a single line, break it before an operational sign or an equal sign. For appearance, and unless the structure of the equation suggests that you do otherwise, the first line of the broken equation should begin at the left margin and the last line should end at the right margin just before the equation number. Where the structure of a long equation is clearly sequential (as when a series of quantities is added), the left sides of successive lines are sometimes aligned vertically for easy identification of the successive parts and to provide a better balance on the page.
5. Some long equations may require more than a single page. In such cases, there is often no alternative to continuing an equation on a second page. But unless it cannot be avoided, do not continue an equation from one page to the next. Keep it all on one page if you can, even if you have to rephrase some of your text or modify spacing a bit.

## Numbering

Displayed equations are numbered to facilitate development and to provide easy reference in the text and elsewhere. There are many variations in practice, but the following is a common system:

1. Number all equations in a single consecutive series of Arabic figures beginning with the first equation in the text and proceeding through the last equation in the last appendix.
2. Place the equation number in parentheses located flush with the right-hand margin on the last line of the equation.
3. If an equation is repeated later in the text, it retains the number originally assigned.
4. Within the text, refer to equations as follows:

   This is accomplished by substituting Eqs (3), (17), and (21) into Eq (62) to produce . . .

   The word "Equation" may either be fully written out or abbreviated, but the form should be consistent throughout the text.

The most common variations from this system of numbering are:

1. Equations in each appendix are given prefix letters corresponding to the appendix in which they appear, and those in each appendix are numbered consecutively in a separate series. Thus, equations in Appendix A are numbered (A-1), (A-2), (A-3) . . .; equations in Appendix B are numbered (B-1), (B-2), (B-3) . . .; and so forth. This is often convenient in theses with many equations or when there are many equations in appendixes. When an unusually large number of equations are used in the text, a similar system is sometimes used in the text itself. The equations in a section are given prefix numbers corresponding to the section in which they appear (2-1, 2-2, 2-3 . . .). This system may become awkward and should be used only where it is actually needed.

2. Equation numbers are placed in parentheses on the same line as the equation but flush with the *left-hand* margin. Numbers for multi-lined equations are placed on the same line as the *first* line of the equation.

3. Only the most important equations or those referred to later in the text are numbered. Intermediate equations in a development are not numbered.

4. Intermediate equations within a series are given decimal numbers or suffix letters as the main equation is developed. Thus Eqs (2.0), (2.1), (2.2), (2.3), and (2.4) might lead to the development of Eq (2.5), or Eqs (2a), (2b), and (2c) might be used in developing Eq (2d).

## Identification of Symbols

Obviously, if the reader does not know what each symbol represents, he cannot understand either individual equations or development built upon them. Guidelines for identifying symbols are as follows:

1. Identify each symbol used. This is usually done either in sentence form or in list form immediately after the equation in which the symbol is introduced.

2. Wherever possible, use the accepted standard notation in your field. If $\Delta$ normally represents stress in your field, use it. Don't unnecessarily confuse your reader by using $\theta$ .

3. If there is much notation, or if many symbols appear in early pages and then not again until much later, place a list of symbols in your prefatory material. This will save your reader the chore of continually flipping back and forth through pages of text looking for definitions of your symbols. If you use a list of symbols, make it easy for the reader to find the one he wants when he needs it. See the discussion of lists of symbols an page 64 and sample pages in Examples 20 and 21.

## Words and Punctuation

Here are just a few rules to provide consistency in introducing, joining, and ending equations:

1. Use a colon after a grammatically complete introductory statement. Do not punctuate after grammatically incomplete introductions.
2. Dangling modifiers are likely to appear in statements introducing equations. While the meaning is usually clear, dangling modifiers are grammatically incorrect. If your readers are grammatical purists, they will find fault with them.

   WRONG:
   Having simplified both Eqs (2) and (4), the term $\theta_2$ was introduced to produce the following:
   (The term $\theta_2$ did not do the simplifying; you did.)
   RIGHT:
   After Eqs (2) and (4) were simplified, the term $\theta_2$ was introduced to produce the following:
3. Place connecting or sequence words between equations at the left-hand margin.
4. In most conventions, you should not punctuate after a displayed equation even though it ends a clause or sentence. In other conventions, you should. Determine the preference of your department on this point and follow it.

## A NOTE OF CAUTION

Some universities require that all equations be either fully typed or fully handlettered—they will not accept copy in which the modes are mixed. Find out what is required before you begin. If you are going to have yours typed, be certain that your typist has *all* of the symbols she needs before she starts. (Sometimes transfer symbols are permissible, but the ones you need are not always available; if they are permissible and available, get them before the bookstore runs out.)

If you are going to handletter your equations, be certain that your ink is acceptable, and use a lettering guide. Also, pay particular attention to spacing because *a handlettered equation usually fills more space than the same equation does when it is typed*. Try lettering a few lines of equations, and measure the space required. Then tell the typist how many lines she should space vertically for each line of equations to be added. (Remember to include spaces above, below, and between equations as well as the spaces for the equations themselves.) If you don't, you're likely to have some very crowded pages and will probably have to have some retyped.

Finally, if you have many equations, you are far better off having them typed than trying to handletter them. It won't cost much more, the pages will look much better, and you will save a good bit of time just when you need it most for other things. You will probably also save yourself the trouble of having some of your pages retyped.

NOTE: There are dozens of small variations in practice in the presentation of equations, especially in internal spacing and the use of brackets. As indicated earlier, conventions vary among professional fields, among professional journals, and among departments. If your department has a preference on a given point, follow it.

with a vortex street, a computation of the corresponding laminar wake
will shed some light on the temperature gradients and will give an estimate
of the width of the wake.  It is assumed that the flow outside the wake has
negligible temperature fluctuations.  The temperature variance equation,
assuming that the second derivatives in the x and z directions are small
when compared to the other terms of the equation, can be written as

$$U \frac{d}{dx} (\tfrac{1}{2}\theta^2) + V \frac{d}{dy} (\tfrac{1}{2}\theta^2) + W \frac{d}{dz} (\tfrac{1}{2}\theta^2) = k\theta \frac{d^2}{dy^2} (\theta) \tag{14}$$

where $\theta$ is the temperature difference, k is the thermal diffusivity, and
U, V, and W are the mean velocities in the x, y, and z directions, respectively.

The continuity equation is

$$\frac{dU}{dx} + \frac{dV}{dy} + \frac{dW}{dz} = 0 \tag{15}$$

The identity

$$\theta \frac{d}{dy} \left( \frac{d\theta}{dy} \right) = \frac{d}{dy} \left( \theta \frac{d\theta}{dy} \right) - \left( \frac{d\theta}{dy} \right)^2 \tag{16}$$

can be combined with Equations 14 and 15 to yield

$$\frac{d}{dx} (\tfrac{1}{2}\theta^2 U) + \frac{d}{dy} (\tfrac{1}{2}\theta^2 V) + \frac{d}{dz} (\tfrac{1}{2}\theta^2 W) = k \frac{d^2}{dy^2} (\tfrac{1}{2}\theta^2) - k \left( \frac{d\theta}{dy} \right)^2 \tag{17}$$

Integrating across the wake in the y direction gives

$$\int \left[ \frac{d}{dx} (\tfrac{1}{2}\theta^2 U) + \frac{d}{dz} (\tfrac{1}{2}\theta^2 W) \right] dy = -k \int \left( \frac{d\theta}{dy} \right)^2 dy \tag{18}$$

The temperature profile of the wake was approximated by

$$\theta = \Theta_m e^{- (y^2/\delta^2)} \tag{19}$$

EXAMPLE 5.    EQUATIONS *Terms defined in sentence form following Equation 14.*

III. The Scalar Potential

The solution of the scalar Poisson equation

$$\nabla^2 \Phi(\vec{r}) = - \frac{\rho(\vec{r}_o)}{\varepsilon_o} \tag{3.1}$$

in the space exterior to a charged, conducting sphere, surrounded by a charge distribution $\rho(\vec{r}_o)$ may be written using Green's functions in the following fashion (Ref 5:18):

$$\Phi(\vec{r}) = \iiint G(\vec{r}|\vec{r}_o)\rho(\vec{r}_o) \, dV_o + \varepsilon_o \iint \left[ G(\vec{r}|\vec{r}_s) \frac{\partial \Phi}{\partial n_s} - \Phi_s \frac{\partial G}{\partial n_s} \right] dA_s \tag{3.2}$$

where

$\vec{r}$ is the location of the field point

$\vec{r}_o$ is the location of the source point

$\vec{r}_s$ is the location of the boundary point

$\Phi_s$ is the potential of the boundary surface

$dV_o \equiv r_o^2 \sin \theta_o \, dr_o \, d\theta_o \, d\Phi_o$ is a unit source volume

$dA_s \equiv a^2 \sin \theta_s \, d\theta_s \, d\Phi_s$ is a unit surface area

$\partial/\partial n_s \equiv [-\partial/\partial r_o]_{\vec{r}_o=\vec{r}_s}$ is the normal derivative directed into and evaluated at the boundary surface

In this problem the potential will be specified on the boundary (Dirichlet boundary conditions), so that $G(\vec{r}|\vec{r}_o)=0$ will be required when $\vec{r}_o=\vec{r}_s$ .

The task of the next two sections will therefore be to determine the potential of a conducting sphere as a function of the charge distribution on and in the space surrounding it, and to construct a Green's function which complies with the required boundary conditions.

EXAMPLE 6. EQUATIONS *Note: 1. Separate series of equation numbers used in each section of the report. 2. Definition of terms in list form following Equation 3.2.*

the closed form solution to the integral is used in this study.

The pitch component of the base motion disturbance is given in Eq (3), and is repeated here for convenience.

$$\Phi_{\omega_q}(\omega) = \frac{.1(1400)^2}{(\omega^2+1.5^2)(\omega^2+1400^2)} \quad (rad/sec)^2/Hz \tag{3}$$

Equation (3) can be written as

$$\Phi_{\omega_q}(\omega) = \frac{.1(1400)^2}{(1.5+j\omega)(1.5-j\omega)(1400+j\omega)(1400-j\omega)} \tag{A-17}$$

or

$$\Phi_{\omega_q}(\omega) = \left| \frac{\sqrt{.1}(1400)}{(1.5+j\omega)(1400+j\omega)} \right|^2 \tag{A-18}$$

Substituting Eq (A-18) into Eq (A-16) gives

$$\Phi_{\theta_e}(\omega) = \left| \frac{\sqrt{.1}(1400)}{(1.5+j\omega)(1400+j\omega)} \cdot \frac{\theta_e(j\omega)}{\omega_d(j\omega)} \right|^2_{\theta_1=0} \tag{A-19}$$

Letting $s = j\omega$ and $y = \theta_e$, and substituting Eq (A-19) into Eq (A-2) yields

$$\theta_{e_{rms}} = \left[ \frac{1}{2\pi j} \int_{-j\infty}^{j\infty} \left| \frac{\sqrt{.1}(1400)}{(s+1.5)(s+1400)} \cdot \frac{\theta_e(s)}{\omega_d(s)} \right|^2_{\theta_i=0} ds \right]^{\frac{1}{2}} \tag{A-20}$$

This equation is of the form

$$\theta_{e_{rms}} = \left[ \frac{1}{2\pi j} \int_{-j\infty}^{j\infty} \left| \frac{c(s)}{a(s)} \right|^2 ds \right]^{\frac{1}{2}} \tag{A-21}$$

EXAMPLE 7.  EQUATIONS  *Note: 1. Equations given alphabetical prefixes in appendix. 2. Well-balanced and easily readable page produced by an excellent typist.*

$$2G_x(s) = \frac{(K/A_e)(s+12)(s+67)}{(s+11.8373)(s+190.379)(s^2+200.392s+23546.1)} \overset{\Delta}{=} \frac{N_x(s)}{D_x(s)} \tag{D-1}$$

Writing $H'_{eq}(s)$ from Fig. 21 yields

$$H'_{eq}(s) = \frac{1}{2} \left| k_2 + A_e s \left| k_3 + \frac{(s+402)}{6(s+67)} \right| k_4 + \frac{12(s+1)}{K(s+12)} k_5 \right| + \frac{k_6}{2G_x} + \frac{s}{2K_c G_x(s+\beta)} \tag{D-2}$$

Substituting the definition from Eq (D-1) into Eq (D-2) gives the numerator of $H'_{eq}(s)$ as

$$N'_{H_{eq}}(s) = [k_2+k_3 A_e s][N_x K_c(s+\beta)] + k_4\left[\frac{KK_c}{12} s(s+402)(s+12)(s+\beta)\right] \tag{D-3}$$
$$+ k_5[K_c s(s+402)(s+1)(s+\beta)] + k_6[K_c D_x(s+\beta)] + k_7[sD_x]$$

Defining

$$K/A_e \overset{\Delta}{=} K_a \tag{D-4}$$

and expanding the factors of Eq (D-3) results in

$$N'_{H_{eq}}(s) = k_2\{(K_a K_c/2)[s^3+(79+\beta)s^2+(804+79\beta)s+804\beta]\}$$
$$+ k_3\{(A_e K_a K_c/2)[s^4+(79+\beta)s^3+(804+79\beta)s^2+804\beta s]\}$$
$$+ k_4\{(A_e K_a K_c/12)[s^4+(414+\beta)s^3+(4824+414\beta)s^2+4824\beta s]\}$$
$$+ k_5\{K_c[s^4+(403+\beta)s^3+(402+403\beta)s^2+402\beta s]\}$$
$$+ k_6\{K_c[s^5+(402+\beta)s^4+(402+403\beta+K_a/2)s^3$$
$$+(39.5K_a+402\beta+\beta K_a/2)s^2+(39.5\beta K_a+402K_a)s+(402\beta K_a)]\}$$
$$+ k_7[s^5+403s^4+(402+K_a/2)s^3+39.5K_a s^2+402K_a s] \tag{D-5}$$

Writing Eq (D-5) in terms of a polynomial in (s) gives

EXAMPLE 8.    EQUATIONS   *Equation (D-5) broken and stacked to empha-size sequence of components added.*

# 15

# Illustrations

While the main burden of communication in the thesis is carried by the text, some things can be presented faster, more clearly, or more exactly by illustrations than by the written word. In such cases, illustrations should be used. A photograph may be the best means for showing the results of destructive testing, a graph may be the clearest way of representing variance of a quality with time or temperature, and a mechanical drawing may be the most effective way to show precise sizes and relationships in fine detail. Where they add to the precision or the effectiveness of communication, illustrations should be used. But the illustrations in the report should be functional; they should help the reader understand the matter illustrated. They should never be included just to "pretty up" the report.

## PLANNING AND GENERAL FORMAT

A little care in the planning and preparation of illustrations can add substantially to the appearance and clarity of the report as a whole. The following suggestions should be helpful:

1. Be certain to read and fully understand any departmental and university specifications concerning the design and reproduction of illustrations before making them. Discuss any contemplated departure, however small, from these specifications with your advisor and with the appropriate people in the graduate school. The specifications usually allow considerable latitude, but outright violation can delay acceptance of the final draft of the report until it is altered to meet them.
2. Sometimes photographic and reproduction services are available through the department or the university, often at nominal cost. If

illustrations are to be enlarged or reduced, or if multiple copies are needed, the extent of such services should be determined in advance.

3. As nearly as possible, try to maintain a generally uniform style and layout for each kind of illustration; be consistent on small points of format and detail. (Graphs, for instance, should look pretty much alike.) This uniformity creates a good impression on the reader, as things match and seem to belong together as parts of a whole.

4. Illustrations are usually boxed—a square or rectangle is drawn around each to produce a balanced form on the page—and figure or table numbers and titles are placed outside the box. When several associated illustrations are placed on a single page (as with a sequence of oscilloscope traces or a set of test samples), they may be enclosed in a single box. The coordinate axes and grids of a graph may make further boxing unnecessary (or even clumsy), and photographs and tables are often left unboxed.

5. As nearly as possible, an illustration should be complete and understandable by itself. It should support or amplify the text, and the text may discuss, interpret, or draw upon the illustration. But it should not be necessary to refer to the text to understand the illustration. All illustrations should be clearly labeled, so that the reader can identify important components easily. He should not have to wonder which part of the apparatus is which or which curve represents data taken on a given test run.

6. If an illustration is reduced or enlarged photographically, all printing on it will be reduced or enlarged proportionately. Obvious though this may be, it is sometimes forgotten and labels turn out to be either overwhelmingly large or unreadably small.

7. The most common failing of illustrations in theses is that they are too complicated; they contain too much unnecessary material that contributes nothing toward attaining the purpose of the illustration and may, in fact, distract and puzzle the reader. (Individual threads drawn on screws or pictures of the room in which an apparatus was set up usually add nothing.) Keep your illustrations simple. They should show the reader whatever he is supposed to see as quickly as possible and without the clutter of irrelevant detail.

NOTE: Sample figures and tables are included throughout the appendix and as Examples 46 through 69.

## Numbering

Each illustration should be numbered and given an exact title. All visual aids except tables are usually numbered in a single consecutive series of Arabic figures (Figure 1, Figure 2, and so forth) in the order in which they appear in the report, from the first figure in the introduction through the last figure in the last appendix. The figure number and title should be placed below the figure, outside the box, with the title immediately following the figure number. Some schools prefer to have the figure number begin at the left-hand margin of the illustration and others prefer that the figure number and title be centered under the illustration. In either case, be consistent throughout the report. If a sequence of small illustrations is contained in a single box, a single title and figure number are placed below the box, but additional numbers or letters and subtitles may be placed below the individual members of the group.

Tables are numbered in a separate series. Uppercase Roman numerals are usually used, and the table number and title are placed above the table (usually centered). Like figures, tables are usually numbered in a single consecutive series in the order in which they appear in the report.

Sometimes a separate series of numbers with alphabetical prefixes is used in numbering figures and tables in each appendix. Figures in Appendix A might be numbered A-1, A-2, A-3 . . . and those in Appendix B numbered B-1, B-2, B-3 . . . Tables in Appendix A might be numbered A-I, A-II, A-III . . . This sort of system is used when there is an unusually large number of figures and tables or when there are many in individual appendixes. Occasionally a separate series is used for the illustrations in each section of the report. (Figures in Section III would be numbered 3-1, 3-2, 3-3 or 3.1, 3.2, 3.3, and so forth.) While this is unusual, it might be convenient in some joint theses or in an exceptionally long one with an especially large number of visual aids. When certain similar illustrations should be used in clearly delineated sets, suffixes are sometimes used—Figure 1-A, Figure 1-B, Figure 1-C.

## Titles

The identifying title of each illustration should be placed immediately following the figure or table number. (In some practices, table numbers are centered immediately above the titles.) The title should be complete enough to tell the reader just what is being illustrated and, where appropriate, what he is to understand from the illustration. (If the illustration was not included to show the reader something, it should have been omitted.) Thus, "Figure 6. Block Diagram" does not identify the figure exactly—it could be a diagram of almost anything. "Figure 6. Block Diagram of the Control System of the E-92B Converter" is more specific. When a reader looks at the list of figures or list of tables at the front of the report to find an illustration of interest, he should be able to identify the one he wants from its title and turn directly to it.

## Size

Illustrations should be large enough to show whatever they are supposed to illustrate clearly. If details of a large subject are important, additional views or balloon enlargements of critical portions should be used. A small crowded drawing crammed with labeling or "call outs" (lines leading from parts of the illustration to labels at the edge) can mislead and confuse the reader more than it helps him, and a graph on which the scale interval is too small may disguise significant perturbations in the curve. Insets or "runarounds" (small illustrations with text running along one side as well as above and/or below them) may sometimes be effective, but they cause unnecessary difficulty in typing. Usually, when an illustration is not as wide as the page, it is best to center it horizontally on the page and leave the space on either side blank. Very little usable space is lost, a cleaner page is produced, and the typing is considerably simplified.

When an illustration is too wide to fit easily on the page, it may be rotated 90 degrees counterclockwise from its normal orientation. When this is done, the top of the illustration should be at the left (binding) margin of the page and the bottom of the illustration at the right (free) margin. Thus, the completed report is rotated 90 degrees clockwise to view the illustration. The figure or table number and title should be in their normal positions with respect to the illustration when rotated for viewing, and any wording should be readable with the page thus rotated.

If a given illustration is too large to fit easily on a standard page (8½ by 11 inches with a usable area of 6 by 9 inches when standard margins are maintained), it may be put on a foldout. Foldouts should normally be prepared and bound so that they open to the right and (if necessary) up rather than downward. In this way they may be opened and viewed conveniently. (Try visualizing how you would view one if it opened downward.) Generally, it is desirable to avoid using foldouts or, at any rate, to avoid using any more than absolutely necessary. They are bulky, they complicate reproduction, and readers do not refold them properly. After several uses, they are likely to be torn or lost. In designing them, special care must be exercised to ensure that any local specifications regarding sizes and sequence of folding are followed.

## Placement

Illustrations should be placed wherever they will be most convenient for the reader. As they are used to support and illustrate the text, they should usually be placed near the text they are intended to support. If an illustration is less than a full page in size, it may be placed on the same page as the text it illustrates. In such cases, it is usually good practice to place the illustration at the top of the page and the text below it. This produces a better balance (appearance) than the reverse. Full-page illustrations are usually placed on the page immediately following the text they support. If several pages of text are involved, the illustration is placed after the first. If a series of illustrations (as those showing oscilloscope traces, test samples, intermediate processed data, or similar materials) would interrupt the text, one or two representative samples may be placed in the text and the rest grouped in an appendix. This shows the reader what the illustrations are like while at the same time allowing him to proceed comfortably through the text without having to leaf through a dozen or more illustrations to find the end of a sentence. When he is ready to examine the series of illustrations in detail, he can find it in the appendix. The placement of foldouts is essentially the same as that of page-sized illustrations. But if a foldout is to be used for reference over a lengthy portion of text or at several places in the text, it may best be placed in an appendix. Thus it may be folded out and referred to continuously as several pages are read.

## Reference to Illustrations

Most illustrations are mentioned in the accompanying text, and some practices require that each be referred to directly. References may be made as parenthetical remarks within sentences—"(see Figure 6)"—or they may be made in full sentences—"Data generated on the third test run is listed in Table IV." If the illustration referred to is not on the same page as the reference, the page immediately following it, or the three or four pages immediately preceding it, the page number is usually included in the reference—"(see Figure 16, page 42)." In some practices, the word "Figure" is written fully in making references; in others, the abbreviation "Fig." is used (this saves exactly two typewriter strokes). The form used should, of course, be consistent throughout the report.

Although each illustration should have an exact title and should be fully labeled, it is customary to indicate its significance when referring to it. This may save the reader some confusion if the significance of the illustration to the text is not immediately apparent. (You know what you want him to see, so tell him.) Thus, "The relative positions of the major components are shown in Figure 8" or "The sharp increase in heat with higher speeds is evident in Figure 19" directs the reader's attention to the pertinence of the illustration to the immediate discussion. This can be especially useful if an illustration is separated from the reference by several pages. The reader may not want to stop reading and locate an illustration in the appendix. If he is told that a given illustration is a wiring diagram or a logic diagram, he may prefer to continue with the text and look at the illustration later. But if he is told only to "see Figure 27 on page 68," he may stop to locate the illustration, only to discover that it contains raw data that is not of immediate interest to him.

## PHOTOGRAPHS

Photographs can be used very effectively to show sizes, shapes, relationships, and details of physical objects. Photographs are, of course, direct visual representations of their subjects. In addition to their obvious uses in showing apparatus, equipment, structures, and geographical features, they are often used to present raw data directly—schlieren photographs; oscilloscope traces; the effects of heat, stress, or impact upon test materials; and similar test results. It is sometimes quicker and easier for a reader to see and to understand what he is supposed to understand from a photograph than from a drawing or from verbal description. So the need for tedious verbal description or highly detailed drawings—both of which are more difficult and time-consuming to produce and more subject to error and misinterpretation—may be eliminated.

Further, photographs have a documentary quality that cannot be matched by other means. And in some cases photographs supply an immediate visual impact which communicates something of the quality of the subject as well as exact detail in precise relationships.

Some of the practical limitations affecting the use of photographs include:

1. The object must exist (you can't take a picture of something that has not yet been built) and must be accessible.
2. Unless the subject is disassembled and parts are cut, a photograph will show only the outside surfaces.
3. Professional help and special equipment may be needed. If special cameras or extensive photography is required, this may be both inconvenient and expensive.
4. If the subject is modified, a new photograph may be necessary. (Drawings, on the other hand, can usually be altered.)
5. Unless special precautions are taken, copies made on many of the common copying machines will lose definition—details will fade and the photograph on a page will become a series of dark blobs. This does not happen with simple line drawings. It is a major disadvantage of photographs that should not be passed over lightly.

## A Few Tips

1. If you are not familiar with the photographic equipment and facilities available to you, have someone (perhaps a laboratory technician) explain them to you. This may enable you to use special kinds of illustrations—stop-action, high magnification, infrared, schlieren, and others—that you were not aware of.
2. Get someone who is experienced in using the equipment to take your photographs for you. If this is not possible, be certain that you understand the capabilities, limitations, and operation of equipment before using it. Where possible, take a few test shots before taking photographs for actual use. This can save considerable lost time (and money) in retaking pictures that are unusable. If it is at all possible, see the prints of important photographs of equipment before altering the equipment for further use on the project. Otherwise, you will have to return the equipment to its original condition if the photograph must be retaken. And if photographs are to be used to present raw data, unusable photographs may necessitate duplication of a test run or, at the least, unprofessional excuses in the text.
3. Eliminate extraneous distractions from the picture. If a piece of apparatus is to be photographed, put it on a table by a white wall and photograph only the equipment concerned. If it cannot be moved, hang a white sheet behind it to mask out nearby clutter. Be certain that the photograph shows only what you want the reader to see, and not eight other things that he will wonder about.

4. Try to get a high degree of contrast between light and dark in the picture—this will allow some leeway for faulty reproduction. Effective use of lighting and contrasting backgrounds will help.

5. Use close-ups or blow-ups when small or critical portions of an object are to be shown. A 6-by-9-inch photograph of an airplane doesn't show much about the structure of the landing gear.

6. Where it would be helpful to the reader, indicate the approximate size of the subject by placing a familiar object in the picture—a coin, a ruler, or even a human being (if the subject is large).

7. As a rule, take a few more pictures than you think you will need. You can't always be certain just how effectively given details will appear until you see the prints, and you never know when a given exposure simply will not turn out well.

8. Label or key important items in the picture. If words or symbols are to be added to the face of the photograph, it is usually good practice to type them on white paper, cut them out (leaving a ⅛-inch white border around the typing), and attach them with rubber cement. If arrows are to be placed on the picture, be certain to draw white lines on dark areas and black lines on white areas.

9. If a photograph is to be enlarged or reduced, remember that any lettering already on it will also be enlarged or reduced. Generally, it is best to add the symbols or lettering after the enlargement or reduction has been made.

Photographs can be very helpful to your reader, and some kinds of things can hardly be presented effectively by any other means. But many of the things that could be presented by photographs are more effectively presented by drawings or schematics. Block diagrams, for example, may be better than photographs in showing the parts of an experimental set-up and the relationships between them. They allow simplified presentation of only the significant information—the things that the reader should see—without the clutter of extraneous lumps, dents, and gouges. Some advisors suggest that photographs be used only where absolutely necessary. So don't get carried away. The thesis is a special kind of technical report, not a picture magazine.

## DRAWINGS AND DIAGRAMS

Various kinds of drawings and diagrams are used to show sequences, schematics, exploded or cutaway views, logic sequences, circuits, and myriad other special graphic effects which may be difficult or impossible to attain photographically or for which a photograph simply may not be effective. The varieties of drawings and diagrams that may be used are limited only by the imagination of the author, and specific conventions which apply to given types vary. Like photographs, their visual impact often makes them much easier for the reader to grasp and understand than lengthy verbal description.

But for many subjects, drawings and diagrams have certain general advantages over photographs:

1. Unlike photographs, they may be used to show nonexistent things or things which are not available for photographing.
2. They may easily be used to show the arrangement of interior parts through cutaway, sectional, or exploded views.
3. Dimensions and tolerances may easily be shown.
4. Unnecessary or confusing detail may be omitted. Generalized representations need include only essential detail. (As has been noted, drawings often illustrate equipment set-ups more effectively than do photographs.)
5. Usually, they can be modified easily.
6. No special equipment is necessary to make them.
7. There is usually little or no loss of definition when they are reproduced or re-reproduced.
8. Very simple drawings and diagrams may be quicker and easier to produce than comparable photographs.

But when compared to photographs, there are some common disadvantages, too.

1. They may contain errors which would not appear in photographs.
2. If they are at all complicated, it may take much longer to make them than to make comparable photographs.
3. They are not documentary in the same sense as photographs.

## A Few Tips

1. If your department or university requires the use of a particular kind of ink or pencil in drawings and diagrams, be certain that you use it.
2. Do not include too much detail in drawings or sketches. Keep them simple. Close detailing can be very time-consuming and too much detail may actually lessen the effectiveness of some illustrations by distracting the reader from what is essential.
3. Where it is used, lettering should be large and uniform. Sloppy lettering may easily spoil the effectiveness of an otherwise excellent drawing.
4. Use the symbols, scaling, and dimensioning techniques that are standard in your field.
5. Transfer art is available for most of the common forms and symbols used in many fields. In addition to the common mathematical and chemical symbols, these include geometric forms, cross-hatching, bullets, arrows and arrowheads, electronic symbols and components, architectural forms, and myriad other such aids that can reduce the time required to make drawings and add to uniformity and professionalism.

# GRAPHS

Graphs are used to show the way in which one or more quantities vary with another. They attract attention, and the information contained in them is easily grasped, compared, and remembered. Extremes, periodicity, maximums and minimums, scatter of data, rates of change, inflection points, and trends are all immediately evident on well-designed graphs. Values may readily be compared, and proportions, convergences, and divergences are evident at a glance. Where it is desirable, values other than those plotted can easily be identified. While there are many specialized kinds of graphs for both technical and nontechnical users, line graphs (or curves) are by far the most commonly used in theses in science and engineering, and the suggestions presented here are focused primarily on them—though the same general principles may be applied to others. A data plot without a curve may, of course, be useful, and a curve should not be drawn unless there is sufficient data to justify it. (When there are only two or three data points, almost any shape of curve could be drawn to connect them.) Where a graph is used, the following suggestions should be helpful in designing and producing it. But first a word of caution: *Don't try to put too much information on one graph.* Sometimes it is effective to put several curves on a single grid for direct comparison (as the performance of a number of samples on a common test). But if too many curves are put on a single graph or if several different scales are used on each axis, the result may be confusing and ineffective, and the selection of the scales or placement of the curves may be downright misleading. More is lost than gained. It may become difficult to distinguish curves from one another—especially if they are close together, if they are generally parallel to one another, or if they cross one another several times. In such cases, it is usually better to place separate graphs together in a series (possibly on the same page) for easy comparison. An effective sequence to follow in making a graph is described in the following paragraphs.

1. **Choose the Proper Paper.** Many sizes and styles of graph paper are available, and the right grid should be chosen to display the information concerned or significant results may be distorted. The most common forms of grid are rectangular, semi-logarithmic, logarithmic, and polar; but various special grids are also available for specialized uses in individual technical fields. Generally, close grids are used when the values to be displayed have a high degree of accuracy and interpolation is possible between plotted points. A wider (or medium) grid is used to indicate that the data is not highly accurate or is insufficient to warrant interpolation. No grid at all may be used when a graph is intended only to display trends or proportions and individual values should not be taken from the curve. In such cases, tick marks are usually placed at intervals along the coordinate axes to indicate scale values.

NOTE: If you intend to use commercial graph paper and expect to reproduce copies of your graphs, be certain that the grid will reproduce by the means

you intend to use. Some grids (especially blue ones) simply will not reproduce by some reproduction processes. Try running a copy of a piece of the
graph paper you intend to use before you invest time and effort in making
graphs on it.

**2. CHOOSE THE COORDINATE SCALES.** A graph is often designed so that the
lengths of the sides of the area within the coordinate axes maintain approximately a 2:3 ratio. This is the proportion of the sides of the usable space on
a thesis page (6 by 9 inches on an 8½-by-11-inch piece of paper) and it produces a pleasing appearance on the page. Where practical, the horizontal axis
(abscissa) is usually used to represent values of the independent variable, and
the vertical axis (ordinate) to represent values of the dependent variable. In
most cases, the graph should be designed so that the curve(s) produced will
cover most of the horizontal and vertical area within the scale; thus, a single
curve should not lie entirely within the top or bottom sixth of the space with
all of the remaining area left blank. Exceptions occur, of course, when the
point to be made is that all values are high or low, when a particular scale is
conventional for a given application, or when a graph is one of a series made
on the same scale for comparison. Particular care should be exercised in
choosing the scale to be certain that a false impression will not be given the
reader. It is always possible to make insignificant differences appear large
simply by using a very small scale or to make substantial differences seem
small by using a very large scale.

If the graph is to be drawn on graph paper, it is usually good practice
to cut out the portion that will be used and rubber-cement (not glue) it to a
piece of bond paper. Then add the coordinate axes (usually along the bottom
and left sides of the grid). These should be drawn slightly heavier than the
heaviest line on the grid. Thus, all of the area outside the grid is blank, and
labeling and numbering are neater and easier to read than if they were written across grid lines outside the axes. Further, the effect is much more professional.

**3. LABEL THE COORDINATE AXES.** Labeling and numbering usually appear at
the bottom and left-hand side of a graph, though they may occasionally be
placed on three or even all four sides. The variable on each axis should
be fully identified (if only symbols or abbreviations are used, a reader may be
forced to find the descriptive text to determine their meaning), and units
(dynes, ohms, volts, abvolts, meters, centimeters, millimeters, milliliters,
minims, inches, degrees centigrade, years, and so forth) should always be
indicated. Units may seem obvious as you make a graph, but they are not
always obvious to the reader, so don't let him wonder. The grid or tick marks
should be numbered at convenient intervals just outside the axes. Use units
that will be convenient for the reader to work with (1, 2, 3, 5, and their
multiples are commonly used; 6.3, 13, and 83 are not, as they are inconvenient
for most purposes) and that will correspond with the grid (don't use units of
9 to identify major divisions when each is subdivided on the grid into 10
lesser divisions). The precision of the information on the graph is often indi-

cated by the interval between numbers on the scale as well as by the grid size. Thus, greater precision would usually be expected on a graph on which intervals of 1 were used and each line labeled than on a graph on which each fifth line was labeled and there were intervals of 100 between numbers.

**4. PLOT THE DATA.** Care should, of course, be taken to place all points properly. If they are to be visible on the completed graph, they should be drawn neatly—preferably with a template. If different sets of points are intended to be distinguishable from one another on the completed graph, the symbols used should be simple and readily identifiable. Those most commonly used are ○, □, △, +, ●, ■, and ▲ (use a template to draw them). When copies of a graph are made by some of the most common methods of reproduction, very small symbols may become blurred or filled in so that all symbols look about alike on the copies and differentiation is lost. So it is important that the symbols be drawn large enough to remain distinguishable when reproduced. The points plotted are usually covered or erased when theoretical curves and curves representing mathematical relationships are drawn.

**5. DRAW THE CURVE.** The curve itself may be laid out with French curves or by other means, and it may be point-to-point or smoothed (if smoothing can be justified), but the line drawn should be noticeably thicker than any of the grid lines so that it is clearly distinct. Otherwise it may be difficult to follow, especially when running almost horizontal or almost vertical. If the curve is smoothed, it need not pass through the points, but approximately equal numbers of points should fall on each side of it. No particular effort need be made to make it pass through the end points as they are often at the limits of accuracy of the data taken. Broken lines, dashes, and dots are sometimes used to distinguish curves on a common grid. Where this is done, the breaks in the line should be large enough to ensure that they will not become filled in when the curve is reproduced. If one curve in the group is more important than the others, it should be drawn with a solid line; and as the curves decrease in importance, they may be drawn with progressively greater numbers of breaks in the line.

**6. ADD NECESSARY LABELS AND CAPTIONS.** Any typing or lettering placed directly on the face of the grid is likely to be difficult to read (especially if the graph is reproduced) and to detract from the graph's appearance. It is usually good practice to type any necessary labels, captions, or legends on white paper and then cut them out (leave a ⅛-inch border around all typing) and attach them to the face of the grid with rubber cement (not glue). Such attachments should be cut in regular geometric shapes—usually rectangles, sometimes circles. Material added in this way is easy to read, and this contributes to the appearance of the graph.

**7. PROOFREAD.** Take the time to proofread the graph to make certain that all scales are complete, units are identified, and curves are labeled. Insufficient proofreading is a common fault on graphs and obvious errors can make the author look foolish.

## Digital Plotters

If a digital plotter (such as those manufactured by Houston Instruments, Zeta Research, California Computer Products, Gould, and others) and suitable subroutines are available, you may be able to produce some or all of your graphs directly by computer. Subroutines are usually available for axes, scales, grids, a wide variety of symbols, smoothed or straight-line curves, boxing, and necessary labeling. Sizes and orientation may easily be altered within the limits of the plotter. If many graphs are to be made in a series, if points are generated numerically, or if unusually large numbers of points are to be plotted on individual graphs, the plotter may be the fastest and most accurate means of preparing the graphs. Further, minor perturbations that might otherwise be missed may be identified. The output should be acceptable without modification for use in most theses, but it may be necessary to go over axes or curves by hand and make them heavier to meet special university requirements.

NOTE: If necessary subroutines are not available and you are not too familiar with the plotter and its idiosyncrasies, it may be better to plot graphs by hand (even if there are quite a few to make) than to attempt to write the needed subroutines. A great deal of time can be spent in attempting to produce workable routines.

## TABLES

Tables are a convenient means of presenting quantities of related information compactly. They attract attention, are easy to construct (no special paper, instruments, or ability are necessary), and facilitate concise and orderly presentation of both qualitative and quantitative information for comparison and analysis. Information on several dependent variables may be presented simultaneously without confusion. Generally, there are two kinds of tables: text tables and formal tables.

A text table is a small table, usually containing no more than three or four columns and three or four rows. It may appear in the middle of a paragraph (it may even be part of a sentence), and it is set off from the running text by an extra vertical space or two above and below it. It has no table number, title, headnotes, footnotes, or rules (lines). Thus, it has no formal identification: it is dependent on the text for its meaning and is referred to simply by page number should reference to it be necessary later. Text tables permit easy comparison of information that would otherwise be buried in the text, and they are a very convenient means of avoiding repetitious phrasing and awkward syntax.

A formal table is a larger table used to present greater quantities of information—the more common kind of table. It has a table number and title, and it should be complete and understandable in itself; it should not depend upon the text for its meaning. Formal tables that contain no rules are said to be open; those that have a few internal rules but no full box are said to be semi-closed; and those that are boxed and contain both horizontal and vertical rules are said to be closed.

Care should be taken in designing any table, and it should be done with the reader in mind. The information contained should be pertinent as well as related. Columns and rows should be arranged in a sequence that will seem sensible to the reader and that will be easy for him to use. Wherever possible, columns or rows containing information that will be compared should be near each other. Alternative arrangements of columns and groupings of stub entries (the stub is the left-hand column in which information in the rows is identified) should be considered to find the form that will be simplest to use. (Try to use your table as your reader will—see if you can find information quickly and make important comparisons easily.)

Some of the common conventions for the preparation of formal tables are as follows:

1. The title should be exact, but it should not run on forever. If more than eight or ten words are needed to identify the content, a subtitle is often used.
2. A headnote is occasionally used at the top of the table to present information that applies to the whole table (identify units used throughout, dates of the information, number of significant figures, rounding, and so forth).
3. If possible, all wording in column headings should be read from left to right, not up or down or diagonally, as the reader uses the table. As columns may be narrow, symbols and abbreviations are sometimes used in column headings. (Avoid them if you can.) Any symbols and abbreviations that may not be well-known to all readers should be identified in footnotes to the table. Special care should be taken to center headings in their boxes, because badly centered headings are common and detract from overall appearance.
4. If entries in the stub fall into natural groups or categories, group headings may be helpful.
5. If there is much space between the words in the stub and the entries in the first column, leaders (a series of spaced dots) may be used to guide the reader's eye from the stub entries to the column entries to simplify reading.
6. If there is much textual discussion of the table with reference to particular entries, rows and columns may be numbered to facilitate reference from the text to the table. If this is done, special care should be taken to ensure that column and stub headings do not become inexact. Don't depend on the textual discussion for partial identification of columns or rows; the table must be comprehensible without it.

7. If there are many rows in a table, a space may be skipped after each seven or eight entries to make it easier to follow individual rows across the table. This can be a great help to the reader and reduces misreading.

8. If any numbers in a column contain decimals, all should be aligned on the decimal points. If all are whole numbers, they should be aligned on the units (right-hand) digit. If a column is composed wholly of decimal numbers less than one (none has an associated whole number), a zero should be placed before the decimal point of the first number in the column. In some practices, zeros are placed before the first number in each group in the column (where groups are separated by vertical blank spaces as suggested above) or before all numbers in the column. NEVER add unwarranted zeros to the end of a decimal number just to give it the same number of digits as other decimals in a column.

9. There should be no unexplained blank cells (a cell is the intersection of a column and a row where an entry is placed) in the table. If no data is available to fill a cell, several periods or a dash should be placed in the cell, and the reason for the absence of data should be explained in a footnote. If this is not done, the reader may wonder whether the blank was caused by an error in typing and proofreading.

10. Footnotes should be used to provide any necessary further identification or discussion of column or stub heads or explanations about information contained in any of the cells (or the lack of information in blank cells). Superscript letters are usually used in the body of the table to identify the items footnoted, and the footnotes (similarly identified) are placed immediately below the table and considered a part of it.

## ILLUSTRATOR

If you have many illustrations or if they are at all complex, it may be worthwhile to have someone else prepare them for you—especially if time is running out. This will cost you something (usually it isn't too expensive) but you will probably get much better-looking illustrations than you might have made yourself, and you will be relieved of what can be a very tedious and time-consuming chore. (It *always* takes longer to make illustrations than you think it will.) A good illustrator who knows what you want can produce drawings, sketches, diagrams, or graphs in much less time than it would take you. If you have a series of illustrations with common characteristics—such as a series of graphs on a common grid—an experienced illustrator can sometimes turn them out almost like pretzels coming off a continuous belt. If you decide to use an illustrator, give him the whole job if you possibly can. When an illustrator prepares some drawings and the student prepares others, there are usually obvious differences in both style and quality which detract from the unity and appearance of the report. So if you have many illustrations, consider using an illustrator. You must, of course, be certain that there is no university rule against it, but there seldom is, just as there is no reason to require that you punch your own computer cards or type your own thesis.

Illustrators may be a little more difficult to locate than typists. You might get suggestions from your thesis advisor or departmental secretary. Secretaries and faculty members in engineering drawing, architecture, industrial design, commercial art, or other departments dealing with graphics may provide leads; sometimes students in these departments earn extra income by doing small jobs for other students or for small publishing companies. Occasionally notices will be found on departmental bulletin boards. And the university publications department is likely to have several illustrators in its graphics section. But avoid going directly to a company in the business of technical illustration. Although their work may be excellent, the cost will be much greater. Try to get a professional illustrator who "moonlights" work apart from his regular job or a competent student illustrator. If you do use an illustrator, the time and effort you save and the quality of the finished illustrations will probably be worth the cost.

Arrangements made with an illustrator and the procedures followed in getting material to him and from him parallel those involved in dealing with a typist. As soon as you decide that you will need an illustrator, locate and contact a good one. In your discussion with him, remember that, like the typist, he will need to know what the job will consist of and when he will get it so that he can set aside the time and do it properly. The more information you can give him about the job in the beginning, the better his estimate of time and cost will be. Typists can usually estimate time quite accurately from the number of pages to be typed, but an illustrator needs to know how complicated drawings, graphs, or diagrams are going to be and how much detail is wanted, as well as how many there will be. So determine as nearly as possible the number of illustrations needed and bring rough sketches of the kinds needed when you go to see him. From these he will be in a position to make a rough estimate of the time it will take to produce them and the cost involved. (The greater the amount of detail, the greater the cost; this is further reason to eliminate unnecessary detail from your drawings.)

The time between submission of the first and final drafts is usually short. So if many illustrations are to be made for the final draft, the illustrator must often start before the completed first draft is given to the faculty advisor for review and comment. This means that illustrations must be planned in advance, but it should not be difficult to do this if a reasonably complete outline has been made and portions of the draft have been written. But you should show rough sketches or layouts of any large or complicated illustrations to your faculty advisor for comment before they are given to the illustrator. This can save expensive revision (and there may not be time for it!) when the final draft is prepared.

When you give the job to the illustrator, take the time to go over it with him, illustration by illustration. Give him a sketch of each illustration to be made and any other available material that will clarify what is to be done, and be certain that he is aware of any university specifications concerning illustrations. Because he may have done several similar jobs before, the illustrator is often in a position to make helpful suggestions. Listen to what he has to say, as he may well improve illustrations and save you money. Be certain that he understands the views, layout, shading, amount of detail, line thickness on axes and curves, and all details about the illustrations to be made. If he is to put wording, numbers, or symbols on illustrations, make sure that they are correct and in the proper places on the sketches, because the illustrator will make exactly what you tell him to make. He may not understand your terms or symbols, so what he sees is what you get. And be very clear about the sizes of illustrations and the borders around them. These can become critical if, as often happens, the typist starts the final draft before the last illustration is completed—she has to know exactly how much space to leave for each illustration. All in all, it is a lot easier to spend half an hour going over sketches with the illustrator than it is to correct illustrations once they have been made.

If you give the entire job to the illustrator at the same time, he should be in a position to establish a fairly firm price. This may differ somewhat from the original estimate, as you probably forgot to tell him a good many things when you first discussed the job with him. Once he has seen the whole job, the illustrator knows exactly what is needed and he can better judge how long it will take him to do it.

Even more than the typist, the illustrator needs time to do the job well, so don't bother him daily to find out how much he has done. Give him a chance to work. But small points are likely to require clarification as he progresses, so give him your telephone number. You will probably pick up portions of the job as they are completed, and each illustration should then be proofread carefully with special attention to making certain that numbers, words, and symbols are correct, that points are properly plotted on graphs, and that the necessary details are there to show what you intend. Any illustration on which correction is necessary should be returned to the illustrator within two or three days. If the mistake was yours, you may have to pay for the correction. But if it was a small one, you probably won't.

Illustrators sometimes complain that students don't know what they want in their illustrations, that they don't give exact instructions, and that they don't allow enough time to do the job. In such cases, the quality of the work may very well suffer. But with a little planning, you can get a first-rate job in plenty of time and without too much expense.

# 16

# Closing Thoughts

While this is not a particularly long book, it may seem from the length of the discussion that master's theses in science and engineering are almost overwhelming projects; but they aren't, or anyway they shouldn't be. Thousands of students undertake them every year, and most complete their projects successfully and as scheduled. It takes a sound general background in your field, careful planning, thorough analyses, and a lot of hard work to complete a project successfully; and a little inspiration and a touch of luck along the way can help.

This book is intended to acquaint you with some of the major things that must be done on your thesis project, whatever your technical field may be, and to provide suggestions about how they might be accomplished. Because individual projects, advisors' preferences, and local practices differ so much, no book can present full detail that will apply in all cases. But most of the general guidelines presented here should be helpful on most projects.

In closing, three of the matters discussed earlier should be touched upon again. Obvious though they may be, they are also critical to the successful completion of any project. While other aspects of the project may vary and corners may be cut on many suggested practices, the following generally hold true for all cases. First, keep in touch with your advisor throughout the project and pay attention to what he says. Determine what you need to cover before going to see him, be on time for appointments, don't try to bluff or mislead him, and don't waste his time by forcing him to question you at length to find out how much you have accomplished and what your problems are. He will not withhold important information, but if he sometimes seems to be vague, remember that you are supposed to demonstrate resourcefulness and the capability of carrying out an independent research effort. He is not supposed to supply you with prepackaged answers to all of your problems; if he does, he is doing you a disservice. If he asks seemingly unnecessary questions about minor points, remember that it is his responsibility to make certain that you thoroughly understand the problem you undertook to solve, the theory underlying your approach, and the implications of what you do. When he does make a suggestion, give it your full attention. He wants you to solve the problem efficiently without wasting too much time on side issues or approaches that won't work.

Second, throughout the project you should plan what must be done, determine a schedule for accomplishing it, and then make every effort to meet your schedule dates. As nearly as possible, you should do some work on the project every day. Keep in mind that time lost at the beginning can never really be made up (except by postponing the completion date), and that you should always leave yourself a little leeway towards the end of the schedule—things often take longer than you think they will. You may not know exactly what will come up to put you off schedule, but you can almost be certain that something will.

Finally, don't make major issues of really trivial points. Not only does this show a lack of perspective, but it can waste time and effort that could much better be applied to your research. If a given requirement seems pointless or unreasonable, you may want to inquire about it or make sure that you really understand what is wanted. But if no waiver is allowed, don't press too hard—do what is asked of you. While victories may occasionally be won in such matters, they seldom result in any benefit to the student concerned. Your object should be to complete a sound research project, submit an effective report, and earn the MS degree.

In the course of completing your thesis project, you will learn a great deal about your general field, about the specific problem attacked, and about planning and carrying out research. But you will also learn that research isn't always as simple and direct as it may seem from the reports, articles, and papers that result from it. Despite careful analysis and planning, there are always unanticipated problems. Things go wrong unexpectedly, and what should take only a few hours may take several days or several weeks. The research worker cannot do all that he wants to do and cannot always do it when he wants to. What seems to an outsider to be a simple, straightforward solution is not always so obvious or so simple and straightforward to the one who has to develop it. This is something to know. It applies generally to all research, and it cannot really be fully appreciated simply by reading about other people's projects or by exchanging witty remarks about them. You have to carry out a project or two yourself to understand what is involved. Further, there is a real personal satisfaction in completing a worthwhile project. This, too, is something to know. All of this is implied when a thesis project is defined as a "learning experience."

# Appendix: Sample Thesis Pages

The examples included in this appendix were selected to illustrate the ways in which the authors presented materials typically used in thesis proposals and thesis reports. The sample report pages are not intended to represent all possible kinds of content or approaches to presentation, but to be representative of some that are commonly used. As has been indicated in the text, each author must select the content, organization, and presentation that will most effectively tell a qualified reader what his problem was, how he went about solving it, what he found, and what it means.

The examples are all taken directly from thesis proposals and thesis reports. A few have been modified slightly for illustrative purposes.

NOTE: Examples 1 through 8 appeared in the text. This appendix starts with Example 9.

THESIS PROPOSAL

STUDY OF SURFACE CURRENTS ON SIMPLE
CONDUCTING SHAPES EXPOSED TO NUCLEAR
BURST X-RAYS

Background

The various electromagnetic phenomena associated with nuclear bursts
cause many important effects which, in some cases, may extend considerably
beyond the range of the primary effects (blast and heat). One such phenomenon is the emission of soft X-rays which, at high altitudes, may propagate
over long distances and seriously affect the performance of electronic
equipment aboard high-flying aircraft or satellites. These X-rays may
either cause direct radiation damage to the components, or give rise to
large current surges within the system due to the emission of electrons
from the surfaces of components.

The increasing complexity and sensitivity of the electronic equipment produced in the decade following implementation of the nuclear test ban
treaty has provided considerable impetus for research into these problems.
Since field testing is impossible under the terms of the treaty and laboratory simulation has its limitations, it is important that simple theoretical
models of X-ray-induced surface currents be obtained to explain and extend
the laboratory results.

Problem

The problem addressed in this thesis will be the development of a
theoretical model of the electrical currents produced on the surfaces of
simple conducting shapes (spheres and cylinders) by the surface emission
of electrons. Since these surface currents will be determined by the
electric and magnetic fields present at the conducting surface, it will be
necessary to determine the self-consistent motion of the emitted electrons.
This theoretical model should be amenable to computer solution.

Assumptions and Limitations

Theoretical complications and practical requirements will necessitate
the imposition of certain assumptions on the problem.

1. This problem can be effectively treated by applying classical
   electromagnetic theory to particles with nonrelativistic energies.
   This assumption is consistent with observation since the imping-
   ing X-rays have an upper energy limit near 50 kev.

2. The conducting surface will be assumed to be a perfect conductor;
   that is, it will always be an equipotential. This is also a good
   assumption since the emitted electrons are slow (non-relativistic),
   and the relaxation times associated with real conductors is on the
   order of $10^{-18}$ seconds.

EXAMPLE 9.    THESIS PROPOSAL    *Theoretical Project*

3. The electrons will be emitted as a discrete pulse in time, normal to the surface, and with a distribution in energy.  This is in conformity with observation.

4. The conductor and emitted electrons will form a complete system; that is, no consideration will be given to external fields or mediums.  Although a real-world problem would necessarily involve such complications, their variety precludes inclusion in a general theoretical model.

5. No consideration will be given to the mechanism of electron emission (Photoelectric and Compton effects).  Its inclusion would involve quantum effects which would appear to contribute little to the macroscopic problem.

6. Symmetry around the azimuthal angle may be assumed for the sphere. In the cylindrical case, separate solutions may be derived for end emission and side emission, and the general solution obtained by superposition.

## Summary of Current Knowledge

The fields generated by the emitted electrons in the presence of a conducting shape obey the Maxwell equations:

$$\nabla \cdot \vec{E} = \frac{\rho}{\varepsilon_o} \qquad\qquad \nabla \times \vec{E} = -\frac{\partial \vec{B}}{\partial t}$$

$$\nabla \cdot \vec{B} = 0 \qquad\qquad \nabla \times \vec{B} = \varepsilon_o \mu_o \frac{\partial \vec{E}}{\partial t} + \mu_o \vec{J}$$

The motion of these electrons will, in turn, be determined by their initial values of position and velocity, and the Lorentz Force Law:

$$\vec{F} = m\vec{v} = e\ (\vec{E} + \vec{v} \times \vec{B})$$

A solution, therefore, exists in principle, but it is generally complicated in practice.

Answers to problems requiring the determination of fields generated by known distributions of charge and current have been developed by antenna theorists.  And electron tube technology has produced an extensive literature on the determination of electron trajectories by known, impressed fields.  The problem of the simultaneous and self-consistent mutual interaction of charges and fields, however, has not been solved except in the simplest cases.  The solution to this problem must, therefore, return to first principles, though it may borrow certain analytical techniques from related fields.

## Approach and Standards

The general approach proposed consists of using the scalar and vector potentials  (Q and A) such that:

$$\vec{E} = -\nabla Q - \frac{\partial \vec{A}}{\partial t} \quad , \qquad\qquad \vec{B} = \nabla \times \vec{A}$$

Substituting these into the Maxwell Equations, and introducing the Lorentz Gauge

$$\nabla \cdot \vec{A} = - \varepsilon_o \mu_o \frac{\partial Q}{\partial t}$$

produces the inhomogeneous wave equations

$$\nabla^2 Q - \varepsilon_o \mu_o \frac{\partial^2 Q}{\partial t^2} = - \frac{\rho}{\varepsilon_o}$$

$$\nabla^2 \vec{A} - \varepsilon_o \mu_o \frac{\partial^2 \vec{A}}{\partial t^2} = - \mu_o J$$

These equations may be solved using scalar and dyadic Green's Functions respectively  to produce integrals over the source distributions and the boundaries involving retarded time.  These integrals exist in principle, but it is not practical to compute them in an extended calculation.

The second term on the left in each of the wave equations, however, is on the order of $(\frac{v}{c})^2$ times the first.  For electron energies below 50 kev, $(\frac{v}{c})^2$ will be less than .05.  For a first approximation, therefore, these terms may be ignored and quasi-static solutions to the resultant Poisson Equations may be produced in terms of Green's Functions without involving retarded times.  These integrals are amenable to computer solution, and by application of Runge-Kutta techniques, the resultant fields may be used to compute the electron trajectories.

The problem, therefore, is essentially one of constructing the required Green's Functions for spheres and cylinders, and matching them to the proper boundary conditions.  The approximate electron trajectories may then be computed along with the resultant surface currents.

Since the underlying purpose of this study is only to obtain an approximate theoretical model from which scaling rules may be derived for real hardware, an exact solution is not necessary.  In general, the calculations may be improved simply by refining the computer grid, and the error involved in neglecting the second terms in the wave equations may be checked by one sample calculation involving retarded times.  In this context, accuracy to within 10% in the final answer will be considered adequate.

Support

The successful solution of this problem will require the use of the CDC 6600 computer, and adequate computer time has been allocated to this project. The only experimental input required in this otherwise theoretical problem is the energy distribution of the emitted electrons.  This has been determined at the Air Force Weapons Laboratory and has been made available.  No further requirement for laboratory support is anticipated.

THESIS PROPOSAL

EXTENSION OF KABRISKY MODEL OF
HUMAN PATTERN RECOGNITION TO
TEMPORAL DOMAIN

Background

The analysis and subsequent recognition of visual patterns by the human brain has been the subject of considerable study.  The motivating idea behind studies of the process of human pattern recognition is that knowledge of this process will lead to a model that can be used to perform many of the visual tasks (photo reconnaissance, EKG interpretation, etc.) unique to humans.  If development of such a model is economically feasible, it should release a significant amount of highly trained manpower for work in other important areas.

One such model, proposed by Kabrisky, has met with considerable success in recognition of static, non-time-varying images.  The Kabrisky theory suggests that the cortex performs a Fourier or Fourier-like transform on the input pattern.  The Fourier operator transforms an input pattern to a frequency domain.  In so doing, it computes the coefficients of the spatial frequencies which, when linearly combined, reproduce the input pattern.  While Fourier models of human perception processes have been shown to be very useful for static patterns (those which do not vary with time), there really is no particular reason to believe, other than intuitively, that such models would apply equally well for time-varying patterns.  However, a number of research reports give evidence that some Fourier-like process is occurring in the temporal domain.  If the Kabrisky theory is to be used to model the complete human pattern-recognition process, it must be determined whether it is valid for time-varying patterns.

Proposal

This project will be an exploratory investigation into extending the Kabrisky two-dimensional Fourier transform model of the human visual system to include the temporal dimension.  The purpose will be to determine whether the Kabrisky model is valid for time-varying patterns.

Scope

The investigation will consist of an analysis of the Fourier transform model using three dimensions, two representing space and the third representing time.  The specific patterns, taken from similar psychological experiments, will be simulated on a 7 x 7 array with the speed of motion equal to 7 cyc/deg, which is above the flicker-fusion point.  For simplicity, the patterns simulated will consist of various curved and straight paths that might be associated with smooth motion.  This investigation will not include a study of the effect of either random or non-random aperiodic motion, nor will it include a study of the effect of variations in pattern intensity.

EXAMPLE 10.    THESIS PROPOSAL  *Experimental Project*

## What Is Already Known?

Several psychological experiments have developed data which can be correlated with the results of the proposed experiment.  In these experiments, temporal patterns have been presented to humans who put them in rank order.  The pattern looking the most like a standard pattern was put at the top of the list, and the pattern looking the least like the standard pattern was put at the bottom of the list.  If the extension of the Kabrisky model to the temporal dimension is to be justified, it must result in a similar ordering of the same patterns.

## Procedure

A temporal pattern will be simulated by moving a spot across the spatial dimensions of an array, one element for each successive time element.  This will be similar to the pattern generated by successive frames of a motion piecture depicting a ball moving across the screen.  Since the spot is an impulse in both spatial dimensions, the only attribute of the input pattern which will appear as a magnitude variation in the transform will be the motion of the spot.

Next the Fourier transform of the pattern of motion will be taken and its location in n-space calculated, where n is the number of elements in the array.  Finally, the Euclidian distance between this pattern and a standard pattern will be calculated,  and the results will be compared with those of similar psychological experiments performed by humans.

The correlation, or lack of correlation, of this data with that of similar experiments involving humans will indicate whether or not temporal changes are acted upon by the Fourier transform in the same manner as are spatial frequencies.  If there is a correlation, it will indicate that extension of the Kabrisky model into the temporal dimension would be justified, and further investigation will be warranted.

## Criteria

Once the Euclidian distance from the standard pattern is calculated for each temporal pattern, the patterns will then be ordered from smallest to greatest.  If there is to be a correlation between data developed in this study and that of the other experiments, this ordering should correlate with a similar ordering from the psychological experiments.

## Assumptions

1.  It is assumed that a speed of motion above 5 cyc/deg will result in the moving spot appearing to have continuous motion.  This assumption is based on the outcome of similar psychological experiments and on the fact that the flicker-fusion point is at 5 cyc/deg.

2.  Correlation of data from this study will justify the extension of the Kabrisky model into the temporal domain.  The justification for this assumption is that if the Kabrisky model performs the same operation on data as does the human visual system, then it must be assumed to be a good model until proven otherwise.  Of course, this study will not cover all the temporal visual tasks performed by a

human; but success of this study might spawn further experiments designed to test the extension of the Kabrisky model into the temporal dimension.

3. The Euclidian distance is associated with human subjective evaluation of similarity and dissimilarity of patterns. The assumption is based on the fact that the Fourier transforms of similar patterns are located closer (in terms of Euclidian distance) to each other in n-space than are the Fourier transforms of dissimilar patterns. This is implicit in the Kabrisky model and will be tested in this investigation. It remains to be seen whether or not it is valid.

## Materials and Equipment

This investigation will require a computer and a flying-spot scanner. The CDC 6600 will handle the calculations, and the Aeronautical Research Laboratory has volunteered the use of their flying-spot scanner. Since they are also interested in the outcome, there will be no charge for its use. The computer is needed to calculate the Euclidian distances and the flying-spot scanner is needed to digitize the Fourier transform of the patterns. Dr. Kabrisky has been generous enough to permit use of his program, which will require only slight modifications. I will be able to handle the modifications in the software myself. The study will require one hour of CPU time on the CDC 6600, and arrangements have been made for its use.

EFFECTS OF NEUTRON RADIATION ON

ALUMINUM-GALLIUM-ARSENIDE LASERS

THESIS

Presented to the Faculty of the School of Engineering

of the Air Force Institute of Technology

Air University

in Partial Fulfillment of the

Requirements for the Degree of

Master of Science

by

Thomas E. Walsh, Jr., B.S.

Capt                    USAF

Graduate Engineering Physics

March 1978

EXAMPLE 11.    TITLE PAGE

## Preface

The purpose of this study was to design a supercritical airfoil test model which would be used to investigate the effects of cooling on boundary layer stability in subsonic flow. Previous investigations have indicated that transition to turbulent flow is delayed by cooling.

This report is limited in scope to model design and the specification of test parameters. I believe that this work will be found complete and self-sufficient by the student who undertakes the actual testing of the model. Anyone who is interested in determining the heat transfer of flow over an arbitrary body with constant surface temperature should find the computer program in Appendix A to be useful.

I would like to thank my advisors, Dr. J. E. Hitchcock of the Air Force Institute of Technology and Dr. A. W. Fiore of the Flight Dynamics Laboratory at Wright-Patterson AFB, Ohio, who have given timely guidance essential to the completion of this study. Deep gratitude is also expressed to Mr. F. W. Spaid, Senior Scientist at McDonnell Douglas Research Laboratories, for his effort in providing me with experimental pressure distributions. And finally, I wish to acknowledge my gratitude to my wife, Donna, for her inspiration and her effort in typing this thesis.

Ray G. Pope

EXAMPLE 12.     PREFACE

## Acknowledgments

Captain Armen Mardiguan of the Air Force Weapons Laboratory proposed this project. I am deeply indebted to him for supplying the lasers for the project and for giving his support throughout its course.

Gratitude is also due to the Department of Energy (DOE) for funding the reactor operation through the Reactor Sharing Program.

Special thanks is extended to Brian Hajek and the staff of the Ohio State University Nuclear Reactor Laboratory for their invaluable assistance with the irradiation and activation aspects of this research.

A very strong debt of gratitude is also owed to my faculty advisors, Drs. George John, Robert Hengehold, and G. Richard Hagee. Their willingness to help when I needed it and to let me work independently at other times was greatly appreciated.

Finally, I want to express my appreciation to my wife, Sandra, for her encouragement throughout the project.

Thomas E. Walsh, Jr.

EXAMPLE 13.    ACKNOWLEDGMENTS *Acknowledgments used in place of Preface.*

## Contents

**EXAMPLE 14.    TABLE OF CONTENTS**  *Theoretical Project*

Contents

TABLE OF CONTENTS

EXAMPLE 15.    **TABLE OF CONTENTS**  *Experimental Project*

List of Figures

**Example 16.   LIST OF FIGURES**

<u>List</u> <u>of</u> <u>Figures</u>

(Continued)

## List of Figures

**EXAMPLE 17.    LIST OF FIGURES**

List of Tables

EXAMPLE 18.    LIST OF TABLES

List of Tables

EXAMPLE 19.    LIST OF TABLES

<u>List of Symbols</u>

| | |
|---|---|
| $a$ | Wing lift curve slope |
| $AR$ | Aspect ratio |
| $b$ | Wing semispan – feet |
| $b_e$ | Effective span – feet |
| $b_v$ | Vortex span – feet |
| $B$ | Wind tunnel test section width – feet |
| $c$ | Chord – feet |
| $c_r$ | Wing root chord – feet |
| $c_l$ | Location of moment center – feet |
| $C$ | Wind tunnel test section cross-sectional area – feet$^2$ |
| $C_D$ | Three-dimensional drag coefficient |
| $C_{D_i}$ | Induced drag coefficient |
| $C_{D_o}$ | Zero lift drag coefficient |
| $C_{D_u}$ | Uncorrected drag coefficient |
| $C_L$ | Three-dimensional lift coefficient |
| $C_{L_\alpha}$ | Lift curve slope |
| $C_{L_c}$ | Corrected lift coefficient |
| $C_{L_u}$ | Uncorrected lift coefficient |
| $C_M$ | Three-dimensional moment coefficient |
| $C_{M_\alpha}$ | Static stability derivative |
| $d$ | Vertical distance of model from wind tunnel test section centerline – feet |

**EXAMPLE 20.   LIST OF SYMBOLS**

| | |
|---|---|
| $D$ | Drag - pounds |
| $D_B$ | Balance drag - pounds |
| $D_{B_O}$ | Wind-off balance drag - pounds |
| $D_{B_U}$ | Buoyancy drag - pounds |
| $D_U$ | Uncorrected drag - pounds |
| $e$ | Span efficiency factor |
| $g(x)$ | Function related to lift per unit chord in Lawrence technique |
| $g'(x)$ | $\frac{d}{dx}[g(x)]$ |
| $H$ | Wind tunnel test section height - feet |
| HSEP | Horizontal separation, % wing root chord |
| INC | Angle of incidence of the canard - degrees |
| $k(x)$ | Function proportional to lift ahead of station x |
| $K_D$ | Slope of drag calibration curve |
| $K_L$ | Slope of lift calibration curve |
| $K_M$ | Slope of moment calibration curve |
| $K_Q$ | Slope of dynamic pressure calibration curve |
| $K_1$ | Body shape factor |
| $K_3$ | Body shape factor |
| $\ell_r$ | Reference length - feet |
| $\ell_t$ | Semichord length - feet |
| $L$ | Lift - pounds |
| $L_B$ | Balance lift - pounds |
| $L_{B_O}$ | Wind-off balance lift - pounds |

*(The list continues for 2 pages.)*

Notation

Roman Letter Symbols

c    –    Specific heat (BTU/$lb_m$-F)

D    –    Spectral dispersion (microns/cm)

$D_h$    –    Hydraulic diameter (ft)

d    –    Distance (cm)

h    –    Thermal conductance (BTU/hr-$ft^2$-F)

I    –    Irradiation (units as noted in text)

k    –    Thermal conductivity (BTU/hr-ft-F)

l    –    Length (ft)

M    –    Mach number

P    –    Power (cal/sec)

q    –    Thermal flux (BTU/hr-$ft^2$)

R    –    Radius (km)

T    –    Temperature (K)

t    –    Thickness (ft)

V    –    Voltage

Greek Letter Symbols

α    –    Absorptivity

β    –    Coefficient of volumetric expansion

ε    –    Emissivity

λ    –    Wavelength (microns)

μ    –    Viscosity ($lb_m$/hr-ft)

ν    –    Kinematic viscosity ($ft^2$/hr)

ρ    –    Density ($lb_m$/$ft^3$)

σ    –    Stefan-Boltzmann constant (BTU/hr-$ft^2$-$R^4$)

**EXAMPLE 21.    LIST OF SYMBOLS**

Abstract

A wind tunnel test model of a supercritical airfoil was designed to investigate the wall cooling effect on subsonic boundary layer stability. A DSMA 523 airfoil section was employed. The model was designed to have surface temperature instrumentation and a liquid nitrogen cooling system.

Heat transfer, aerodynamic loads and stresses, and instrumentation were analyzed for the proposed test conditions. A computer program was developed to analyze the forced, convective heat transfer over a two-dimensional body with a constant wall temperature. The program utilized an integral method to compute local Stanton numbers. Local heat flux and total heat flow were predicted for a Mach number of 0.7, Reynolds numbers of $0.923 \times 10^6$ and $1.673 \times 10^6$, and cooling ratios from 1.000 to 0.824. Stress analysis was performed by application of beam-bending theory with appropriate simplifying assumptions. Construction drawings and specified test conditions for Mach numbers of 0.3, 0.5, and 0.7 are presented.

EXAMPLE 22.    ABSTRACT   *Design Project*

<u>Abstract</u>

Double heterojunction aluminum-gallium-arsenide laser diodes were irradiated in a nuclear reactor to determine the effects of neutron radiation.  Two types of lasers were used:  RCA C30127 and Laser Diode Laboratories LCW-10.  Both are capable of continuous operation at room temperature.

Both types of diodes showed significant decreases in power output at neutron fluences of $10^{14}$ n/cm$^2$.  Linear increases in threshold current and linear decreases in external quantum efficiency were observed.  There was no significant change in bias voltage versus forward current or in the spectral composition of the outputs of the diodes at neutron fluences up to $10^{15}$ n/cm$^2$.

Formulas were developed to predict the changes in threshold current, external quantum efficiency, and power at a constant current above threshold.  Damage coefficients for these formulas were derived from the irradiation data.

Unusual discontinuities were observed in the power output versus input current curves of some diodes.  Neutron irradiation tended to enhance these anomalies.

EXAMPLE 23.    **ABSTRACT**  *Experimental Project*

APPLICATION OF STATE-VARIABLE AND CONDITIONAL FEEDBACK METHODS
TO REDUCE THE POINTING ERROR OF A TWO-AXIS BEAM DEFLECTOR

I.  Introduction

Technological advances have made practical the transmission of information by way of optical communication links.  No unusual difficulty is encountered in aiming a fixed point-to-point link; but a problem arises when one or both of the terminals are mounted on a moving vehicle.  In this situation, the system must be mounted on gimbals to allow changing the pointing direction.  Two gimbals are sufficient to give the two degrees of freedom required for azimuth and elevation tracking.  However, a third gimbal is normally necessary to effectively isolate the system from the motion of the base.

In addition to the error introduced by base motion, the tracking capability of any pointing system is limited by the dynamics of the system itself.  Thus, the pointing error in a given situation is the combined total of the dynamic tracking error and the base motion error of the elevation and azimuth channels, and is usually expressed as an rms value.

A simplified drawing of a two-axis, gimbaled, planar-mirror beam deflector is shown in Figure 1.  Base motion makes an undesirable and uncontrolled contribution to the line-of-sight (LOS) output angle.  Depending on the application of the system and the nature of the base motion disturbance, the pointing error of the typical system under consideration in this study has been calculated to be nearly one milliradian (Ref 3:6).

EXAMPLE 24.    INTRODUCTION  *Design-Theoretical Project*

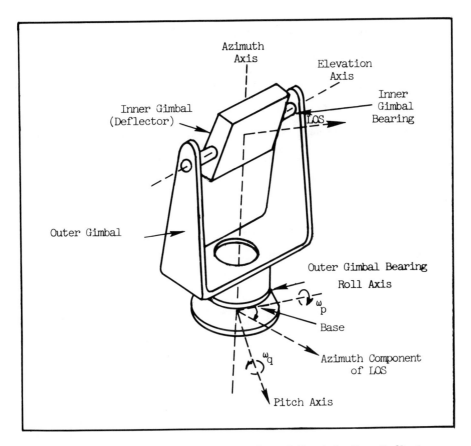

Figure 1.    Simplified Representation of Two-Axis Beam Deflector
(Adapted from Ref 3)

Because of the isolation characteristics inherent in an additional

gimbal, a three-axis pointing system has a high degree of base motion immunity.

However, because of the complexity of the three-gimbal system, it is desirable

to reduce the disturbance error of the two-axis system to allow its use where

possible in applications where a third gimbal would otherwise be required for

isolation.

In a previous investigation of this problem by Comfort at the Sieler

Research Laboratory (Ref 3), the invariance method of compensation (Ref 4:531)

was used.  This method requires that the disturbance be measured and applied to an available point within the system in such a way that the disturbance is effectively cancelled.  The calculated rms error, assuming perfect measurement of the disturbance compensated by a physically realizable network, was 13 microradians.  However, when the imperfect characteristics of a typical measuring device (rate integrating gyro) were considered, the accuracy was degraded to about 30 microradians of rms error in the elevation channel. Although there was a substantial improvement over the uncompensated system, the error was still larger than that for a three-axis system.  Dynamic tracking error of the system was not considered in the investigation.

## Problem

The problem investigated in this study is the independent application of the conditional method (Ref 5) and state-variable feedback techniques (Ref 8:355) to reducing the system disturbance response while maintaining or improving the dynamic tracking capability.

The analysis and design comprising this study are limited to the elevation channel, except where inclusion of the azimuth channel is required for completeness.  Therefore, unless otherwise indicated, all references to the "system" will refer only to the elevation channel.  A detailed description of the overall system is presented in Chapter II.

## Assumptions

The statistical base motion disturbance used in evaluating the system is assumed to be representative of the actual operating conditions, and the two components, $\omega_p$ and $\omega_q$, are assumed statistically independent.  For purposes of this study, the power spectral density functions given by Comfort for base

motion are used and are assumed to represent stationary random processes
having zero mean.  They appear in Chapter II of this report as Eqs (2) and
(3).

The parameters of the basic system are assumed to be accurate and constant, and the system is assumed to be linear.  Since it is known that some
of the quantities are not directly measurable, they must be simulated in
any physical realization of the state-variable feedback design solution.
Additionally, the conditional method requires synthesis of compensators based
on transfer functions of the basic system.

It is assumed that the diagram in Fig. 2 (page 8) represents the
actual system, and the assumptions made in the derivation of the gimbal
dynamic equations (Ref 3:13) are considered valid.  These include the assumptions that the gimbals are rigid and perfectly balanced about their respective
principal axes, and that bearing friction is negligible.  Further, gyro
cross-coupling between the azimuth and elevation channels is neglected.

Although the tracker output described in Chapter II is discrete, it is
treated as being continuous for purposes of this project.  The torque disturbance is computed by Comfort to be about one microradian, and is therefore
considered negligible.

## Design Basis

The degree of merit of the design solutions is measured with respect
to the basic system as compensated by the invariance method in Ref 3.  This
necessitates a complete analysis of the basic system to permit the desired
comparisons.  Also, in order to verify the disturbance response given in
the previous study and to establish the validity of the computational method
used in this report, the base motion disturbance rms error of both the basic

system and the invariance compensated system (where perfect measurement was assumed) are calculated. Whereas Comfort used numerical integration to determine the disturbance error, this study uses a computational algorithm which gives the rms error from the system parameters and power spectral density in s-domain form.

Development

Analysis of the system is presented in Chapter II. The root loci of the elevation channel are plotted, and the closed-loop transfer function is used to determine the time response and base motion disturbance response. The target simulation for testing the dynamic tracking ability is derived in Appendix B, and is used in the analysis of the basic system.

In Chapter III, the conditional feedback method of compensation is applied to the basic system; Chapter IV contains the state-variable design. Again, the time responses and base motion disturbance error are determined. The various results are compared in Chapter V, and the conclusions and recommendations are presented in Chapter VI.

## II.   Historical Survey

The phenomenon of Raman light scattering has been known for a number of years.  The process was first experimentally observed in 1928 by C. V. Raman using the light from a mercury arc lamp scattered by vibrational states in ice and other common substances.  The phenomenon was, however, of minor technological significance until the development of laser sources.  Laser light, being highly intense and monochromatic, made feasible the observation of many Raman processes which were impossible to observe with ordinary light.  In this chapter the development of one such Raman process, that of spin-flip in semiconductor compounds, will be traced from its theoretical prediction to its most recent application as a mechanism for producing tunable laser radiation in the infrared portion of the electromagnetic spectrum.

### Stimulated Raman Scattering

The first indication that Raman scattering might be directly applied to laser technology came in 1962 when Woodbury and Ng[Ref 59] succeeded in producing stimulated Raman scattering from molecular excitations in a nitrobenzene Kerr cell.  The possible application of this phenomenon was immediately apparent:  the production of new laser frequencies from essentially fixed-frequency laser sources.  The success of Woodbury and Ng prompted immediate attempts to obtain stimulated molecular Raman scattering from other substances; this was subsequently achieved in organic liquids [Ref 18], gases [Ref 29], and solids [Ref 17].  In addition, since the Raman process was also known to occur from energy exchanges with quantum particles, these processes also fell under investigation.

### Landau-Raman Scattering

In 1966, Wolff [Ref 55] proposed that an as-yet-unobserved Raman process might occur in semiconductor crystals placed in a strong magnetic field.  According to his one-electron model, incoming quanta

EXAMPLE 25.   REVIEW OF THE LITERATURE

$n_{\omega_0}$ would be Raman scattered in transitioning mobile carriers (electrons or holes) between magnetically generated Landau levels. His work dealt specifically with the process whereby a carrier's Landau quantum number increased by two $(\Delta n = 2)$. Although Wolff did not consider electron spin, later the same year Yafet [Ref 62] and Kelly and Wright [Ref 22] extended the theory to include the effects of spin as well. It was shown that for an InSb-like compound, the processes $\Delta n = 0$ and $\Delta n = 2$ accompanied by a "spin-flip" $(\Delta s = -1)$ should also be expected. Furthermore, unlike the $\Delta n = 2$ process, the spin-flip transition $\Delta n = 0, \Delta s = -1$ was shown not to require nonparabolicity in the band structure; in fact, it was shown to have its largest cross section when the band structure becomes parabolic as the magnetic field drops to zero. Thus, the spin-flip process was expected to be stronger than the ordinary $\Delta n = 2$ process at normally attainable field intensities.

The first experimental observation of Landau-Raman (L-R) scattering came toward the end of 1966 when Slusher, Patel, and Fleury [Ref 48] reported the observation of spontaneous L-R scattering in n-type InSb. Using a Q-switched $CO_2$ laser, they observed both the $\Delta n = 2$, $\Delta s = 0$ and $\Delta n = 0$, $\Delta s = -1$ processes. In addition, the process $\Delta n = 1, \Delta s = 0$, not previously predicted, was also observed. As predicted, the $\Delta n = 0, \Delta s = -1$ spin-flip transition produced the more intense Raman line.

With this first confirmation that L-R scattering in semiconductors was a viable and potentially useful phenomenon, additional research, both experimental and theoretical, was strongly encouraged. As might be expected, the majority of this research was applied specifically to spin-flip scattering $(\Delta n = 0, \Delta s = \pm 1)$ since it proved to be by far the strongest of the L-R processes. Other compounds in which the spin-flip Raman (s.f.R.) process has been observed include InAs [Ref 42], PbTe [Ref 43], CdS [Ref 50], ZnSe [Ref 19], CdSe [Ref 51], and CdTe [Ref 51]. In the theoretical area, the original theory of Wolff [Ref 55] and Yafet [Ref 61] was further extended by Wherrett and

Harper [Ref 54] and by Makarov [Ref 27] who modeled the spin-flip
process using Fermi-degenerate statistics and thus accounted for the
carrier-concentration and magnetic-field dependence of the s.f.R.
scattering intensity.  Blum [Ref 5] generalized the original cross-
section calculations made by Wolff to include the effects of Coulomb
interactions and to allow for a certain amount of arbitrariness in
energy band structure.

The Spin-Flip Raman Laser

    In the earliest theoretical work on L-R scattering, Wolff [Ref 55]
recognized the possibility of producing stimulated L-R omission from
a semiconductor compound.  He subsequently proposed [Ref 56] that a
magnetically tunable laser could be constructed using the $\Delta n = 2$
process, provided that a semiconductor could be pumped to stimulation
in this mode.  For the pump, Wolff proposed the 10.6-$\mu$ $CO_2$ laser
capable of producing several megawatts of output power; for the semiconductor, he proposed n-type InSb with its narrow bandgap  ($\approx 0.25eV$)
and large-magnitude g-factor ($\approx -50$).

    Although spontaneous L-R scattering was achieved [Ref 48] shortly
after Wolff's original prediction, it was not until 1970 that any type
of L-R scattering could be coaxed into stimulated emission.  This was
finally achieved at the Bell Telephone Laboratories by Patel and Shaw
[Ref 39] using, in accordance with Wolff's suggestion, a Q-switched
$CO_2$ laser as the pump and an InSb crystal, in the form of a 2.5 X 2.5
X 4.0-mm parallelepiped, as the Raman-active medium.  They observed
stimulated L-R emission which was tunable from 11.7$\mu$ at  B = 4.8T to
13.0$\mu$  at  B = 10.0T .  Unlike the process $\Delta n = 2$  envisioned by Wolff,
this emission was the result of the  $\Delta n = 0$, $\Delta s = -1$ (Stokes) spin-flip
transition.  A power output of  $\approx 1W$  was achieved in the stimulated
s.f.R. line with a conversion efficiency of  $\approx 5 \times 10^{-4}$ ;  an estimated
linewidth of  $< 0.05$ cm$^{-1}$  was reported.  In a later report, Patel and
Shaw [Ref 40] reported a tenfold increase in output power and a
measured linewidth of  $< 0.03$ cm$^{-1}$.   To demonstrate the applicability

of the s.f.R. laser, Patel and co-workers [Ref 41] used the device to study the absorption spectrum of NH.

Since its initial operation, numerous improvements and extensions have been added to the s.f.R. laser. In Europe, Allwood and co-workers [Ref 3], using the greater amplification available in the collinear scattering configuration (Fig 4), were able to produce stimulated anti-Stokes ($\Delta s = +1$) and second-Stokes scattering. Working independently of Allwood, Patel [Ref 36], and Shaw and Patel [Ref 47] reported similar successes. This achievement of stimulated emission in the anti-Stokes and second-Stokes processes effectively increased the s.f.R. laser tuning range to 9 - 16μ.

In attempts to increase the output of the s.f.R. laser, Allwood and co-workers [Ref 4] applied quarter-wave layers of PbTe and ZnS (95% reflectance) to the InSb crystal surfaces to reduce spectral reflection losses; a power output of ≈10W was achieved with a conversion efficiency of ≈1%. Aggarwall and co-workers [Ref 1], using a transversally-excited, high-pressure 10.6-μ $CO_2$ laser in the Q-switched configuration, achieved output powers on the order of 1 KW in the Stokes line, 30 W in the anti-Stokes line, and 1 to 3 W in the second-Stokes line.

5.3μ Operation. The earliest observations of stimulated s.f.R. emission in InSb were made using the Q-switched or "giant pulse" mode of the $CO_2$ laser. Q-switched operation was necessary due to the almost complete lack of resonance enhancement (see p 27). In fact, at 10.6μ the pump frequency was only about 45% of that associated with the crystal's bandgap. Thus, without the benefit of a resonance condition, the threshold power requirements were on the order of 200W [Ref 40:1284]. Toward the end of 1970, the significance of resonance enhancement was pointed out rather dramatically when Mooradian and co-workers [Ref 31] achieved operation of the s.f.R. laser, using a 5.3-μ CO laser as the pump. The cross-section enhancement resulting from operation at ≈90% of the InSb bandgap reduced the observed threshold for stimulated emission

*(The section continues for 4 pages.)*

II.    <u>Requirements Definition</u>

The conditions specifying how the VCASS software is to be constructed will be presented in this section.  No particular hardware, such as input or output devices, will be specified since these details will be determined in a later stage of the design.

The four accepted goals of the discipline of software engineering are modifiability, efficiency, reliability, and understandability (Ref 1:92).  These goals were the constraints used in selecting the analysis and design techniques for the design of the VCASS software. The techniques selected are SofTech's structured analysis for the formal functional specifications and Yourdon and Constantine's design method for the software design (Ref 23:18-23).

<u>Functional Specifications</u>

The system to be designed is to simulate VCASS.  It should accept inputs from an aircraft-representative vehicle whose type, threat, and weapons dynamics can be altered; it should provide synthesized out-of-the-cockpit instrumentation, visual scenes, and targets.

The software portion will have two basic modes of operation, Exerciser and Operational.  The Exerciser mode allows the user to interact with the system to build and modify the formats for the aircraft symbology displays.  During this mode of operation, the system will output messages to the user in response to the options and parameters entered.  These symbology displays are then used under the Operational mode to evaluate the pilot's perceptions.    The software design for the Exerciser mode of operation is not contained in this thesis but is

EXAMPLE 26.    DESIGN REQUIREMENTS

being designed as a separate subsystem called the Symbology Exerciser
of the VCASS simulator.  The design of the Symbology Exerciser can be
found in Ref 9.  This thesis defines the interface between the Symbology
Exerciser and the VCASS simulator.

In the Operational mode, the system functions as an aircraft simulator.  Flight control and target inputs will be processed, according
to pre-set parameters, to update aircraft instruments, symbology displays,
and background imagery.  There are four main functions that will be
performed in this mode.  They are  (1) process configuration parameters,
(2) produce the plant dynamics,  (3) update the aircraft displays, and
(4) perform operational recording.  The first function is an initialization step only, while the next three functions are continuously repeated in a "real-time" environment.  A brief description of each of
these functions follows.

Process Configuration Parameters.  When the system is put into the
Operational mode, a message is output to the user questioning configuration parameters.  The user then interacts with the system by supplying
the required parameters for system options, vehicles, weapons, cockpit,
target, environment, and display formats.  The user can choose to enter
all parameters or only a partial set of parameters.  System default
parameters are used for all parametrs undeclared by the user.

A frequent user of the system will not have to be prompted by the
system for the parameters; the system will allow the user to input a
command and the parameters at the same time.  The system will also be
capable of obtaining the parameters from a specified storage device.

*(The section continues for 6 pages.)*

III.   Theory of Spin-Flip Raman Scattering

The theoretical aspects of s.f.R. scattering have been treated in depth by a number of authors.  Only those aspects of s.f.R. theory which are applicable to CdTe or to semiconductors very similar to CdTe are discussed here; and, in general, no attempt is made to perform the rigorous derivations leading to results already published.  It is assumed, with some qualification, that s.f.R. scattering in CdTe parallels that observed in InSb, a compound whose s.f.R. scattering characteristics have been the subject of the majority of work done in the s.f.R. field.

Both CdTe and InSb crystallize in the zincblende structure and thus have a marked similarity in the shapes of their respective energy bands-- the electron dispersion relations touched upon briefly in Chapter I. Any differences which are evident, notably band-gap width $E_g$ and electron-effective-mass, $m^*$, arise from the compounds' constituent elements being in different chemical groups.  CdTe is a II-VI compound; InSb, a III-V. Typically, the II-VI compounds exhibit a greater degree of ionicity [Ref 52:178] in the chemical bond than do the III-V compounds, and thus tend toward larger band gaps.  Electron-effective-mass differences arise from the variations between the two in their respective band curvatures. Like InSb, CdTe is a direct-gap semiconductor with the conduction-band minimum and various valence-band maxima occurring at $\bar{k} = (0, 0, 0)$ , the $\Gamma$-point in the first Brillouin zone [Ref 13].  Thus, each compound has only one gap energy of any importance.  Also, since the bands near $\Gamma$ are very nearly spherical (in $\bar{k}$-space) in both compounds, there is only one conduction-electron-effective mass to consider; that is, $m^*$ is isotropic near $\Gamma$.  In both compounds, the $\Gamma$-point electron wave functions

EXAMPLE 27.   THEORY

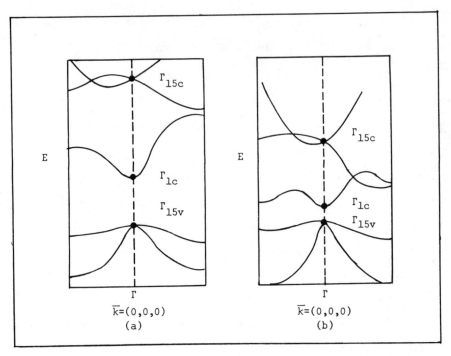

Fig 3.   Energy Band Diagrams: a) CdTe, b) InSb (From Ref 13)

are s-like in the conduction band and p-like in the valence band.  As a result, their valence bands are triply degenerate at $\Gamma$ .  As with InSb, this degeneracy is partially lifted in CdTe due to spin-orbit inter- actions and results in a split-off valence band having an energy which is lower than the other two bands by an amount $\Delta_v$, the so-called spin-orbit splitting.  For CdTe,  $\Delta_v \simeq 0.93$ eV  [Ref 53]; for InSb,  $\Delta_v \simeq 0.90$ eV [Ref 21].  The band structures of the two compounds, centered on $\Gamma$ , are illustrated in Figure 3.  The split-off valence band is not shown because of a lack of published data on its specific contour.

Since experimental determination of the CdTe g-factor was one of the immediate goals of the thesis project, this chapter begins with comment regarding the expected value of this parameter based on previous theoretical and experimental investigations.  This is followed by sections on polarization selection rules, the phenomenon of resonance enhancement, tuning constraints on the s.f.R. emission and, finally, the concept of the quantum limit condition.

### CdTe g-factor

For the free electron, the g-factor is defined as the ratio of the spin magnetic moment to the spin angular momentum and has a value $g_o = 2$ [Ref 61].  However, for an electron occupying a conduction-band state in a semiconductor such as CdTe, it has been shown [Ref 45] that the g-factor, $g^*$, differs from $g_o$ because of the coupling of the conduction band to the spin-orbit-split valence band.  Roth, Lax, and Zwerdling (RWZ) [Ref 45] have shown that $g^*$ for InSb can be given by

$$g^* = 2 \left( 1 - \frac{2\Delta_v}{3m_o E_g (E_g + \Delta_v)} \left| \Gamma_{1c} \left| P_x \right| \Gamma_{15v} \right|^2 \right) \tag{5}$$

where $\left\langle \Gamma_{1c} \left| P_x \right| \Gamma_{15v} \right\rangle$ is the momentum matrix amplitude between the states $\left| \Gamma_{1c} \right\rangle$ and $\left| \Gamma_{15v} \right\rangle$ , representing the s-like conduction band and the p-like valence band, respectively, and $m_o$ is the electron rest mass. In the absence of valence-band spin-orbit splitting, that is, $\Delta_v = 0$ , $g^*$ reduces to the free-electron value of 2.

In developing Eq (5), RLZ neglected the spin-orbit splitting taking place also at $\Gamma_{15c}$ of Fig 3b since in InSb the energy gap between $\Gamma_{15c}$ and $\Gamma_{1c}$ is much larger than the corresponding gap between $\Gamma_{1c}$ and $\Gamma_{15v}$. Unfortunately, this liberty cannot be taken with CdTe since these two gaps are comparable in size.  To include the effects of spin-orbit splitting at $\Gamma_{15c}$, Piper [Ref 44] has derived the relation

*(The section continues for 11 pages.)*

II.   <u>Development</u> <u>of</u> <u>Observer</u> <u>Theory</u>

This chapter presents the basic theory of the operation of an observer driven by any system which is linear, time-invariant, and deterministic.  All measurements of the state vector are assumed to be noise free.  This observer theory was originally presented in 1964 by Luenberger (Ref 7:74-80) and later expanded (Ref 9:596-602).

<u>General</u> <u>System</u> <u>Description</u>

A system, restricted by the above assumptions, is governed by the state equation

$$\dot{x}(t) = Ax(t) + Bu(t) \tag{1}$$

where

x is an n X 1 state vector

u is an r X 1 control vector

A is an n X n matrix

B is an n X r matrix

The matrices A and B in Eq (1) are constant for the time-invariant system, but the state and control vectors are, of course, functions of time.  For notational convenience the time arguments are omitted from all equations throughout the remainder of this section.

A feedback design which assumes that the entire state vector can be measured is described by

$$u = Kx \tag{2}$$

where K is an r X n matrix of constant feedback coefficients.  A control solution of this form can be obtained by several well known

EXAMPLE 28.   THEORY

techniques for the type of system under consideration. Determination of a full-state feedback control as in Eq (2) is the first step in the control synthesis procedure, even if the full state vector is known to be unavailable. For all applications in this discussion, it is assumed that a solution of Eq (2) is known.

For systems with incomplete state measurement, a vector y can be defined by

$$y = Cx \qquad (3)$$

where

        y is an m X 1 measurement vector

        C is an m X n constant gain matrix

The purpose of adding an observer to such a system is to use both the available measurements, as defined by Eq (3), and the system model represented by Eq (1) to provide a reasonable estimate of either the state vector or the full-state feedback control.

## Derivation of Observer Equations

An observer is a linear system driven by the measurement vector y and the control vector u. The state equation is written as

$$\dot{z} = Fz + Gy + Lu \qquad (4)$$

where

        z is a v X 1 observation vector

        F is a v X v observer model matrix

        G is a v X m measurement distribution matrix

*(The section continues for 5 pages.)*

V.    Equipment

The experimental apparatus used for the CdTe scattering experiments will be described here in five sections.  These include  1) the pump laser,  2) the superconducting magnet and magnet dewar,  3) the focusing and collecting lenses,  4) the spectrometer system, and  5) the sample holders.  A plan view of the entire apparatus is shown in Figure 7.

For spin-flip scattering, a CdTe sample is mounted at the center of the magnet and irradiated with the pump laser.  Scattered light is then collected at right angles to the pump beam, directed into the mono-chrometer, and detected at the photomultiplier.  The photomultiplier output is processed with a lock-in amplifier and displayed on a strip-chart recorder.  The recorder output appears as a plot of light intensity versus wave number.  For room-temperature optical phonon scattering, the magnet and dewar were removed, and the CdTe sample was mounted on a brass or aluminum stand which was set on a laboratory table at the same position normally occupied by the magnet.

Pump Laser

As a source of pump radiation, a Holobeam series 250 Nd:YAG laser was used, the term "Nd:YAG" referring to the laser's neodymium-doped yttrium aluminum garnet ($Y_3Al_5O_{12}$) lasing rod.  The laser can be operated in either cw or pulsed mode at 1.06u.  Nominal maximum output power for the device is 40 W for cw operation; however, peak powers of up to 20 KW are possible in the Q-switched, or "giant pulse," mode.  Checks made with a Brewster's-angle polarizer indicated that the beam was preferentially polarized at 30° to the vertical.  To produce vertical or horizontal

EXAMPLE 29.    EQUIPMENT

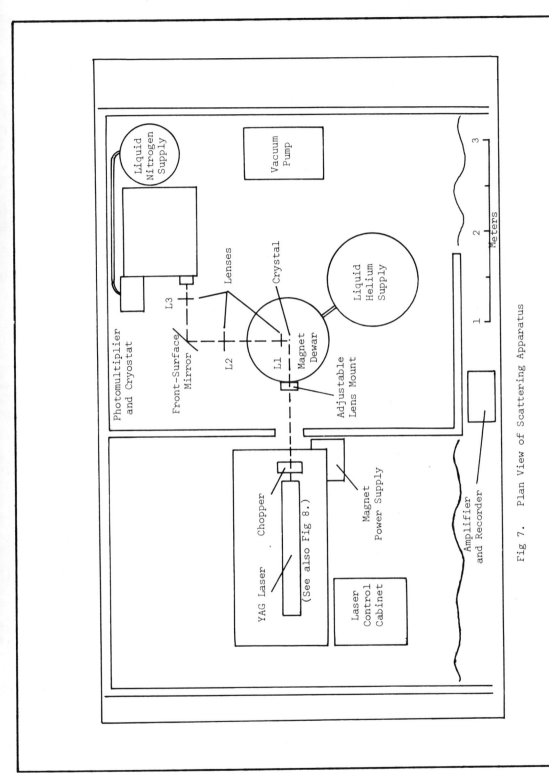

Fig 7.    Plan View of Scattering Apparatus

linear polarization, an intracavity Brewster's-angle polarizer was used. Laser modes could be restricted to the lowest-order longitudinal set TEM$_{ooq}$ by placing an aperture inside the optical cavity.  The laser is shown in Figure 8.

Laser Head.  The laser-head assembly houses a 50mm-long Nd:YAG rod and two 2.5-DW krypton pump lamps.  Deionized water supplied from a heat exchanger is pumped to the laser head, passes through a system of jackets and couplings inside the head, and carries away heat from the Nd:YAG rod and pump lamps.

Q-Switch.  In order to generate large pulses of output power, an acousto-optical Q-switch was used.  The Q-switch is placed on the laser's optical rail between the front mirror and the laser head.  Inside the Q-switch, acoustic wave fronts generated in a fused-quartz transmission block act to momentarily deflect the laser beam as it passes through the switch.  This deflection is only about 1°, but results in a brief power loss of about 30%.  This is sufficient to decrease the cavity gain to the point where lasing stops; and, during this brief hesitation, population inversion within the laser rod climbs to the enormous magnitudes required for the production of a "giant pulse."  It is thus possible to produce short bursts of power of about 250-ns duration which may rise to several kilowatts.  The pulse recurrence frequency (PRF) is variable from 0.4 to 24 KHz.

Control Cabinet.  The laser head and Q-switch are connected to a control cabinet which houses the 6-KW power supply, Q-switch rf drive, and heat exchanger components.  Electrical cables and water lines pass

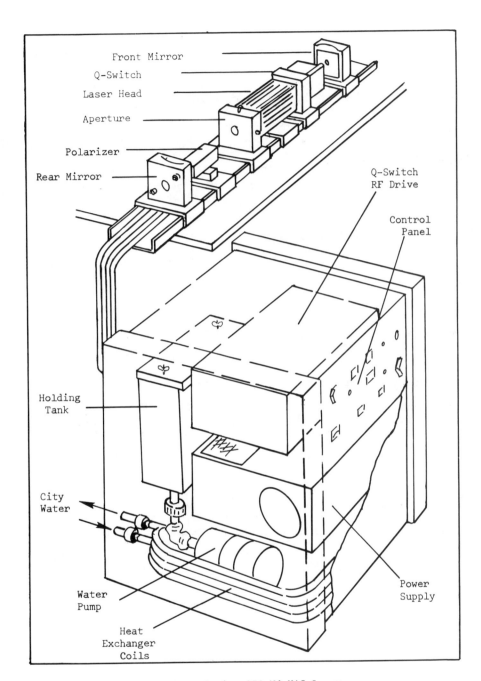

Front Mirror

Q-Switch

Laser Head

Aperture

Polarizer

Rear Mirror

Q-Switch
RF Drive

Control
Panel

Holding
Tank

City
Water

Water
Pump

Heat
Exchanger
Coils

Power
Supply

Fig. 8.   Holobeam Series 250 Nd:YAG Laser

from the rear of the cabinet and into the trough of the optical rail. Cables and water lines are of sufficient length to allow placement of the cabinet within about five feet of the rail.

Superconducting Magnet and Magnet Dewar

To produce the large magnetic flux densities required for s.f.R. scattering, an RCA type SM829 superconducting magnet was used. To facilitate magnet cooling during operation, the device was housed in a specially built liquid-helium dewar flask. The magnet and magnet dewar are shown in Figure 9.

Superconducting Magnet. The RCA type SM2829 superconducting magnet is essentially a Helmholtz coil wound with $Nb_3Sn$ superconducting ribbons. The magnet is capable of producing a magnetic flux density of 10T homogeneous to within 1% within a 2.54-cm-diameter spherical volume at the center of the magnet. Coil current may be varied up to a maximum of 91A with a field-to-current ratio of 0.11T/A over the entire current range. The flux density can be computed directly from the field-to-current ratio; however, to provide an independent reading of the flux density, a magneto-resistive sensing coil has been wound around the magnet's bore. When the coil is operated at 50ma, the voltage developed across its terminals is proportional to the magnetic flux density with a ratio of 0.525T/mV.

Access to the center of the magnet is through any of three othogonal bores: a 5.87-cm-diameter longitudinal bore, a 3.02-cm-diameter transverse bore, and a 3.02-cm-diameter vertical bore. Once the magnet is

*(The section continues for 7 pages.)*

### III.   Equipment and Procedure

The detection system consists of a sample chamber, two detectors, support electronics, and a gas-handling system.  The components of the system and the procedure for handling samples are described in this chapter.

Sample Chamber

The sample chamber is designed to freeze the xenon gas sample uniformly;   provide maximum source-to-detector geometries for two detectors; and allow one detector to observe most electrons, while shielding electrons from the other detector.

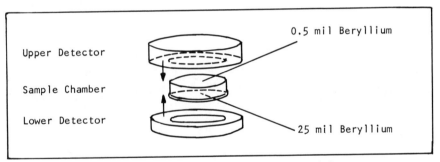

Figure 6.   3-Dimensional View of Sample Chamber and Detectors.

The chamber (Figure 6) is a flat, hollow cylinder of stainless steel, capped with two beryllium end "windows" of differing thicknesses.  The thicker window (0.025 in.) allows the lower detector to record only electromagnetic energy while stopping electrons with energies less than 350 keV.  The thinner window (0.0005 in.) allows electrons with energies greater than 40 keV to pass through, and thus allows the upper detection

EXAMPLE 30.   EQUIPMENT AND PROCEDURE

system to record a combined spectrum of electrons and electromagnetic radiation.  The stainless steel wall of the chamber is flared to provide an edge for a vacuum-tight seal between the windows and the chamber.

The 2-cm-diameter windows of the chamber are designed to match the surface area of the 300 $mm^2$ Si(Li) detector used by Rowe.  The thickness (0.2 in.) of the chamber was designed to improve the window-to-total-surface ratio, providing a better theoretical geometry factor for both detectors than that used by Rowe (Figure 5).

Unlike Rowe's chamber (Figure 5a), the new sample chamber cannot be connected directly to a cryostat because it is sandwiched between the two planar detectors.  The chamber is cooled to near-liquid-nitrogen temperatures ($\sim$95°K) by edge contact with the two detectors (see Figure 5b).

Upper and Lower Detectors and Electronics

Two lithium-drifted silicon detectors face the chamber through the beryllium end windows.  The detectors and the electronics used to produce a signal from each are described in the following paragraphs.

Both detectors were made by Kevex Corporation and are planar Si(Li) detectors with an active area of 300 $mm^2$.  The upper detector has a sensitive depth of 2mm, and faces the thin beryllium window.  The sensitive depth makes it less efficient for x-rays and gamma rays, but is thick enough to detect electrons with energies up to 1500 keV.  The detector is cooled by contact with the chamber and a copper cylinder connected to the cryostat rod, as shown in Figure 7.  It is connected to the preamplifier by a segment of low-impedance, braided cable through the side of the detector assembly.  The preamplifier is an Ortec Model 118A, specifically

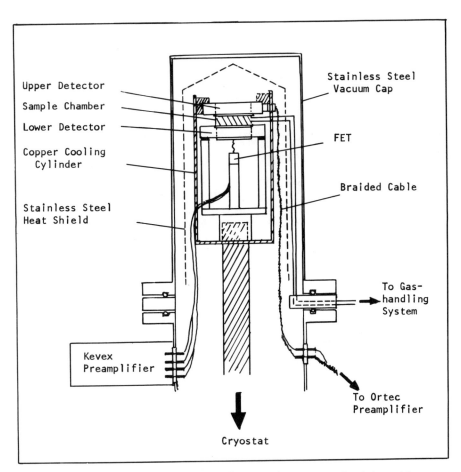

Figure 7.    Cross-sectional View of Detection System Head Assembly.

designed for cooled, low-leakage detectors.  The preamplifier signal is
amplified and shaped in an Ortec Model 451 Linear Amplifier.  The detector is operated at +400 volts with a Power Designs, Inc. Model AEC-500
Power Supply.

The lower detector is the x-ray kit used by Towe (Ref 11:13).  The
larger sensitive depth of 5mm makes the detector more efficient for
detecting x-rays.  For example, the lower detector has an intrinsic

*(The section continues for 4 pages.)*

VII.    Experimental Procedure

Because the general sequence of the experimental procedure was described in part in Chapter V, only specific information regarding the operation of the scattering apparatus and the collection of data is presented here.  A short section on the CdTe optical phonon scattering is included at the end of the chapter.

Apparatus Preparation

Preparation for each s.f.R. run was accomplished over a two-day period.  If no significant problems were encountered, the actual run took place on the third day.

Sample Mounting.  To prepare sample holder A, shown in Figure 13, the crystals were glued in position behind the small focusing lenses using Kleerite rubber cement.  Some mounting was also done using Eastman brand cellulose tridecanoate; however, the rubber cement was found to be more tolerant of low-temperature cycling.  Once the crystals were in place, the sample holder was attached to an aluminum rod and inserted in the magnet's bore through the vertical support stem.

To prepare holders B and C, shown in Figure 14, it was necessary to raise the magnet out of the dewar with a ceiling hoist in order to insert one of the holders in either the transverse or longitudinal bore. While the magnet was out of the dewar, the bore-mounted collecting lens L1 (Figure 7) could be relocated or adjusted.

Magnet Pre-Cooling.  To minimize helium boil-off, it was normal practice to pre-cool the magnet in liquid nitrogen on the evening prior to a spin-flip run.  With the magnet in place and all flange bolts

EXAMPLE 31.    PROCEDURE

secured, the magnet dewar's vacuum cavities (Figure 10) were pumped down to about $5 \times 10^{-5}$ torr. Following this, both the inner and outer dewars were filled with liquid nitrogen to a level just above the top of the magnet. The magnet was then allowed to sit in this configuration overnight.

Helium Transfer. On the morning of the run, nitrogen in the inner dewar was forced out through a transfer tube by means of pressure from a cylinder of nitrogen gas. Once the inner dewar had emptied, it was purged thoroughly with helium gas and, finally, filled with liquid helium from a 200-liter helium dewar. Transfer was accomplished using the pressure from a cylinder of helium gas, and the helium supply was normally left in position beside the magnet during the run.

The liquid-helium transfer is one of the more critical steps in setting up the apparatus. If the nitrogen has not been thoroughly purged from the inner dewar and magnet, nitrogen crystals are likely to form on the inner-dewar walls and may even become thick enough to obstruct the dewar windows.

Photomultiplier Cooling. Three or four hours prior to a run, a 25-liter dewar of liquid nitrogen was vented into the photomultiplier cryostat. An electric heater placed inside the dewar insured a constant boil-off of cold nitrogen gas into the cryostat, permitting low-noise operation of the photomultiplier tube.

Alignment Procedure. The most difficult portion of the experimental procedure centered around the various optical alignments. Since the YAG laser operates in the near infrared, the beam is completely invisible and, therefore, cannot be used as an alignment tool.  To overcome this problem, a Spectra Physics model 133 helium-neon (He-Ne) laser was used for most of the alignment work.  A rough alignment was usually accomplished before or during magnet pre-cooling, and a final alignment was performed after the inner dewar had been emptied and refilled with liquid helium.

To align the pump laser to the crystal, the following procedure was used.  First, a paper target was attached to the front dewar window, and the YAG laser, operated at about 300 mW, was used to burn a small hole in the target.  The laser was then turned off, and the He-Ne laser was positioned on the optical rail behind the YAG's rear mirror (Figure 8).  Since the YAG's optical components exhibit low reflectivity at 6328 A, the He-Ne beam passed completely through these elements and struck  the paper target at the dewar window.  When the He-Ne laser was adjusted so that its beam passed through the target hole, it was essentially collinear with the YAG laser.  It could then be used in lieu of the YAG laser for front-end alignment purposes.

To perform the front-end alignment, the paper target was removed, and the height and orientation of the YAG's optical rail were adjusted until the He-Ne beam was properly positioned onto the crystal.  Fine adjustment was accomplished using the adjustable lens mount shown in Figure 11.

To align the monochrometer to the crystal, the He-Ne laser was attached to an alignment port behind mirror M3 (Figure 12).  Its beam was then directed back through the first half of the monochrometer and out the entrance slit S1.  The beam could then be directed into the

*(The section continues for 3 pages.)*

### IV.  Computer Program Development

Once the analog system had been converted to a set of gains and difference equations, the next task was to write the actual program to use in the Aerospace Multiprocessor.  It was assumed that only one processor was available for flight control.  Therefore the calculations for one axis output were done completely before the calculation of the output of another axis began.  However, each new axis output was stored until all six outputs were ready.  Then they were sent out in immediate succession.

### Data Format and Type of Arithmetic

The first programming task was to determine the format of the data word and the type of arithmetic to be used.  Filter equation coefficients were calculated.  They range in magnitude from 0.000711 to 1.8749.  The highest value of control system gain is 4, and the extreme value of input and output voltage was determined to be 5.0.  Because the Aerospace Multiprocessor has no built-in floating point capability, fixed point, two's-complemented arithmetic was selected with a 32-bit data word.  The primary radix point is located between the 21st and the 20th least significant bits.

### Multiply Subroutine

Since the Aerospace Multiprocessor does not have a built-in multiplication capability, a multiply subroutine based on a routine described in Reference 36 (pages 49-54) was devised.  The product is calculated to double-precision accuracy and is then truncated to a 32-bit word in order to minimize error buildup.

EXAMPLE 32.  **DEVELOPMENT OF COMPUTER PROGRAM**

The flowchart for the first third of the multiply subroutine is shown in Fig. 8.  The subroutine requires that the main program load the multiplicand into the A2 scratch pad register of the LU (Logic Unit) and load the multiplier into the B register of the LU before the multiply subroutine is called.  Also, the value put into the AMPCR (Alternate Microprogram Count Register) by the CALL instruction, which called up the multiply subroutine, has to be put into storage because the AMPCR is needed for other purposes.  Scratch pad registers A3 and A1 are zeroed. A3 and A1 will contain the MS (most significant) byte and the LS (least significant) byte of the double precision product, respectively.

During each multiply routine iteration, the multiplier in the B register is shifted one bit to the right, end off.  When all bits in the B register are zeros, the computer exits the multiply routine.  This requires that at the beginning, the MSB (most significant bit) of the B register must be a 1.  If the multiplier has a value of 0 or greater, then the one's complement of the B register contents is taken to put a 1 into the MSB.  When the multiplier has a value less than 0, the two's complement of both the multiplier and the multiplicand is taken to preserve the sign of the product.  Then the one's complement of the multiplier is taken for use in the remainder of the subroutine.

Decision block 1, Fig. 8, tests the B register contents to determine whether it contains only ones.  If it does, this means the multiplier is zero, and since product register A3 already contains only zeros, the computer returns immediately to the main program.

In the case of a nonzero multiplier, the computer moves on to decision block 2, Fig. 9, where the LSB of the B register is tested.  If it is

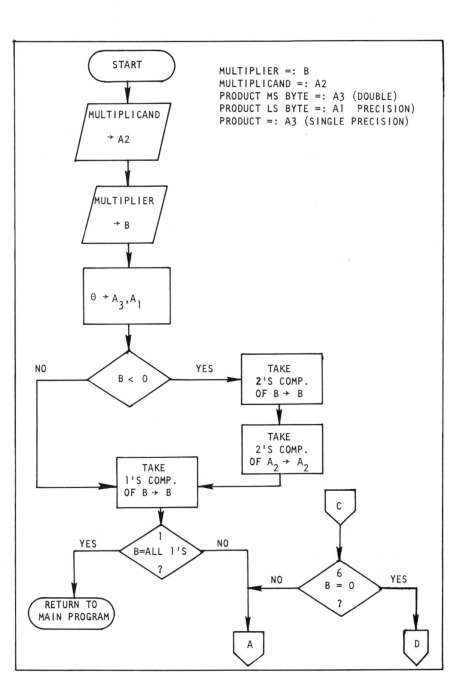

Fig. 8.    Flowchart--First Third of Multiply Subroutine

*(The section continues for 26 pages.)*

IV.    Results

To demonstrate the feasibility of an MNOS dosimeter it was necessary to show that its response to radiation was reproducible.  Once
that was shown, data were required concerning minimum and maximum dose
and the effect of dose rate.  Experimental data were therefore taken on
the effect of radiation and on the effect of time on the MNOS threshold
voltage.  Minimal data were taken on dose-rate effects since the MNOS
is considered dose-rate independent.  Tallon and Vail (Ref 14) indicated
that under proper test conditions the MNOS responds only to total dose
effects.

Time Dependence

Initial tests of the variation of $V_T$ with time indicated a logarithmic dependence.  The curve in Fig. 8 shows the effects of time on
$V_T$ .  On the semi-log axes, the curve is almost linear out to the last
data point at 47 hours.

A linear least squares fit applied to $V_T$ versus $\log_{10}$ (time)
yielded a correlation coefficient of 0.98.  Consequently, data on $V_T$
versus time was only taken for approximately 30 minutes on later MNOS
transistors.  The threshold voltage at later points in time was estimated by extrapolation of the initial data.

Fig. 8 also shows the excellent reproducibility of the data for $V_T$
versus time.  The time history for the transistor was started from the
saturation write point to insure a fixed starting value of threshold
voltage.

EXAMPLE 33.    RESULTS

The MNOS transistors used in this study respond slowly over time. This slow response is an asset in a device which is to be used as a dosimeter. Several hours are often required in experiments to achieve a large total dose.

Radiation and Time Dependence

The dependence of MNOS threshold voltage on the combined effects of radiation and time is shown in Fig. 15. Some 3 hours and 45 minutes were required to accumulate the maximum dose shown, $4.3 \times 10^6$ rads (Si). Radiation exposure was stopped at that time since the change in threshold voltage with further radiation had become minimal.

After the initial $4.3 \times 10^6$ rads (Si) exposure, the transistor was cleared and then written again to saturation. A second radiation exposure repeated the threshold voltage measurements out to 2 M rads (Si). Further checks on reproducibility of data were made with two additional radiation exposures to 640 k rads (Si) each. The data from the first exposure was seen to differ from that of the remaining radiation exposures. The difference was determined to be a systematic error of 0.14 volts. The error was caused by failure to write the device fully into saturation prior to the start of the experiment.

After the constant 0.14 volt error was subtracted from the first set of data, the standard deviation for the data was determined. Application of a single standard deviation to the data indicated a reproducibility of $\pm$ 0.01 volts. This excellent reproducibility held for the remaining five MNOS transistors tested. The data showed such a high degree of precision, $\pm$ 0.01 volts, that discrepant values were immediately apparent.

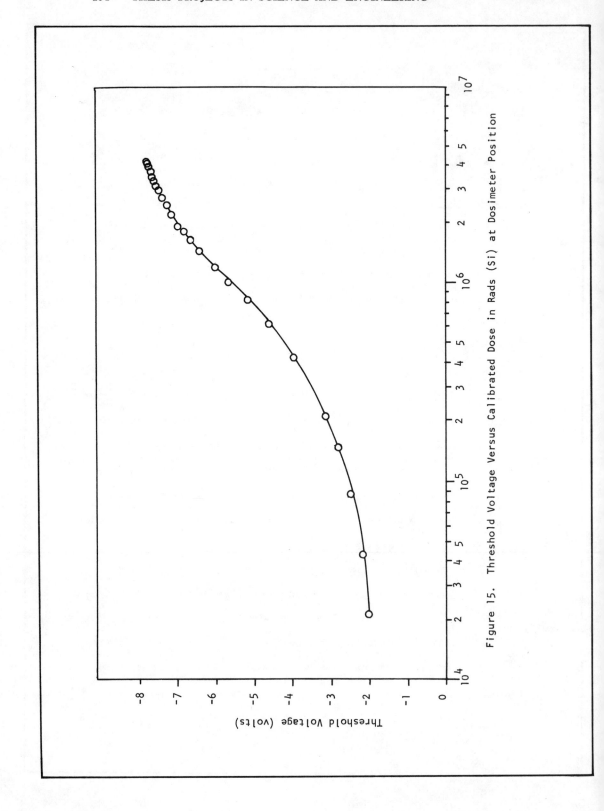

Figure 15.   Threshold Voltage Versus Calibrated Dose in Rads (Si) at Dosimeter Position

Dosimetry Data

In order to use the MNOS as a dosimeter, the effect of radiation alone had to be separated from the previous data which included the effect of time required for exposure to that calibrated radiation dose. Fig. 16 shows the effect of radiation alone on the value of threshold voltage. The curve shows the change in threshold voltage versus calibrated dosage for an MNOS initially written to saturation. Primary radiation effect data for the curve was obtained from a single 4.3 M rad irradiation. The first data points were then confirmed with a second irradiation to a calibrated dose of 640 k rads. After the irradiation tests, a 22-minute nonradiation test was made to determine the effects of time on the threshold voltage. The threshold voltage versus time curve was then extrapolated to provide data covering the time required to achieve the calibrated radiation dose. Then the time-dependent threshold voltage data was subtracted from the radiation effect test data. Fig. 16 represents the result of the subtraction.

Theoretical Curve Fit

The suggested equation for changes in threshold voltage versus radiation, Eq (23), was fitted to the data for Fig. 16. A best value for the radiation effect constant B was found through the use of a nonlinear curve-fitting computer program. With threshold voltage as the dependent variable, a minimum RMS error of 0.018 yielded a value of $B = 8.22 \times 10^{-7}$ rads$^{-1}$ . Fig. 16 shows the excellent agreement between the experimental and calculated data.

Although the devices tested in this study differed from the devices tested by Mariffino et al (Ref 9), the radiation damage constant was

*(The section continues for 6 pages.)*

VI    Discussion of Results

The results of testing the three systems are discussed in the following pages. Results applicable to each objective are presented in the sequence in which the objectives were presented in Chapter V. All tables referenced in this chapter are located in Appendix E, and all figures are in Appendix F.

Verification of Closed-Loop Pole Locations

The closed-loop poles of observer-augmented systems, designed by the algorithms described in Chapter IV, were indeed those of the original system and of the observer (as derived theoretically in Chapter II). Table V contains a list of the closed-loop poles computed for a number of Test System I observer-augmented system designs. The values obtained for the poles of the observer-augmented systems were equivalent (within an acceptable accuracy) to those of the full-state feedback system and the designed poles of the observers. This comparison was made for several observer root locations, for different sets of measured states, and for both major design algorithms.

Table VI contains a similar comparison of the closed-loop poles for several representative observer-augmented systems designed for Test System II. The measurement set $(x_2, x_3, x_4)$ was used for each of the systems listed in the table. The results for this test system again reflected a good comparison with the expected results. As in the cases shown for Test System I, designs for several different observer root locations and the application of both Algorithms I and II are included in the comparison. Note that the results for the system in which the observer root is placed at -16 were less accurate. This was because the

EXAMPLE 34.    DISCUSSION OF RESULTS *Because of the quantity of results, most are placed in appendixes.*

gains required in this design are larger than those required in other

cases ($g_2$ and $g_3$ were approximately ten times as large).  A specific dis-

cussion of the effect of "high" gains on the design results is the subject

of a later section in this chapter.

The closed-loop poles for two observer-augmented systems are com-

pared to those of the full-state feedback system for Test System III in

Table VII.  Again, the results were nearly those values predicted by

theory.  Note that one of the observer-augmented systems shown in the table

used a three-measurement,  third-order observer.  This indicates that the

algorithms can be used without loss of accuracy to design observers of

higher order.

In summary, the closed-loop poles of observer-augmented systems will

indeed be those predicted in the development of Chapter II.  In addition,

it has been verified that the algorithms for designing the observers do

function correctly and provide accurate system designs.  Furthermore, it

is clear that a check of the closed-loop poles of the observer-augmented

system designs is a reasonable method of verifying the accuracy of any

particular design.

## Effects of Varying Observer Root Location

The effects of varying the locations of the observer roots on both

the magnitudes of the design gains and the performance of the observer-

augmented systems obtained from Algorithms I and II will be discussed

in that order.

Effect on Gain Magnitude.  Table VIII contains a tabulation of the

design gains required for a set of first-order observers (obtained from

Algorithm I) for Test System I with the states $x_1$ and $X_3$ measured and the root locations of the observers varied.  The gain $l_1$ was constant over the range of roots in each case, since it was dependent only on $t_4$ which was always equal to $k_4$ .  The other four gains in the design either monotonically decreased or increased as the observer root location was varied between -11 and -30.  In general, the variation of these gains was linear over a range of the observer root locations.  Further examination reveals that the gains $d_1$ and $d_3$ were significantly lower in magnitude than $g_1$ and $g_3$ , and they varied less as the root location was changed.  The gain $g_3$ was the most critical, and the determination of how far from the origin the observer root can be placed will depend on the maximum value of $g_3$ that is practical.  The behavior of certain observer-augmented systems is examined in the next section of the chapter.

Another example of a variation in the placement of the obserber roots for Test System I designs is shown in Table IX.  In this table, the required gains for a pair of second-order observers (designed by Algorithm II) are compared.  Again, $l_1$ was constant since it depended only upon $t_{14}$ which was always equal to $k_4$ .  Again it may be noted that the gains were of higher magnitude for the root placement which was farthest from the origin (-25 in the example).  The two most troublesome gains in this particular design were $g_{13}$ and $l_2$ .  It is clear that a limit would have to be set on how far to the left of the origin the observer root could be placed in order to limit these two gains.

Results for design gains obtained from a study of Test System II exhibited characteristics similar to those found in the cases taken from Test System I applications.  Tables X through XII summarize the required gains for observer designs (obtained from Algorithm I) for three different

*(The section continues for 29 pages.)*

### V.   Application

Several existing computer applications of iterative techniques will iterate toward zeros of a function, but the initial starting values for these schemes may pose a significant problem.  If the initial point is not close to an actual zero, the iterative techniques often diverge.

The theorems and examples presented in this work can be used to locate intervals on which a function has a zero.  If the given function f can be paired with one of the differential equations  L [f] = 0 , and if a trial function u which makes the corresponding functional J [u]  negative on a given interval is found, then a zero of f does exist on that interval.

Examples of common differential equations from a variety of engineering sciences were chosen to demonstrate the breadth of applications possible.  This method may, perhaps, be applied to indicate the existence of zeros of other differential equations before valuable computer time is spent on hit-or-miss searches to find these zeros. In fact, the algorithms obtained can themselves be implemented using numerical techniques on a computer of reasonable size.

EXAMPLE 35.   **APPLICATION** *Application used in place of Conclusion. Project was entirely mathematical development.*

VI    Conclusions and Recommendations

Conclusions

On the basis of the results obtained in the analysis of the basic system and design solutions for the conditional and state-variable feedback methods, the following conclusions are drawn:

1.  Both the base motion disturbance rms error and the dynamic tracking error involved in tracking the simulated target (Appendix B) are excessive for the uncompensated system.

2.  The base motion and tracking errors can be simultaneously reduced by application of a modified conditional feedback configuration or by state-variable feedback.

3.  It is possible to increase the system type and bandwidth by application of state-variable feedback.

4.  The reduction in system errors must be accompanied by a relatively large gain increase. This fact, coupled with the dynamics of the sensors required to physically realize the necessary configurations, may result in errors larger than those obtained in this study. Further, the open-loop synthesis of the control ratio in the conditional method may cause deviation from the desired results.

Recommendations

Based on the assumptions stated initially and observations made during the investigation, the following recommendations are proposed for further study:

**EXAMPLE 36.    CONCLUSIONS AND RECOMMENDATIONS** *Numbered lists used.*

1.  Although the elevation and azimuth channels are similar, the azimuth channel contains a nonlinearity (Ref 3:6) which could be investigated.

2.  Bearing friction was assumed negligible and the azimuth angle was treated as a constant. The derivation of the gimbal dynamic equations (Ref 3:13) could be modified to include bearing friction and a time-varying azimuth angle.

3.  The various states in the state-variable feedback representation are assumed accessible by perfect measurement. One method of synthesizing the inaccessible states is by use of block diagram manipulation; i.e., shifting the feedback elements to accessible states. Since this may result in excessive noise, estimation of the unavailable states by Kalman filtering or Luenberger observer techniques could be considered. In addition, the effect of state feedback on the torque disturbance response should be investigated.

4.  In this study, the tracker output is treated as a continuous signal. Since it is actually discrete, further study in this area would indicate the validity of the original assumption.

5.  The base motion rms error is computed by use of the power spectral density in the frequency domain. Time domain simulation could be made by utilizing a filtered white-noise source possessing the autocorrelation function obtained by taking the inverse Fourier transform of the power spectral density function. The simulation could be accomplished by writing the

system and filter differential equations and solving the

system by use of the MIMIC programming language.  The white-

noise would be obtained from a random-number generating

routine.

VIII    Conclusions and Recommendations

In this study, the ability of a cryogenically-cooled detection system employing two lithium-drifted silicon (Si(Li)) detectors to detect low activities of radioactive noble gases was evaluated. Testing was performed with two isotopes of xenon: $^{133}$Xe and $^{131}$Xi.

The theoretical results of the study indicate that a Si(Li) detection system has the capability of detecting a lower activity of $^{131m}$Xe in the presence of a higher activity of $^{133}$Xe. For instance, if the activity of $^{133}$Xe is 6800 DPM, it would be theoretically possible to quantify 50 DPM of $^{131m}$Xe in 24 hours ($A_Q$ from SPECTRA). Coincidence analysis would reduce this figure to 30 DPM (for the same counting period).

The experimental results demonstrate that the present detection system functions far below its theoretical capabilities. X-ray analysis is complicated by carrier-gas fluorescence that cannot be quantified. Electron analysis is impossible because of the large amount of electron-scattering present. Electron scattering and low efficiencies for detection made coincidence analysis unsuitable.

In contrast, it appears that there is more potential for gamma-ray analysis than was originally thought. A coaxial Ge(Li) detector was used to quantify a mixture of gases that was impossible to quantify by any means in the present Si(Li) detection system.

It is recommended that further studies be directed toward improving a gamma-ray detector to analyze lower activities of radioactive gases. A well-type Ge(Li) detector would increase the detector

EXAMPLE 37.    CONCLUSIONS AND RECOMMENDATIONS  *Numbered lists not used.*

efficiency to approximately 1, and active shielding such as an anti-coincidence umbrella would reduce the background.  It is estimated that the $A_Q$ can approach 20 DPM of $^{131m}Xe$ for a counting time of 24 hours.

It is also recommended that further work be done on the Si(Li) detection system to verify the qualitative findings of this project. Methods can be devised to eliminate the migration of gas in the sample chamber and to also decrease the scatter of internal conversion electrons. Solutions to these problems could lead to a Si(Li) system that would compare favorably with a well-type Ge(Li) system.

Bibliography

1. AR-3. Supporting Your Computer System. Product brochure. Seattle: Electrometric Corporation, 1975.

2. Bridgman, Charles J. and R. A. Shulstad. "An Evaluation of Mass Integral Scaling of Atmospheric Radiation Environments," Transactions of the American Nuclear Society, 24 (11): 406 (November 1976).

3. Carl, Joseph W. and Richard V. Smartwood. "A Hybrid Walsh Transform Computer," IEEE Transactions on Computers, C-22, (7): 669-672 (July 1973).

4. Cohen, Alan M. Numerical Analysis. New York: John Wiley and Sons, 1973.

5. Corwin, Donald L. Hot Wire Measurements of Temperature Fluctuations. Unpublished MS thesis. State College, Pa.: Department of Aerospace Engineering, The Pennsylvania State University, September 1972. (N72-84693)

6. D'Azzo, John J. and Constantine H. Houpis. Feedback Control System Analysis and Synthesis (Second Edition). New York: McGraw-Hill Book Company, 1966.

7. Dolan, Kevin. An Algorithmic Approach for Reducing Kinematically Similar Differential Systems. MS thesis. Wright-Patterson AFB, Ohio: School of Engineering, Air Force Institute of Technology, December 1977. (AD A047 781)

8. Elrod, William C. "The Nature of Turbulence in the Mixing of Binary Gases in Flowing Systems," OAR Research Review, VIII (5): 3-27 (May 1969).

9. Franke, Milton E. and Douglas L. Carr. "Effect of Geometry on Open Cavity Flow-Induced Pressure Oscillation," Progress in Astronautics and Aeronautics, Vol 45; Aeroacoustics: STOL Noise; Airframe and Airfoil Noise, edited by I. R. Schwartz. New York: American Institute of Aeronautics and Astronautics, 1976.

10. Hitchcock, James E. "Laminar Gas Flow and Heat Transfer in a Parallel-Plate Channel with Large Temperature Differences," Journal of Heat Transfer, 3 (11): 469-471 (November 1971).

11. Jones, John, Jr. "Explicit Solutions of the Matrix Equation AX-XB=C," Rendiconti del Circolo Mathematico de Palermo, 23 (2): 245-257 (June 1975).

12. Koski, Walter S. Molecular Beam Studies with F(+) Ions. C00-3283-21. Baltimore, Md: Department of Chemistry, Johns Hopkins University. (N77-24914)

13. Lamont, Gary B., D. B. Ahern, and J. B. Peterson. "Microprocessor Development for a Digital Flight Control System Voter/Monitor," Proceedings of the National Aerospace Electronics Conference. 454-462. Dayton, Ohio: Dayton Section, IEEE, May 1976.

14. Lee, David A. and David R. Andley. "Considerations Related to Ill-Posed and Well-Posed Problems in System Identification," IEEE Transactions on Automatic Control, AC-19 (6): 738-747 (December 1974).

15. Luke, Theodore E. "Nucleation-Site Drift and Depoling in Ferroelectric Bismuth Titanate," Ferroelectrics, 6 (4): 307-312 (September 1974).

EXAMPLE 38.    BIBLIOGRAPHY  Alphabetical sequence. Authors' first names included. Issue numbers of periodicals included.

16.  Lyon, Craig A., Paul A. Shadady, and William C. Elrod.  Propeller Acoustics Research (Isolated Airfoil Noise).  AFAPL-TR-75-78.  Wright-Patterson AFB, Ohio: Aeropropulsion Laboratory, 1975.

17.  "Matrix Analysis of Bifurcated Structures," British Journal of Mathematical Theory, 63 (8): 86-89 (November 1978).

18.  Maybeck, Peter S.  Solutions to the Kalman Filter Wordlength Problem: Square Root and U-D Covariance Factorizations.  AFIT-TR-77-6.  Wright-Patterson AFB, Ohio: School of Engineering, 1977.  (AD A049 704)

19.  Melendez, Kenneth and Joseph Howard.  "Representation Theorems for Unconditionally Converging Operators," Proceedings of the American Mathematical Society, 45 (6): 404-408 (December 1974).

20.  Palazotto, Anthony N. and James A. Cervantes.  "Cutout Reinforcement of Stiffened Cylindrical Shells," A Collection of Technical Papers, No. 78-512.  331-339.  New York: American Association of Aeronautics and Astronautics, 1978.

21.  "Salient Implications of the Laubenthal-Holly Transform," Microbiology Today, 14 (6) 21-23 (February 1979).

22.  Salisbury, John W., Graham R. Hunt, and Salvatore R. Balsamo.  "Compositional Implications of Christiansen Frequency Maximums for Infrared Remote Sensing Applications," Journal of Geophysical Research, 78 (23): 4983 (August 1973).

23.  Shankland, Donn G.  "Particle Identification and Subsidiary Conditions from Correlation Functions," American Journal of Physics, 38 (10): 1239-1244 (October 1970).

24.  Stephan, Brian G. and Charles J. Bridgman.  "Relatavistic Compton Scattering by the Discrete Ordinates Method," Nuclear Science and Engineering, 54 (2): 101-115 (June 1974).

25.  Torvik, Peter J.  "An Analysis of the Pressure Wave Generated in Seated Spinal Impact," Proceedings of the Symposium on Biodynamic Models and Their Applications.  575-620.  AFPL-TR-71-29.  Wright-Patterson AFB, Ohio: Aerospace Medical Research Laboratory, December 1971.  (AD 842 921)

Bibliography

1.  Luke, T. E. and S. E. Cummins.  "Bismuth Titanate-Ferroelastic Distortion and Domain Studies," Ferroelectrics, 7: 323-235 (Oct 74).

2.  Kirschner, F. D. et al.  "Passive Detection of Motion Transverse to the Optical Viewing Axis," IEEE Transactions on Instrumentation and Measurements, IM-24: 248-255 (Sept 75).

3.  Weber, W. B. et al.  Turbine Engine Variable Cycle Selection Program, Phase I Summary.  Report MDC A3570.  St. Louis Missouri: McDonnell-Douglas Aircraft Company, June 1975.

4.  Miller, I. and J. E. Freund.  Probability and Statistics for Engineers. Englewood Cliffs, N.J.: Prentice-Hall, Inc., 1975.

5.  Houpis, C. H.   "A Control System Design Method for a System Having a Plant with Variable Parameters," International Journal of System Science, 6: 607-613 (July 75).

6.  Lamont, G. B. and R. V. Gressany.  "Observers for Systems Characterized by Subgroups," IEEE Transactions on Automatic Control, AC-20: 523-528 (Aug 75).

7.  Kalman, R. E.   "A New Approach to Linear Filtering and Prediction Problems," ASME Journal of Basic Engineering, 82: 35-46 (Mar 60).

8.  Jones, J., Jr.  "Solution of Certain Matrix Equations," Proceedings of the American Mathematical Society, 31: 333-339 (June 72).

9.  Robinson, S. R.  "On the Problem of Phase from Intensity Measurements," Journal of the Optical Society of America, 68: 87-92 (Jan 78).

10. Carl, J. W.  "Digital Signal Processing: An Overview," Proceedings of the National Aerospace and Electronics Conference (NAECON 78) Volume 3.  1320.  New York: IEEE Press, 1978.

11. D'Azzo, J. J. and B. Porter.  "Transmission Zeros of Linear Multivariable Continuous-Time Systems," Electronics Letters, 13: 735-755 (Nov 77).

12. Wright, H. E., D. B. Wilkinson, and W. C. Elrod.  "Progress in the Development of Small, Low Cost Turbojet Engines," Proceedings of the 1978 JANNAF Propulsion Meeting.  CPIA Publication 293.  395-424. Laurel, Maryland: Chemical Propulsion Information Agency, Johns Hopkins University, 1978.

13. Vaughn, G. L. et al.  "Time Domain Design of Frequency-Sampling Digital Filters for Pulse Shaping Using Linear Programming Techniques," IEEE Transactions on Acoustics, Speech, and Signal Processing, ASSP-22: 180-185 (June 74).

14. Wiesel, W. E.  "Fragmentation of Asteroids and Satellites in Orbit," Icarus, 34: 914 (Oct 78).

EXAMPLE 39    BIBLIOGRAPHY  *Items listed in the order in which they were cited in the text.*

15. Fontana, R. E. et al. "Software Engineering Education," IEEE Transactions on Education, E-20: 17-21 (Feb 77).

16. Hengehold, R. L. and F. L. Pedrotti. "Ultraviolet Reflectivity and Electron Energy Loss Spectra of $AgGaS_2$ and $CuGaS_2$," Journal of Applied Physics, 46: 5202-5204 (Dec 75).

17. Merz, R. A. et al. "Rear Stagnation Point Location in a Subsonic Near Wake," Journal of Spacecraft and Rockets, 13: 319-320 (May 76).

18. Hannah, S. R. and A. N. Palazotto. "A Finite Difference Approach Incorporating a Truncated Fourier Series for Solving the Fourth Order Differential Equation Considering Stability Analysis," Proceedings of the Southeast Conference of Theoretical and Applied Mechanics. 851-893. Nashville, Tenn: Vanderbilt University Press, 1978.

19. Maybeck, P. S. et al. "Application of an Extended Kalman Filter to an Advanced Fire Control System," Conference on Decision and Control. 1192-1195. New York: Institute of Electrical and Electronics Engineers, 1977.

20. Reeve, W. H. and J. L. Stinson. Software Design for a Visually-Coupled Airborne Systems Simulator (VCASS). MS thesis. Wright-Patterson AFB, Ohio: School of Engineering, Air Force Institute of Technology, March 1978. (AD A055 226)

21. Nielsen, P. E. "The Role of Discrete Plasma Initiation Sites in the High-Intensity Laser Irradiation of Surfaces," Applied Physics Letters, 27: 458 (Oct 75).

22. Truxal, J. G. Introductory System Engineering. New York: McGraw-Hill Book Co., 1972.

23. Baker, A. J. and P. D. Manhardt. Finite Element Analysis of Low Speed Viscous and Inviscid Aerodynamic Flows. NASA-CR-2908, COMOC-77TR-2. Knoxville, Tenn: Computational Mechanics Consultants. (N78 - 10029/4GA)

APPENDIX D

Zero-Sensitivity Method

A method of obtaining a system in which the sensitivity functions
for plant parameter variations are zero is based on a technique developed
by Truxal (Ref 13:410).  Although the design is not based on state-
variable methods, it does represent a means by which the plant dynamics
may be isolated.  An example will be worked using the plant described in
Chapter II.  The plant will include the integrator, the actuator, and the
aircraft dynamics.

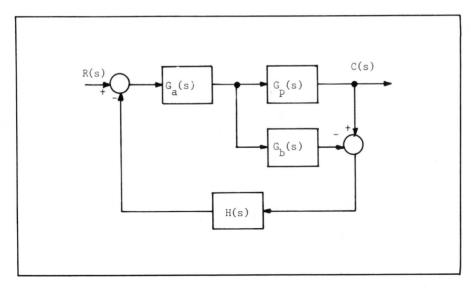

Figure D-1.    Two-Loop System

Figure D-1 shows a two-loop system, including the plant $G_p(s)$ and
three controller transfer functions:  $G_a(s)$, $G_b(s)$, and $H(s)$.  The closed-
loop control ratio $C(s)/R(s)$ is given as

EXAMPLE 40.    APPENDIX  *Detailed explanation of a method used. Equations are given prefix letters corresponding to appendix letter.*

$$T(s) = \frac{C(s)}{R(s)} = \frac{G_a(s)G_p(s)}{1 + G_a(s)G_p(s)H(s) - G_a(s)G_b(s)H(s)} \qquad (D-1)$$

The sensitivity function described in Chapter III is calculated for changes in the plant $G_p(s)$. The expression is given by

$$S_{G_p}^T = \frac{1}{1 + G_p G_a H/(1 - G_a G_b H)} = \frac{1 - G_a G_b H}{1 + G_a H(G_p - G_b)} \qquad (D-2)$$

where the transfer functions are functions of s, but the notation is omitted for convenience. It may be noted that $S_{G_p}^T$ can be made equal to zero if

$$G_a G_b H = 1 \qquad (D-3)$$

If controller transfer functions are selected to satisfy Eq (D-3), the system will be insensitive to changes in the plant. If Eq (D-3) is satisfied, the control ratio of Eq (D-1) becomes

$$\frac{C(s)}{R(s)} = \frac{G_a(s)G_p(s)}{G_a(s)G_p(s)H(s) + [1 - G_a(s)G_p(s)H(s)]} = \frac{1}{H(s)} \qquad (D-4)$$

The reason the sensitivity of $C(s)/R(s)$ to $G_p(s)$ is zero is that $G_p(s)$ is in tandem with essentially infinite gain. With $G_a(s)G_b(s)H(s) = 1$, there is a feedback loop with a gain of +1 (Ref 13:410).

To apply the above technique, let the transfer function $G_b(s) = 1$ so that Eq (D-3) becomes

$$H_a(s) = \frac{1}{H(s)} \qquad (D-5)$$

As seen from Eqs (D-4) and (D-5), the system's response is now determined

*(The appendix continues for 2 pages.)*

Appendix A

Synthesis Strategy

In this appendix the method of taking the phonemic representation
of what is to be "said" and converting it to an acceptable form for the
Model 4516 synthesizer is presented.  The representation of the desired
utterance includes phonemes, stress marks (ST), word boundaries (blanks),
pauses (period, question mark, or comma), and a terminal symbol (END).
The inputs to the Model 4516 are the 24 parameters introduced in
Chapter III which include 10 pole or zero frequencies and their associated bandwidths, two volume controls, a pitch period duration, and a
threshold for voiced fricatives.  Some of the rules and methods which
follow were derived directly from Rabiner (Ref. 14).  His work is the
starting point for this discussion.

## Phoneme Characteristics

Each phoneme has a unique steady state characterization.  This
characterization includes the first three formant target frequencies
($F_1$, $F_2$, $F_3$), the voiced amplitude ($A_V$), noise amplitude ($A_N$), a frequency
range ($\Delta 1$, $\Delta 2$, $\Delta 3$) around each of the formant targets, and a duration.
The formant targets for stops and fricatives are virtual targets; the
formants do not actually reach the targets because voicing is replaced
by voiceless sound (fricatives) or amplitude drops (stops).  The frequency ranges are used to determine when a transition to a new phoneme
is complete.  When all three formants have moved to within hertz of
the specified target and the additional duration requirements are met,
the transition is defined as complete.  In the case of a nasal or

EXAMPLE 41.    APPENDIX  *Detailed analysis of an approach and specific
method used.*

fricative, the characterization must also include the frequency and
bandwidth of the nasal pole and zero or the fricative pole and zero.
Table V presents the formant targets, amplitudes, frequency ranges,
and the additional durations of the various phonemes.  The diphthongs,
affricatives, and aspirant are not included for reasons which will be
discussed later.

Formant Motion

In connected speech the speaker moves from one phoneme to another
in a continuous manner.  Although some phonemes are known to influence
others two or three removed, the principal effects are produced by the
adjacent phonemes.  Transitions, in this strategy, are a function of only
the two adjacent phonemes.  As one might expect, they are smooth and
continuous.  Rabiner's strategy of using a critically damped second
degree differential equation to control motion in the frequency space
has been used.  He chose a second degree equation because it provided a
good fit to the observed data.  He made it critically damped because
only a single time constant is necessary to completely characterize the
response to a forcing function.  Since he found that this algorithm
worked very well, it was used in this study.  The equation is

$$x(t) = Af + (Ai-Af)\exp(-t/\tau) + Vi + \frac{(Ai-Af)}{\tau} \; t \; \exp(-t/\tau) \tag{3}$$

where

$x(t)$ = formant value as a function of time

$\tau$  = time constant in ms

$Ai$  = formant target of previous phoneme

$$Af = \text{formant target of current phoneme}$$
$$Vi = \text{velocity of the formant at } t = t_0$$

For computer simulation of this method, the equation was Z-transformed, using impulse invariant technique (to preserve the time response to an impulse) to obtain the following difference equation

$$x(nT)=2kx(nT-T)-k^2x(nT-2T)+(1-k)^2F(nT-T) \tag{4}$$

where

$$T = \text{sampling time (PER)}$$
$$x(nT) = \text{formant position at time } nT$$
$$k = e^{-T/\tau}$$
$$\tau = \text{time constant in ms}$$

and

$$F(nT) = \text{formant target at time } nT$$

Formant data is used to define intrinsic phoneme durations and is the basic mechanism from which all timing is controlled.

Time Constants

Each formant may move from one target to the next at different rates; thus, a time constant is necessary for each formant in the transition. In this implementation there are 31 basic phonemes, so there are 961 possible combinations. Since three formants are controlled for each phoneme, there are 2883 possible time constants. However, use of certain approximations and phoneme groupings made possible a reduction of the number of time constants to a more workable 371.

TABLE V

PHONEME CHARACTERISTICS

| Phoneme | $F_1$ | $F_2$ | $F_3$ | $A_V$ | $A_N$ | $\Delta 1$ | $\Delta 2$ | $\Delta 3$ | DURATION |
|---------|-------|-------|-------|-------|-------|-----------|-----------|-----------|----------|
| IY | 270 | 2290 | 3010 | 100 | 0 | 40 | 40 | 110 | 50 |
| II | 390 | 1990 | 2550 | 88 | 0 | 50 | 50 | 90 | 20 |
| EE | 530 | 1840 | 2480 | 60 | 0 | 50 | 55 | 90 | 20 |
| AE | 660 | 1720 | 2410 | 45 | 0 | 40 | 40 | 75 | 50 |
| UH | 580 | 1190 | 2390 | 40 | 0 | 50 | 50 | 50 | 20 |
| AA | 730 | 1090 | 2442 | 38 | 0 | 25 | 40 | 80 | 50 |
| OW | 570 | 840 | 2410 | 28 | 0 | 40 | 40 | 80 | 50 |
| UU | 440 | 1020 | 2240 | 43 | 0 | 50 | 50 | 65 | 30 |
| OO | 350 | 1300 | 3900 | 85 | 0 | 40 | 45 | 55 | 50 |
| ER | 450 | 1275 | 1700 | 47 | 0 | 30 | 20 | 30 | 50 |
| BB | 150 | 600 | 3000 | 20 | 0 | 50 | 75 | 120 | 20 |
| PP | 150 | 800 | 1750 | 0 | 0 | 50 | 40 | 80 | 20 |
| MM | 280 | 900 | 2200 | 120 | 0 | 17 | 17 | 40 | 30 |
| DD | 440 | 1300 | 1700 | 20 | 0 | 50 | 50 | 160 | 20 |
| TT | 440 | 2200 | 3000 | 0 | 0 | 50 | 30 | 100 | 10 |
| NN | 280 | 1300 | 2000 | 120 | 0 | 17 | 17 | 100 | 30 |
| GG | 220 | 1300 | 1450 | 20 | 0 | 50 | 50 | 100 | 20 |
| KK | 220 | 1300 | 3300 | 0 | 0 | 50 | 30 | 70 | 20 |
| NG | 280 | 1700 | 2600 | 120 | 0 | 17 | 17 | 100 | 50 |
| FF | 175 | 900 | 2400 | 0 | 50 | 20 | 34 | 80 | 20 |
| VV | 175 | 1100 | 2400 | 65 | 35 | 10 | 15 | 40 | 20 |
| TH | 200 | 1400 | 2200 | 0 | 99 | 20 | 28 | 68 | 00 |
| TE | 200 | 1600 | 2200 | 50 | 90 | 10 | 15 | 100 | 00 |
| SS | 200 | 1300 | 2500 | 0 | 40 | 20 | 28 | 50 | 50 |
| ZZ | 200 | 1300 | 2500 | 50 | 90 | 20 | 30 | 50 | 20 |
| SH | 175 | 1800 | 2050 | 0 | 99 | 10 | 34 | 100 | 50 |
| ZH | 175 | 1800 | 2000 | 50 | 40 | 10 | 40 | 100 | 20 |
| WW | 300 | 610 | 2200 | 45 | 0 | 25 | 40 | 150 | 00 |
| LL | 380 | 1000 | 2575 | 75 | 0 | 25 | 80 | 150 | 30 |
| RR | 420 | 1300 | 1600 | 50 | 0 | 40 | 80 | 100 | 30 |
| YY | 300 | 2200 | 3065 | 58 | 0 | 25 | 110 | 200 | 00 |
| RO | 295 | 845 | 1315 | 80 | 0 | 30 | 80 | 100 | 00 |

*(The appendix continues for 7 pages.)*

Appendix B

Operating System

The operating system controls the operation of the IFPDAS II prototype hardware.  Execution of the operating system by the CPU results in
initialization of the system and then acquisition, reduction, and storage
of the data.  The operating system selects the proper input sensor, starts
the A/D conversion, and inputs the data for reduction and permanent
storage.  In addition, it ensures that the proper service routine receives
the data.

A flow chart of the operating system begins on this page; a listing
of the program follows the flow chart.

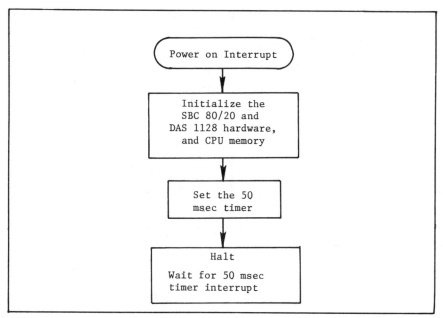

Fig. 19.    Operating System Flow Chart    (Sheet 1 of 9)

**EXAMPLE 42.    APPENDIX**  *Computer Flow Diagram. Computer program*
*follows 9-page flow diagram.*

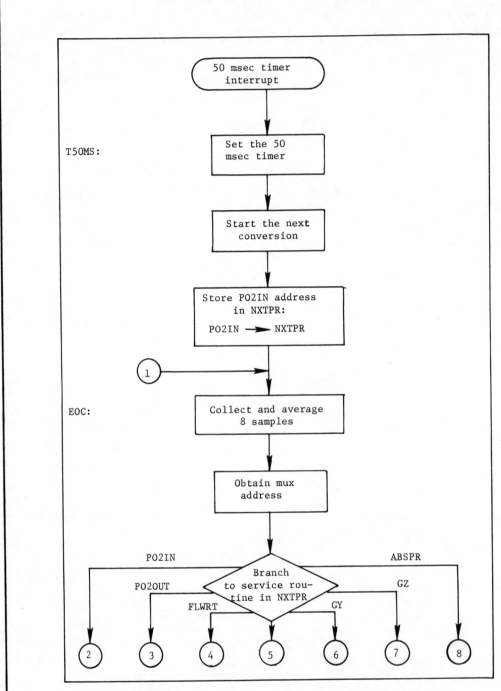

Fig. 19.    Operating System Flow Chart    (Sheet 2 of 9)

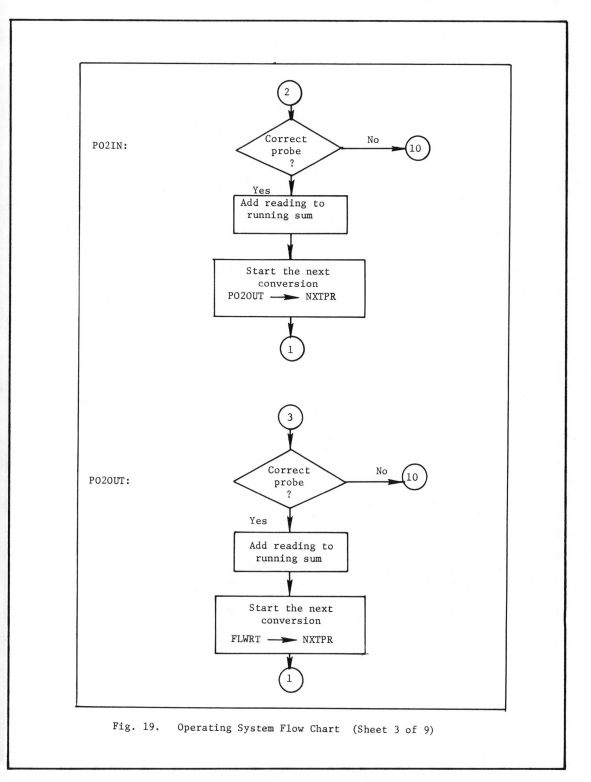

Fig. 19.    Operating System Flow Chart   (Sheet 3 of 9)

*(The appendix continues for 40 pages.)*

Appendix C

IFPDAS II Prototype User's Guide

Data Collection

The IFPDAS II prototype is operated as follows to acquire data:

1.  AC Power – ON to both the Hazeltine video terminal and the
        cassette tape

2.  DC Power – +5 VDC supply: OFF
        all others (–5, +12, –12, +15, & –15 VDC):  ON

3.  Video Terminal – Parity: 1
        Full Duplex
        Baud Rate: 1200
        Clear the screen

4.  Cassette Recorder – Insert tape in Recorder 2 and engage
        Select CONT – OFF LINE – PAGE
        Depress RESET, then REWIND
        Depress INTERLOCK and RECORD buttons
            and wait for tape to stop
            (RECORD button stays lighted)

5.  +5 VDC Supply – ON

The +5 VDC power supply resets the SBC 80/20 hardware and the

operating system starts to execute.  Data will be output to the video

terminal every ten seconds and transferred from the screen to the

cassette tape under program control.  The 8080 CPU directs the writing

of this data, using two control characters.  The CONTROL SHIFT PERIOD

(cs.) character (7EH) tells the Hazeltine that a command will follow.

The PRINT character (1EH) directs the transfer from the screen to the

tape.

When all of the desired data have been recorded:

EXAMPLE 43.   APPENDIX *Operational Procedure*

1.  DC Power - OFF (this terminates the IFPDAS's operation)

2.  Push RESET (the tape will advance momentarily, then stop
    and the RECORD light will go out)

3.  Press REWIND

4.  AC Power - OFF (to both the video terminal and the cassette
    recorder)

The data is now recorded on the cassette tape and is ready for transfer

to the main computer.


Data Transfer

The procedure to transfer the data from the cassette tape to a per-

manent file in AFIT's computer system is as follows:

1.  Video terminal - Parity: 1
                      Half Duplex
                      Baud Rate: 300

2.  Cassette Recorder - Select CONT - OFF LINE - PAGE
                        Depress RESET, then REWIND

3.  Using the terminal, LOGIN and enter EDITOR

4.  Enter:  CREATE, SUPPRESS line numbers (C,S)

5.  After system responds ENTER LINES, depress PLAYBACK on tape
    channel

6.  After the data are transferred, send an "=" to release the
    CREATE mode

7.  List the file and check for errors

The data are now in the edit file.  To store it permanently, the following

commands must be entered:

1.  REQUEST,Q,*PF

2.  SAVE,Q,NOSEQ,O      (NOSEQuence, Overwrite)

3.  CATALOG,Q,DATA,ID=(problem #),RP=(# of days to retain)

The data are now stored on disc for later use by the post-flight data conversion routine.

Data Conversion

The procedure to execute the compiled post-flight data conversion routine (COMPCONVERT), using the file DATA as the data, is as follows:

Enter the following commands:

1.  ATTACH,LGO,COMPCONVERT    (attaches COMPCONVERT as a local file called LGO)

2.  ATTACH,AFITSUBROUTINES,ID=AFIT   (attaches the AFIT subroutines as a local file called AFITSUB)

3.  LIBRARY,AFITSUB

4.  ATTACH,TAPE1Ø,DATA    (attaches DATA as a local file called TAPE1Ø)

5.  REWIND,LGO

6.  REWIND,TAPE1Ø

7.  LGO    (executes the post-flight data conversion subroutine)

When the program execution is complete, a local file called PLOT containing the output graphs has been created.  To send these graphs to AFIT's plotter, enter:

ROUTE,PLOT,TID=BB,FID=(xxx),DC=PT

This routing completes the data conversion process.

APPENDIX C

Derivation of Sensitivity Functions

The definition and use of the sensitivity function was covered in Chapter III. Here, the calculations required to find these functions are presented.

Sensitivity to M. The sensitivity of the closed-loop transfer function to variations in elevator effectiveness is

$$S^M_{M_\delta}(s) = \frac{M_\delta}{M} \frac{dM}{dM_\delta} \tag{C-1}$$

where $M = \dot{\theta}(s)/\dot{\theta}_c(s)$. Let the closed-loop transfer function given in Eq (A-4) be represented as

$$M = \frac{\dot{\theta}(s)}{\dot{\theta}_c(s)} = \frac{6.67 M_\delta (s + 1/T_a)}{s^4 + D_1 s^3 + D_2 s^2 + D_3 s + D_4} \tag{C-2}$$

where $D_1$, $D_2$, $D_3$, and $D_4$ are defined as

$$D_1 = K_i k_4 + 2\zeta\omega_a + 6.67 \tag{C-3}$$

$$D_2 = K_i \left[ -\frac{6.67_\delta}{A} k_2 - 6.67 k_3 + (2\zeta\omega_a + 6.67)k_4 \right] + \frac{2}{a} + 13.34\zeta\omega_a \tag{C-4}$$

$$D_3 = K_i \left[ 6.67 M_\delta k_1 \frac{6.67 M_\delta (1/T + \sigma)}{A} k_2 - 13.34\zeta\omega_a k_3 \right. $$
$$\left. + (\omega_a^2 + 13.34\zeta\omega_a)k_4 \right] + 6.67\omega_a^2 \tag{C-5}$$

$$D_4 = K_i \left[ 6.67 M_\delta (1/T_a) k_1 \frac{6.67 M_\delta (1/T_a)\sigma}{A} k_2 - 6.67\omega_a^2 (k_3 - k_4) \right] \tag{C-6}$$

The terms A and $\sigma$ are defined in Appendix A as the values of $M_\delta$ and $\zeta\omega_a$, respectively, at the nominal flight condition. The derivative of M with respect to $M_\delta$ is

EXAMPLE 44.    **APPENDIX**  *Mathematical Development*        *(The appendix continues*

*for 3 pages.)*

VITA

Joseph Gregory Jolda was born on 12 January 1948 in Worcester, Massachusetts.  He graduated from high school in Webster, Massachusetts in 1965 and attended Northeastern University, Boston, Massachusetts, from which he received the degree of Bachelor of Science in Electrical Engineering in June 1970.  Upon graduation he was employed as an associate engineer for Amperex Electronic Corporation, Slatersville, Rhode Island.  He also taught Mathematics and Circuit Theory at Worcester Junior College, Worcester, Massachusetts.  He entered the Air Force on active duty in September 1970, and received his commission from Officer Training School in January 1971.  He completed pilot training and received his wings in April 1972.  He served as a T-33 pilot with the 67th Tactical Reconnaissance Wing at Bergstrom AFB, Texas, and then as a T-37 instructor pilot with the 37th Flying Training Squadron at Columbus AFB, Mississippi, until entering the School of Engineering, Air Force Institute of Technology, in June 1976.  He is a member of Eta Kappa Nu and Tau Beta Pi.


Permanent address:   Wawela Park

Webster, Massachusetts   01570

EXAMPLE 45.   VITA

Figure 1.    Combustor "A" and Engine

EXAMPLE 46.    PHOTOGRAPH    *Equipment*

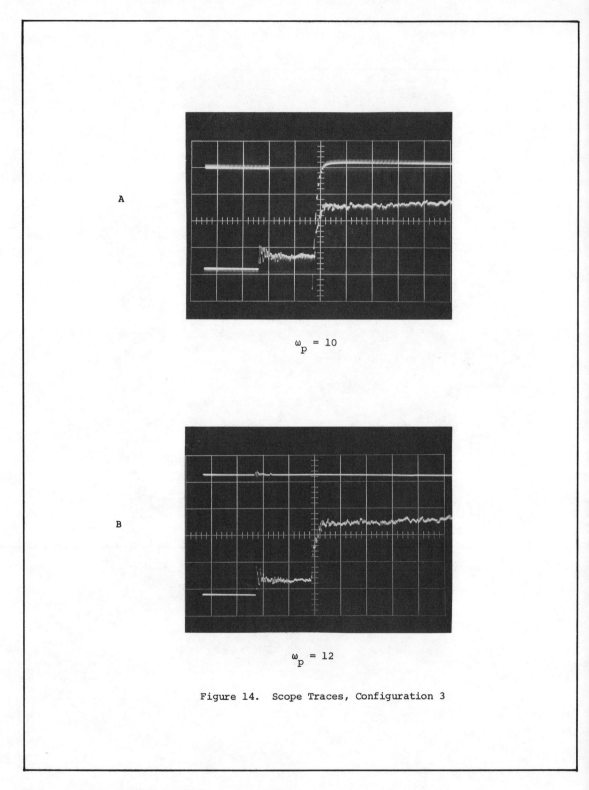

A

$\omega_p = 10$

B

$\omega_p = 12$

Figure 14.   Scope Traces, Configuration 3

EXAMPLE 47.    PHOTOGRAPH   *Scope Traces*

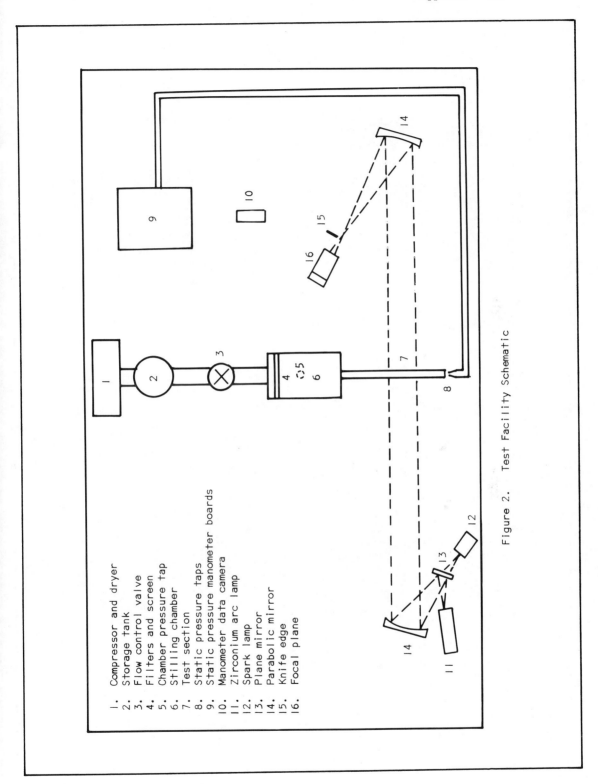

1. Compressor and dryer
2. Storage tank
3. Flow control valve
4. Filters and screen
5. Chamber pressure tap
6. Stilling chamber
7. Test section
8. Static pressure taps
9. Static pressure manometer boards
10. Manometer data camera
11. Zirconium arc lamp
12. Spark lamp
13. Plane mirror
14. Parabolic mirror
15. Knife edge
16. Focal plane

Figure 2. Test Facility Schematic

EXAMPLE 48. DRAWING *Schematic of Test Equipment*

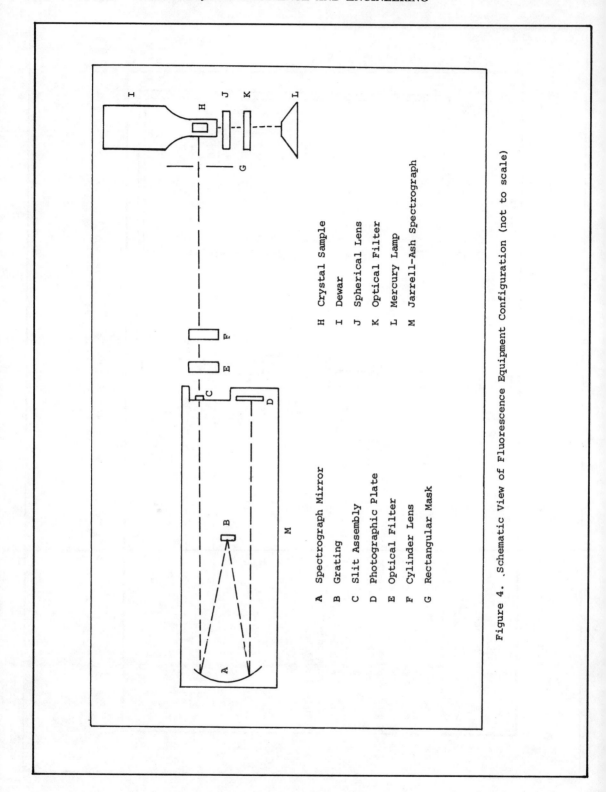

Figure 4. Schematic View of Fluorescence Equipment Configuration (not to scale)

A  Spectrograph Mirror
B  Grating
C  Slit Assembly
D  Photographic Plate
E  Optical Filter
F  Cylinder Lens
G  Rectangular Mask

H  Crystal Sample
I  Dewar
J  Spherical Lens
K  Optical Filter
L  Mercury Lamp
M  Jarrell-Ash Spectrograph

EXAMPLE 49.    DRAWING  *Schematic of Test Equipment*

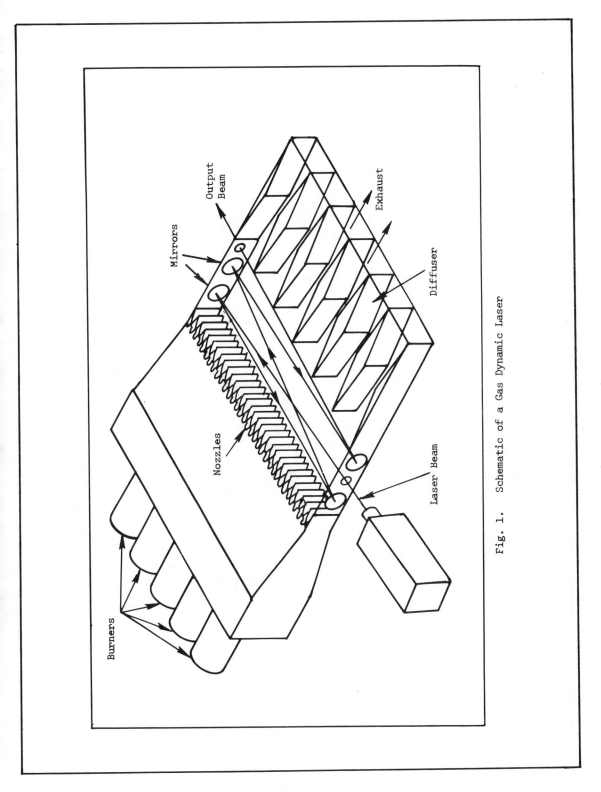

Fig. 1.    Schematic of a Gas Dynamic Laser

EXAMPLE 50.    DRAWING    *Schematic of Test Equipment*

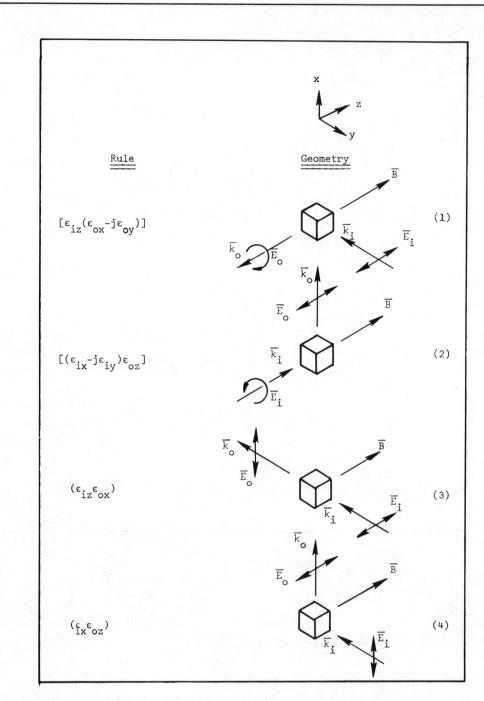

Fig. 4.  Spin-Flip Scattering Geometries

**EXAMPLE 51.**   **DRAWING**  *Scattering Geometries*

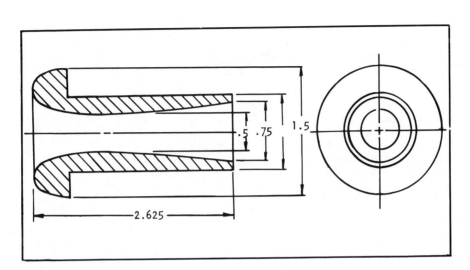

Fig. J-5.  Axisymmetric Nozzle

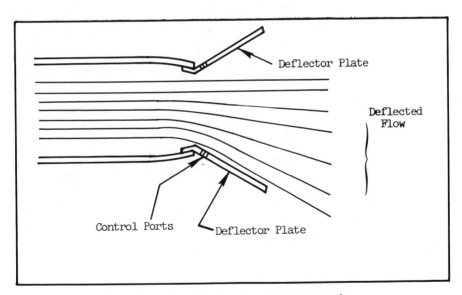

Fig. 14.    The Coanda-Effect Yaw Thruster

EXAMPLE 52.    DRAWINGS  *Details of Equipment*

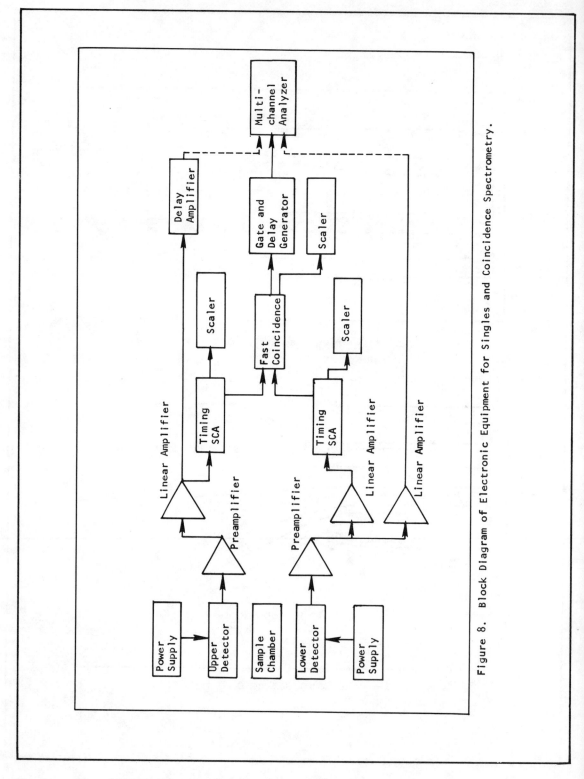

Figure 8. Block Diagram of Electronic Equipment for Singles and Coincidence Spectrometry.

EXAMPLE 53. DIAGRAM *Block Diagram of Test Equipment*

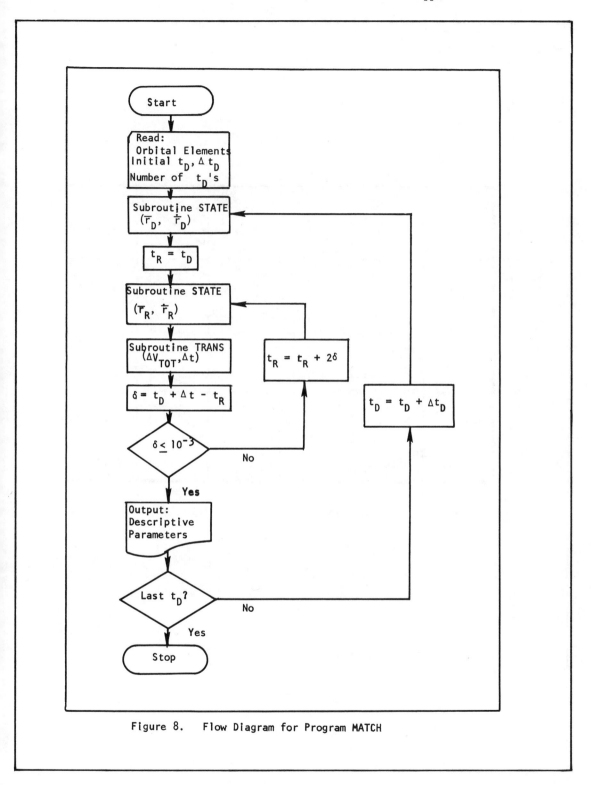

Figure 8.    Flow Diagram for Program MATCH

EXAMPLE 54.    DIAGRAM    *Computer Flow Diagram*

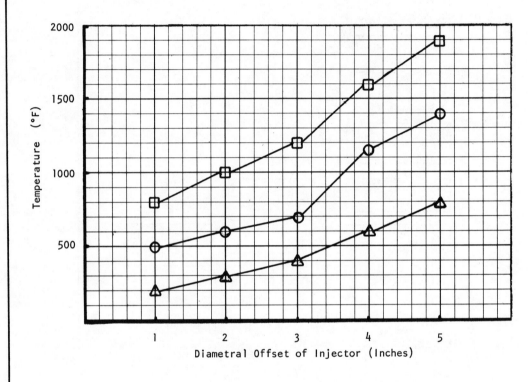

Figure 26.    Test Results - Run 4,    P = 4000 psi

EXAMPLE 55.    GRAPH  *Square Grid—Test Results*

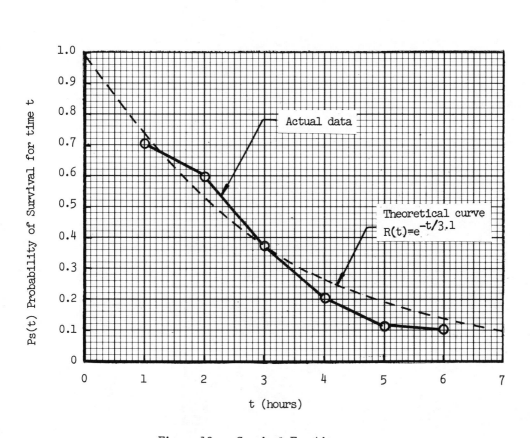

Figure 19.    Survival Function

EXAMPLE 56.    **GRAPH**    *Square Grid—Theoretical Curve vs. Test Results*

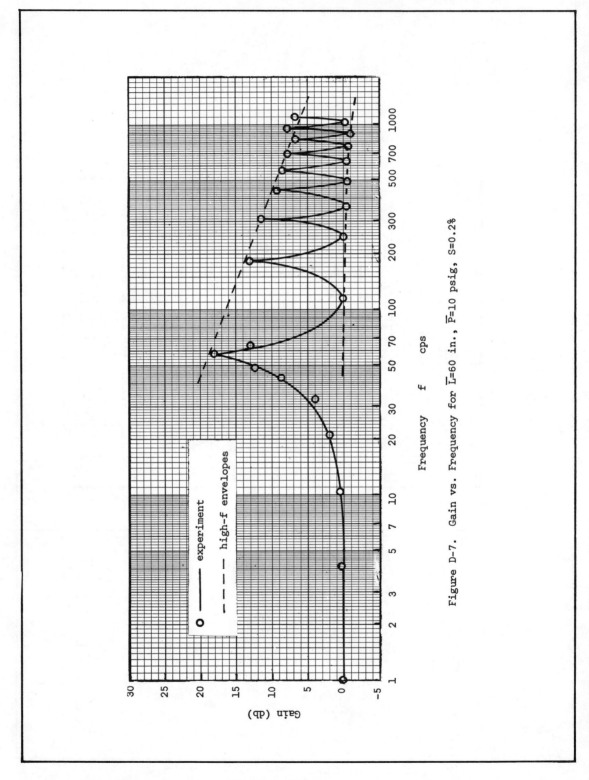

Figure D-7.  Gain vs. Frequency for $\overline{L}$=60 in., $\overline{P}$=10 psig, S=0.2%

EXAMPLE 57.    GRAPH  *Semilogarithmic Grid*

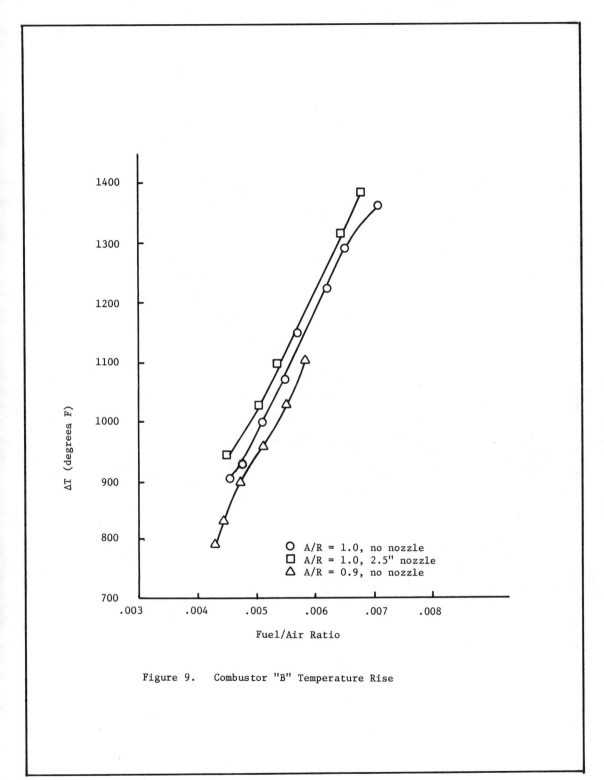

Figure 9.    Combustor "B" Temperature Rise

Example 58.    **GRAPH**    *No Grid—Test Results*

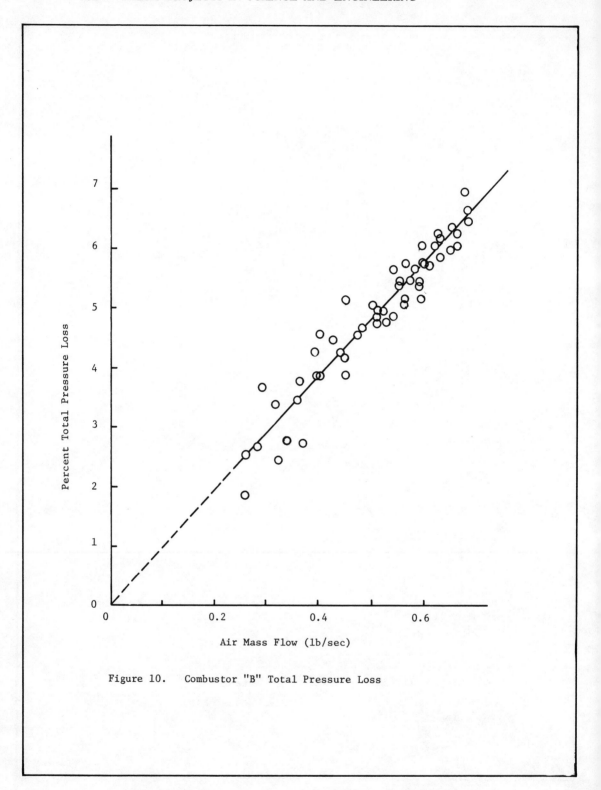

Figure 10.    Combustor "B" Total Pressure Loss

**EXAMPLE 59.    GRAPH** *No Grid—Test Results—Scatter Plot with Trend Line*

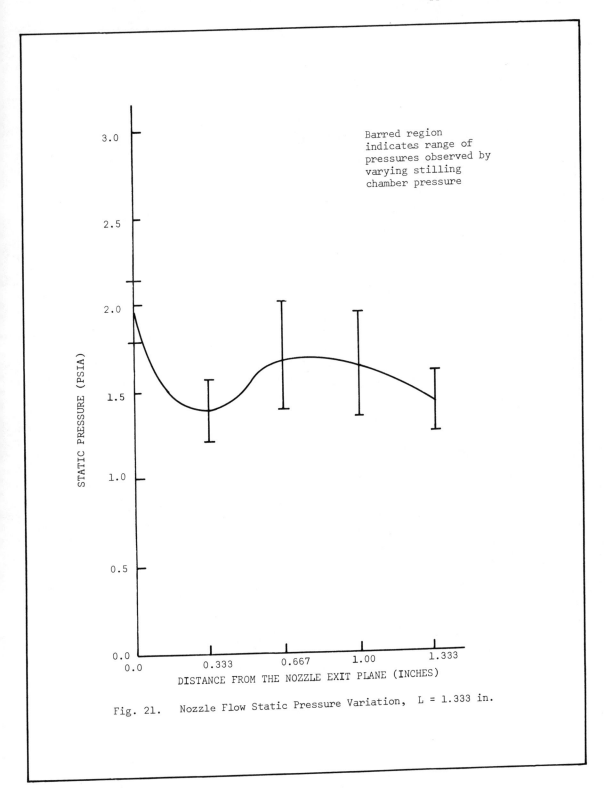

Barred region
indicates range of
pressures observed by
varying stilling
chamber pressure

Fig. 21.    Nozzle Flow Static Pressure Variation,    L = 1.333 in.

EXAMPLE 60.    GRAPH    *No Grid—Curve with Range Bars*

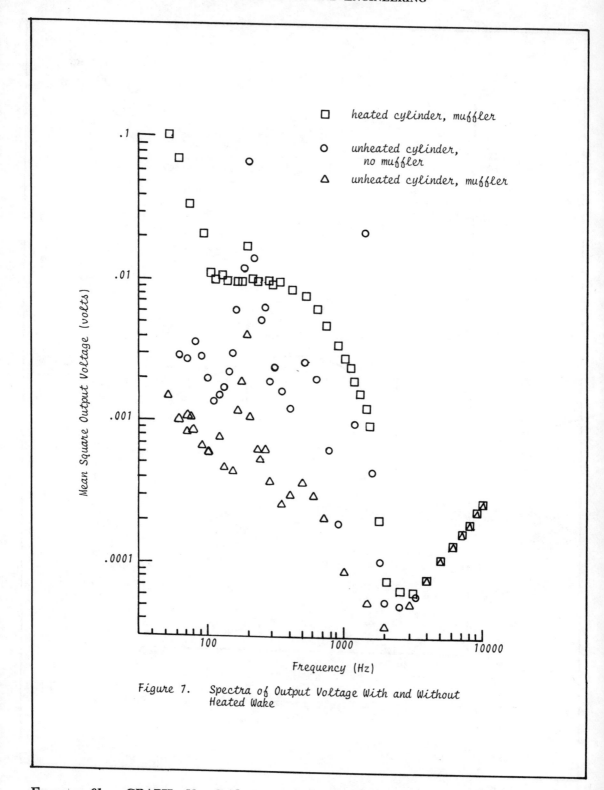

□    heated cylinder, muffler

○    unheated cylinder,
     no muffler

△    unheated cylinder, muffler

Figure 7.    Spectra of Output Voltage With and Without
             Heated Wake

EXAMPLE 61.    GRAPH  No Grid—Log-Log  Scale—Scatter Plot  without Curves

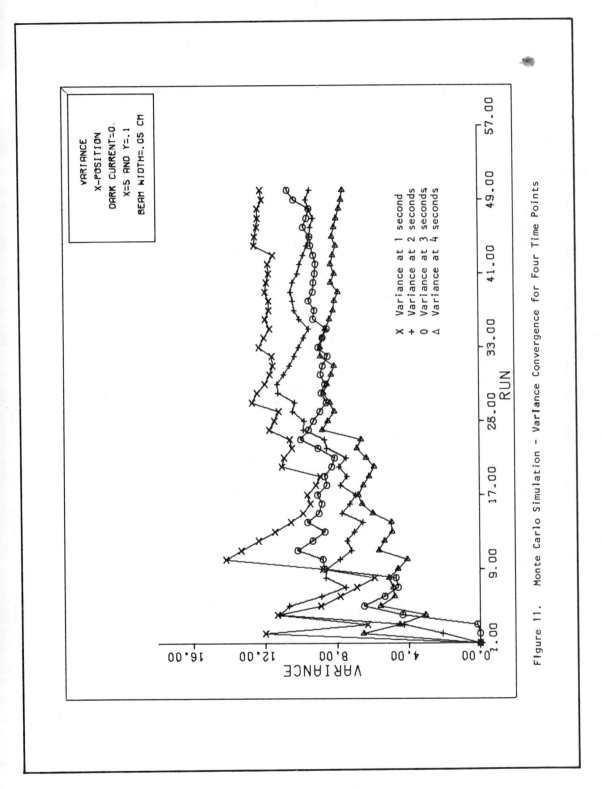

Figure 11.    Monte Carlo Simulation - Variance Convergence for Four Time Points

**EXAMPLE 62.    GRAPH**  *Incremental Plotter Output—Test Results*

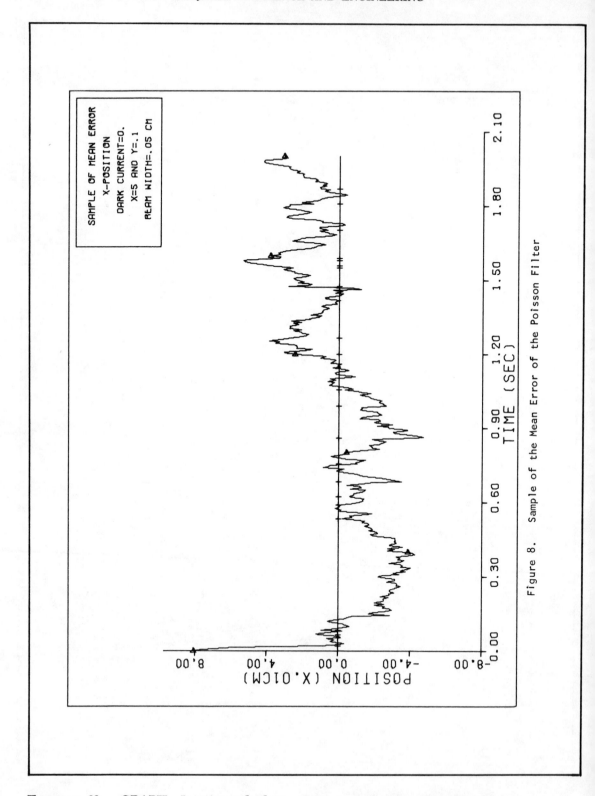

Figure 8.    Sample of the Mean Error of the Poisson Filter

EXAMPLE 63.    GRAPH    *Incremental Plotter Output—Sample of Mean Error*

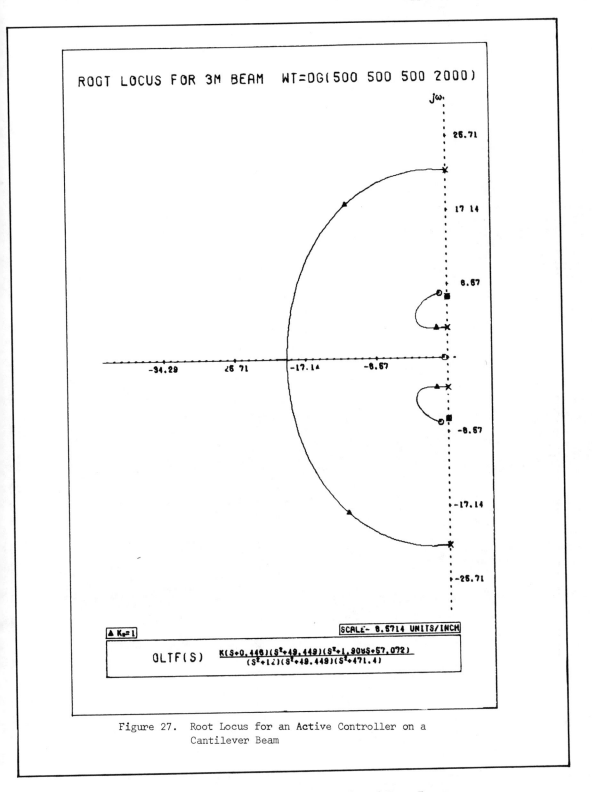

Figure 27.    Root Locus for an Active Controller on a
Cantilever Beam

**Example 64.    GRAPH**    *Incremental Plotter Output—Plot of Root Locus*

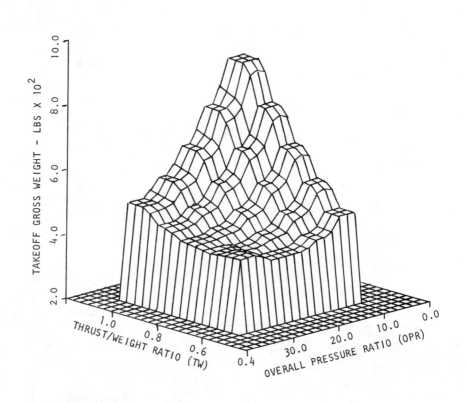

Figure 20.    3-D Plot of TOGW vs. TW and OPR -  Optimized
             Aircraft  (AR=3.5).

EXAMPLE 65.    GRAPH  *Incremental Plotter Output—3-D Plot. Plot has been traced from original output to smooth the lines. Original output contained scales and identification of scales as shown. It could have been used directly without tracing.*

Table I

Parameter Ranges

| Parameter | Desired Range | IFPDAS II Range |
|---|---|---|
| Heart Rate | 50 to 180 ± 2 b/min | 53 ± .1 to 225 ± 2.2 b/min |
| Breathing Rate | 10 to 30 ± 2 b/min | 4.7 ± .1 to 50 ± 1 b/min * |
| Flow Rate | N/S | 0 to 124 ± .25 l/min * |
| Flow Rate Integral | N/S | 0 to 26.2 volt-sec (± .3%) |
| Minute Ventilation Volume | 5 to 35 ± 2 l/min | 0 to 100 ± 2 l/min ** |
| Oxygen Partial Pressure | N/S | 0 to 760 ± 2 mm Hg |
| Absolute Pressure | N/S | 0 to 760 ± 2 mm Hg * |
| G's | -3 to +12 ± .25 G's | -3 to +12 ± .1 G |

N/S = Not Specified

* Assuming accurate probe input and ± 1/2 bit accuracy (± 10 mv)

** At sea level, assuming an accurate probe input

EXAMPLE 66.    TABLE  *Closed*

Table III

Comparison of Intervals Containing Zeros to Actual Zeros
of Bessel Functions $J_n(x)$, n=4,5,10,50

Interval:  [h,kh] = h-kh

| k | n = 4 | n = 5 | n = 10 | n = 50 |
|---|---|---|---|---|
| ∞ | 0 - 9.487 | 0 - 11.619 | 0 - 22.584 | 0 - 111.849 |
| 50 | .184 - 9.216 | .225 ⌐ 11.263 | .436 - 21.822 | 2.159 - 107.955 |
| 20 | .444 - 8.895 | .541 - 10.834 | 1.044 - 20.887 | 5.157 - 103.152 |
| 5 | 1.592 - 7.964 | 1.900 - 9.504 | 3.546 - 17.731 | 17.301 - 86.510 |
| 3 | 2.579 - 7.740 | 2.999 - 8.998 | 5.336 - 16.010 | 25.532 - 76.599 |
| 2 | 4.150 - 8.302 | 4.614 - 9.230 | 7.428 - 14.857 | 33.755 - 67.512 |
| 1.5 | 7.092 - 10.639 | 7.489 - 11.235 | 10.216 - 15.325 | 40.611 - 60.917 |
| 1.1 | 31.851 - 35.037 | 31.979 - 35.177 | 33.026 - 36.329 | 57.169 - 62.887 |

Actual Zeros $J_{n,p}(x)$

| n | p=1 | p=2 | p=3 | p=4 | p=5 | p=6 | p=7 | p=8 | p=9 | p=10 |
|---|---|---|---|---|---|---|---|---|---|---|
| 4 | 7.588 | 11.065 | 14.373 | 17.616 | 20.827 | 24.019 | 27.20 | 30.37 | 33.54 | 36.70 |
| 5 | 8.771 | 12.339 | 15.700 | 18.980 | 22.218 | 25.43 | 28.63 | 31.81 | 34.99 | 38.16 |
| 10 | 14.476 | 18.433 | 22.047 | 25.51 | 28.89 | 32.21 | 35.50 | 38.76 | 42.00 | 45.23 |
| 50 | 57.12 | 62.81 | 67.70 | 72.19 | 76.44 | 80.51 | 84.46 | 88.32 | 92.09 | 95.80 |

EXAMPLE 67.    TABLE  *Closed*

TABLE B-1

Comparison of Desired Target Model and Approximated Simulation

| Time (sec) | Target Angle (Degrees) | | |
| --- | --- | --- | --- |
| | Desired | Approximation | Error |
| 0.000 | 57.296 | 57.296 | 0.000 |
| 0.100 | 55.080 | 55.056 | 0.024 |
| 0.200 | 52.589 | 52.667 | −0.078 |
| 0.300 | 49.778 | 49.898 | −0.211 |
| 0.400 | 46.598 | 46.900 | −0.302 |
| 0.500 | 42.997 | 43.305 | −0.309 |
| 0.600 | 38.917 | 39.142 | −0.224 |
| 0.700 | 34.310 | 34.381 | −0.071 |
| 0.800 | 29.135 | 29.034 | 0.102 |
| 0.900 | 23.384 | 23.147 | 0.236 |
| 1.000 | 17.078 | 16.803 | 0.285 |
| 1.100 | 10.337 | 10.111 | 0.226 |
| 1.200 | 3.285 | 3.204 | 0.081 |
| 1.300 | −3.867 | −3.772 | −0.095 |
| 1.400 | −10.902 | −10.667 | −0.235 |
| 1.500 | −17.620 | −23.646 | −0.285 |
| 1.600 | −23.874 | −29.491 | −0.228 |
| 1.700 | −29.579 | −34.792 | −0.088 |
| 1.800 | −34.707 | −39.504 | 0.085 |
| 1.900 | −39.269 | −43.620 | 0.234 |
| 2.000 | −43.308 | −47.170 | 0.312 |
| 2.100 | −46.873 | −50.221 | 0.297 |
| 2.200 | −50.020 | −52.871 | 0.201 |
| 2.300 | −52.803 | −55.242 | 0.067 |
| 2.400 | −55.271 | −57.477 | −0.028 |

EXAMPLE 68.    TABLE  *Semiclosed*

for the nasal and are returned to the nominal value at the end of the nasal. These shifts take about 50 ms. The nasal pole and zero and their bandwidths are as follows:

|  | NASAL POLE | | NASAL ZERO | |
|---|---|---|---|---|
|  | Center Frequency (Hz) | Bandwidth (Hz) | Center Frequency (Hz) | Bandwidth (Hz) |
| MM | 1300 | 100 | 1100 | 100 |
| NN | 1100 | 200 | 1700 | 200 |
| NG | 1000 | 200 | 2000 | 800 |

If the nasal is preceded by a voiced sound, the shift of the values can be heard because the pole and zero are cascaded with the formant network in the voiced branch...

Table III
Quartz Lamp Bank Data

| $\lambda$(microns) | $V_{245}/V_{int}$ | $V_{305}/V_{int}$ | $V_{355}/V_{int}$ | $V_{420}/V_{int}$ |
|---|---|---|---|---|
| 0.4000 | 1.80 | 6.21 | 11.36 | 22.57 |
| 0.5000 | 1.61 | 3.14 | 4.11 | 7.38 |
| 0.6000 | 0.81 | 1.39 | 2.16 | 3.52 |
| 0.7131 | 0.77 | 1.38 | 1.87 | 2.75 |
| 0.8798 | 0.82 | 1.47 | 1.97 | 2.55 |
| 1.0465 | 0.91 | 1.50 | 2.03 | 2.71 |
| 1.1000 | 1.40 | 1.54 | 2.00 | 2.46 |
| 1.2000 | 1.27 | 1.71 | 1.87 | 2.22 |
| 1.4000 | 1.41 | 1.79 | 2.23 | 2.43 |
| 1.6000 | 1.50 | 1.85 | 2.18 | 2.56 |
| 1.8000 | 1.60 | 2.00 | 2.25 | 2.75 |

EXAMPLE 69.    TABLES  *Text Table and Open Table*

# Index

*Page numbers in bold indicate sample thesis pages.*